STAGING TO SELL

STAGING TO SELL

THE SECRET TO SELLING HOMES IN A DOWN MARKET

BARB SCHWARZ

WILEY

John Wiley & Sons, Inc.

Published by John Wiley & Sons, Inc., Hoboken, New Jersey.
Published simultaneously in Canada.

For general information on our other products and services or for technical support, please contact our Customer Care Department within the United States at (800) 762-2974, outside the United States at (317) 572-3993 or fax (317) 572-4002.

Wiley also publishes its books in a variety of electronic formats. Some content that appears in print may not be available in electronic books. For more information about Wiley products, visit our web site at www.wiley.com.

Library of Congress Cataloging-in-Publication Data:

Schwarz, Barb, 1944-
    Staging to sell : the secret to selling homes in a down market / Barb Schwarz.
        p.   cm.
    Includes index.
    ISBN 978–0–470–44712–3 (pbk.)
        1. House selling.   2. Home staging.   3. Real estate business.   I. Title.
    HD1379.S354 2009
    333.33068'8—dc22

                                                                    2009005641

Printed in the United States of America.

10 9 8 7 6 5 4 3 2 1

I dedicate this book to the women of the real estate and Home Staging industries. You are the women who make the world of real estate go round.

Throughout my travels as I give my Home Staging and real estate training all over North America, I am blessed to meet the most beautiful, talented, graceful, and inspiring women.

You have the creativity and the mind of genius as you Stage, market, and sell homes, and consult with the sellers whom you represent and help.

This book is for you because you are a blessing to all whom you serve.

CONTENTS

PREFACE

This book exists for one simple reason: to share my secrets for selling real estate in today's market. These secrets are the S Factor. What is that? *The S Factor is Staging.*

WHAT IS STAGING?

Staging is preparing a property for sale. I call it the S Factor! And Staging helps homes sell in the shortest time and for the most money possible. But S stands for other things:

- *S* stands for Service. I am all about providing service to the very best of my ability. Service, service, service!
- *S* also stands for System. And in this book I will be sharing with you the secret of my Real Estate System that works for all involved: the seller, the Agent, and the Stager!
- *S* stands for Secret, too. I will be sharing numerous secrets with you that help you sell your home at top dollar, even in a weakened and down housing market.
- And *S* stands for *sold*! And sold is what you want to be. When you list your home for sale or list someone's home for sale as an Agent or Stage someone's home, you want it sold. That is the whole goal. So the S Factor of Staging is to get the house listing and get the home sold. That is what this book is all about.
- *S* is also the first initial of my last name, Schwarz. Because I really did invent Home Staging, *S* stands for Schwarz as well as for Staging.

Many Real Estate Agents through the years have said to me, "This house has been Schwarz'd." These are the Agents who have heard me speak and who have been in my How to List and Sell Residential Real Estate Successfully seminars across the country since 1985.

So the S Factor stands for Staging, Service, Secret, System—and Schwarz, too. Agents like to say, "May the Schwarz be with you," which, of course, gives me lots of joy to hear.

So why is Staging still such a secret? I wish I knew. Few people—especially Real Estate Agents who *should* know what it is—really understand Staging. I invented Home Staging over 30 years ago as an interior designer who then went into real estate. I saw a problem with the way homes looked on the market as they came up for sale. So after many experiences, about which you will read and learn in this book, I came up with the ideas and techniques of my invention of Home Staging. In 1985, I became a professional speaker, author, and trainer, and, in addition to my writings, I have spoken about Staging with people for thousands and thousands of hours at large, anywhere I can share my message. Then in 1999, I started Stagedhomes.com as a part of my training company, Barb Incorporated. Through Stagedhomes.com, I began to train Real Estate Agents and Home Stagers to become Accredited Staging Professionals (ASPs). Agents attend a two-day course to become ASP Agents, learning my Real Estate Program. Home Stagers attend a three-day course to learn my Staging Business Model, becoming ASP Home Stagers, and they learn how to build and run a successful Home Staging business.

Staging is a part of the real estate industry, not the decorating industry. Real estate is the industry in which I invented Home Staging, and without sellers there would be no Home Staging. Without houses to sell and sellers who needed to sell them, I never would have come up with the idea in the first place. Staging, as you will see, is *not* decorating, and decorating is *not* Staging. Staging is my passion, and as much as I continue to educate people about Home Staging, there are still many myths and misunderstandings in the marketplace about it.

This book will teach you the *truth* about Staging and explain a proven program that works! Home Staging *works*

When the market is slow.
When the market is depressed.
When the market is hot.

When the market is not.
In every price range.
In every market area around the world.
With homes, condos, and even vacant land.

WHY STAGING WORKS

Staging works for one very simple reason. The vast majority of buyers can't envision themselves in a property when they look at it. I'm talking about 80 to 90 percent of the population and maybe more! It's just human nature! Buying property is an emotional decision for all but a few cutthroat investors, and this vast majority of buyers need *help* to see a house as a home they can live in. That help is Staging. *Please reread this paragraph and understand its significance.* This is the key to everything. It is why we Stage and why it works. It *is* the secret to success in real estate!

Why can't people envision themselves in most properties for sale? Again, the emotional reaction of normal human beings makes it very difficult for them to see through the way the majority of homes on the market are presented. Most homes have too much clutter in them, are dirty, have wrong colors, and/or are cold and vacant.

Buyers need to mentally move into a property for it to become their home. I can tell you as a former real estate broker that if buyers can't see themselves living in the space, they will walk away, even if it is the perfect place for them. I have seen buyers walk away from a great house hundreds, maybe thousands, of times. I have seen buyers who won't even get out of my car to look at a house because they are so turned off by the street appeal of the property. I can't tell you how many times I have seen buyers walk into a great house, take one look at the inside from the entryway, turn to me, and say, "Get me out of here!" They wouldn't even take a look because of the dirt or clutter!

These are the things that turn off buyers: clutter, a lack of cleanliness, bad colors, and cold emptiness.

Is the secret of Real Estate really that simple? *Yes*!

The trouble is that most people won't accept that fact, especially home sellers and unfortunately many Real Estate Agents who don't really understand the secret. If you are a homeowner reading this, you are probably saying to yourself, "Oh, this applies to other people, not me." Sorry! Even the Taj Mahal needs Staging. Agents who are reading this are probably saying, "Oh, I know what Staging is, and I tell my sellers to clean their house and put things away." Sorry! Most Agents don't really understand Staging, and, worse, even if they do know what to do, they are afraid to tell their sellers! Once you really understand the secret of Staging, there is only one question: *If you were going to sell a property in today's market, why in the world wouldn't you Stage it?!*

This book shares the simple truths and design basics that will turn any house into a desirable home that buyers can mentally move into and want to purchase. All you have to do is *do* it!

Can I prove statistically that Staging works? Absolutely! At Stagedhomes. com we collect information from our network of *Accredited Staging Professionals,* who are both professional Stagers or Real Estate Agents with the ASP designation. Over the years I have seen thousands of emails with wonderful success stories from Agents, Stagers, and homeowners. In a hot market, like the one we've had in most market areas for the last few years, Staged homes sell for more money. On average the sale price has been up to 20 percent higher or even more. There are countless examples of homes selling for 5, 10, even 20 percent or more above similar homes in the same neighborhood or area compared to homes that were not Staged.

STAGING IN A DOWN MARKET

I wrote *Staging to Sell: The Secret to Selling Homes in a Down Market* for today's kind of market, whether hot or not. When the market is hot and there are not so many houses for sale, Staging helps you sell homes for even more money. In a slow market, even in a down market, the market can be flooded with houses for sale. Staging gives you the edge in a market like that, too.

Let's say for an analogy that only 10 houses are for sale in a hot market. All 10 will sell, but the Staged Homes will sell for more money than the other houses, even though the market is hot. But in a down market, instead of 10 houses, 100 houses are for sale, and only 10 of the 100 houses will sell. The other 90 houses are used to sell the 10. Why and how? The 10 houses are sold because the buyer saw the other 90 homes that were not Staged and bought the Staged home instead.

You will hear me say many times that two things sell a home in any market, and this is of course true in a down market. One is price, and the other is Staging. So in a down market, when the prices of two homes are the same, the buyer will almost always purchase the Staged home over the non-Staged home. Wouldn't you? A Staged home is usually better cared for, and it is easier to visualize your furniture and possessions in than the cluttered non-Staged home. And in the down market, when the prices are the same for the same houses in the same neighborhood, you would buy the house that looks better than the others. And even in a down market you may still be willing to pay a bit more to get the house you want. If you don't believe me, just look at the pictures in this book and the real-life stories at the end of it.

Staging makes all the difference in the world, and I will prove that to you in this book in many, many ways. Selling is all about presentation in any market, and this is crucial in a down market more than ever. Staging gives you the advantage as the seller and as the Agent, and the Home Stager makes it all happen. That is why I invented the Home Staging industry, whose professionals make all the difference in the world. That is also true of real estate industry professionals, who need to work with ASP Real Estate Agents, and of Home Staging industry professionals, who need to work with ASP or ASPM Home Stagers, as well. *Staging to Sell: The Secret to Selling Homes in a Down Market* will show you what to do, how to do it, and how to sell your home or listing in any market. You will see not only how to sell in a poor market using these ideas, but also how to sell in a hot market for even more.

More recently, in a slowed market our statistics show that 95 percent of Staged homes *sell* on average in 35 days or less. Homes that aren't Staged on average take 187 days or more to sell, or they simply don't sell at all! If you want to *sell* a home in today's market it *must* be Staged.

This book and my program will make you money! I have made thousands and thousands of dollars for thousands and thousands of sellers, Agents, and Stagers. The program that I have developed through the years and that I am going to share with you in this book is tested and it works! It is a *proven* program. It is a program of great service and marketing. It works! It works in a hot market, *and* it works in a poor market! It works in a buyer's market and it works in a seller's market. It has been put to use successfully by hundreds of thousands of Real Estate Agents all across the United States and Canada in all types of markets and price ranges. It is a detailed program that brings success. You will see that this whole program is based entirely on the secrets of successful service.

WHAT THIS BOOK WILL DO FOR YOU!

I have written this book for you, *whether you are a seller, a Real Estate Agent, or a Home Stager!* I believe that this is the first book—ever—that has been written for all of you together: seller, Agent, and Stager. It is about time someone did it, and who could do it better than I, the creator of the Real Estate Listing and Selling Program and my Staging Secrets Program? I got to thinking one day, "We need a book that allows me to give my honest input to all parties on the listing end of real estate and have a dialog with them." So here it is. In this book sometimes I talk with you as the seller, sometimes I talk with you as the Agent, and sometimes I talk with you as the Home Stager.

Selling a home is a joint venture. We are all needed in the process: sellers, Agents, and Stagers. One without the other is not as effective. I have written this book to show how important each role is and how interdependent all the roles are. There is a reason for each of the roles, and I do not believe in keeping ideas from one group and sharing them with another. No, there is nothing to hide here at all. The seller needs to know what I share with an Agent to see what the Agent should be doing. As a Stager, you need to know both the seller's and the Agent's views so that you can work with both in a productive way. Agents, you need to understand Stagers and how they really can help you and the seller. Stagers, you need to know what Real Estate Agents should be doing to serve their clients and, if not, how you need to help them understand.

Because many sellers do not receive the services they deserve at times, I have written a Seller's Note at the beginning of each chapter. Sellers, pay close attention to these notes. The Seller's Note feature summarizes what I believe you should know about the chapter and what to expect of an Agent and a Stager. As a seller, you have the right to know what to expect and what Agents and Stagers should be doing to serve you. That is why I have added the Seller's Note feature. Also, Agents or Stagers, you will learn from these notes what sellers need to look for, and you will want to make sure that you fit the bill by providing what many other Agents or Stagers do not.

No one person can own the house, list the house, prepare it for sale, write the sale, do the mortgage, do the title insurance, inspect the property, appraise the house, and close the transaction. Even if one person could do all that, it would not be a good idea to try. We have specialists for a reason, and each specialist in real estate has a specific role and job to do. This is also true of the seller, the Agent, and the Stager.

Although the way the business of listing and selling real estate is done is constantly changing, one thing always remains the same: *The best looking houses at the right price sell much more quickly and for more money.* And the Real Estate Agents who provide the best service to clients invariably get the most business and sell the most houses. Even though we are now so computerized as houses are marketed on the Internet, agreements are faxed back and forth, and cell phones are a way of life, service and human communication can still be poor and bring many challenges our way. Service is more important than ever in the real estate industry!

Successful Agents are successful because they follow a program and constantly use it to provide good service. Most of the Agents who drop out of the business do not have or do not follow a program. Sellers get upset without great service and without proper communication from their Agents. And in slow markets, both the seller and the Agent can become very frustrated.

You are the key.

- If you are a seller, you hold the keys to decide whom you work with, how much you pay them, and what you should do to prepare your home for sale.
- If you are the Agent, you have a wonderful opportunity to use the services I share with you in this book and to be rewarded well for doing so.
- If you are a Home Stager, you are needed by both the seller and the Agent in today's market, and you too hold great keys as to how fast the house may sell and how much it may sell for, as you Stage the property for sale.

As the inventor of the Staging Industry and having devoted my whole life to it, I am told daily that the industry is literally changing the entire world of real estate in a very positive way. I want to help you change your life, too, by understanding and seeing the benefits of Home Staging as a seller, as an Agent, and as a Stager.*

---

*If you want to know how to build a Home Staging business, you need to read my *How to Build a Home Staging Business* book (Wiley). And if you want to know even more on Staging a home, then you need to also read my *Home Staging: The Winning Way to Sell Your Home for More Money* (Wiley).

In this book, I am going to put you to work, no matter what role you play in selling a home. I believe that too many people in the real estate industry are not prepared, whatever their role. Too many sellers do not know what to do as they bring their homes on the market for sale. Many people act out of the fear that they will not be able to do what they need to do. Many sellers do not know how to work with Agents or what to expect from them. Agents, in turn, are often not prepared enough to provide what sellers need today. Therefore, no matter which role you are in, I am going to ask you to become better prepared than ever before. This is going to mean exploring some new ideas and using new tools that will well serve you well.

I want to raise the level of awareness and the degree of use of Home Staging to sell homes in today's market and in any market. To sell a home for top dollar in any market, you must prepare it for sale. Selling is all about presentation, and presentation is Staging, and Staging is the name of the game. In a way, real estate can be like a game, and the winners are the owners of Staged homes. Don't gamble in any market by just "trying it," that is, coming on the market overpriced and not Staged. Today's market is *not* the market to try that. Selling in a down market means that you are priced at or better than the market *and* that your home or listing *is* Staged! The secret to selling homes in a down market *is* Staging!

As I have said all these many years in my real estate, Home Staging, and trainer/speaking careers: "The home becomes a house and the house becomes a product because that is where the money is!"

Selling a home for top dollar and Home Staging go hand in hand. One cannot happen without the other.

Now, let's get going to learn the secrets of the S Factor!

BARB SCHWARZ

ACKNOWLEDGMENTS

I want to acknowledge all of the Real Estate Agents and the Home Stagers who have taken my ASP courses and who have become ASPs!

You are the now and the future of Home Staging. I rely on you, through your daily work, to help me carry out my work and vision and mission.

As ASPs, you are the leaders of the industry. I thank you and admire you for becoming ASPs. I truly believe that something special in you saw the specialness in Home Staging and the magic and miracles that it creates.

I congratulate you and honor you and acknowledge you for who you are.

You are the key to the future.

B.S.

STAGING TO SELL

CHAPTER 1

GET SET, GO!

It begins with one single step.

BARB SCHWARZ

SELLER'S NOTE

In this chapter you will read about the importance of the Agent's or the Stager's sharing the truth with you. At first glance you may say, "Well, of course, people share the truth." In general, people do tell the truth. I am not suggesting at all that they don't. What I am saying is that people often don't want to hurt others' feelings, so it is much easier for an Agent—especially Agents—or Stagers not to tell you something that they think you don't want to hear. You the seller need to make it clear to these professionals that you want to hear the truth, not something that they think you want to hear. True professionals come from that place. The key is that they would rather walk away and not serve you rather than tell you something that isn't true. This is especially pertinent in pricing a home or in Staging a property. So read, take note, and make sure that you make it clear as a seller that you want to know what

(Continued)

is actually taking place in the market—and then be ready to hear it because sometimes it is as tough to hear the truth as it is to tell it. And selling a house for top dollar in any market takes speaking the truth about market conditions, appropriate pricing for the property, and what needs to be done to have the property Staged for sale so that it sells!

Whether you are a seller, a Real Estate Agent, or a Home Stager, I ask you, "Do you want to make more money in real estate?" I can hear your answer—a resounding "yes." That's good, because you are looking in the right place. This book can help you make a lot more money than you are now making—if you will trust the ideas and techniques that I will share with you and apply them. You may be saying, as a seller or an Agent or a Home Stager, "Is this a good market to sell in?" My response is always, "Yes, it is a good market to sell in because it is a good market to buy in!"

These techniques work, if you are you are willing to work. And they do take work. There is no other way. They take rolling up your sleeves and digging into projects and marketing to get the property sold. Sellers, as you do your homework to find the right Agent and Home Stager, you will earn the equity that is there for you. Just living in a certain city, state, or country does not mean that we automatically get to sell our house for more money. It takes time and work on your end as a seller, and it takes time and work by the Agent and Home Stager, too.

Agents, my complete philosophy is to serve the seller—first, last, and always! If you do that, the money will follow because, just as sellers receive their equity at closing, you will earn the commissions that you deserve.

Home Stagers, your role is crucial. You provide the creative third eyes that are vital to preparing homes for sale. Too many sellers are overworked and stressed by life today and selling a home at the same time, too; so as a Stager your role is to bring in your creative talent so that the house shows at its very best from the first viewing until the close of the sale.

Now, a lot of real estate salespeople in the real estate industry are doing things the same way they have always done them. For years, Agents have walked into properties, looked around, and said, "Well, gosh. I think you can get about $400,000 for this home. I'm sure I can sell it. Sign here and I'll put an ad in the Sunday paper." The sign goes in the yard, the ad shows up in the Sunday paper, and that's what they call marketing. Those days must come to an end.

When I got into the real estate business many years ago, I saw what I still see today in many cases: a lack of service. I saw that a lot of people did little to market properties they had listed. Unfortunately a lot of Agents in this business still continue to approach real estate that way. But the true professionals in real estate know that the secret to success in our business is to serve the seller—first, last, and always—and to be creative in doing so.

It is called marketing—marketing, marketing, marketing. And Staging is a very critical marketing tool, especially in today's difficult market!

THE RECIPE FOR A GREAT STAGER

Did you know that Real Estate Agents do not have a very good reputation? In a survey conducted by George Gallup Jr. and reported in the *Los Angeles Times*, people were asked how they viewed the honesty and ethical standards of those in various careers. The results of the survey indicated that out of 25 occupations across the country, Real Estate Agents rated among the bottom five. As far as the public is concerned, when it comes to honesty and ethics, we rank right down there with used car and insurance salespeople! This is amazing but true.

I believe a lack of service has cultivated that poor reputation. So the best way to wipe out that poor image is to give sellers and buyers more service than ever. Let me ask the Agents reading this book. Do you work long hours in this business? Of course, you do! Do the sellers you represent know everything you do for them? No, they do not because many times we simply don't tell them! Somehow we expect sellers to know many of the ins and outs of real estate, and, although most sellers *think* they know how the real estate market works, most really do not and need our guidance. My strong contention, throughout this book, is that we need to educate our sellers as to how we work and what we do for them. The key is to tell them up front. Sellers have the right to know, and you have the obligation as an Agent to tell them.

Good service gives any Agent the edge, and it gives the home owner and house a much better chance of selling, selling more quickly, and selling for more money. And the best service you can provide to a seller is to make sure that the seller's home is prepared for sale.

I believe good service is the difference between a good Agent and a poor one, between a successful Agent and a struggling one. If you want to be ahead of the game, serve your sellers professionally and efficiently. I have developed a simple but comprehensive three-step program that can help you do just that. It starts with service when you first meet your potential sellers and goes all the way until the sale closes. And your sellers deserve that kind of treatment.

Leadership is also important. As an Agent and as a Stager, you have to be in the role of leadership; that is what you are being paid to do: lead. To be able to serve your sellers to the best of your ability, you must have control of the situation, in much the same way you have to let your doctor have control over you in order to help you when you are sick. Now, when I talk about control, I'm not talking about being mean or rude; that's not what I mean at all. "Control" doesn't need to be a negative word. Control simply means managing the situation. Control is taking on the role of leadership. And sellers want to work with Agents and Stagers who know what they are doing and who show that they know what they are doing. For if the Agent and Stager cannot lead, then there is little chance that they will lead the buyer as the Agent or the Staging as a Stager. Leaders and persons who are passionate about what they do are the types you want on your side. I've never met a seller who wanted to work with a dud!

As a real estate professional, you can't do your best job or best work if you don't act as a leader. You need to price the home to sell in order to get top dollar for the seller. That means working to price the property right, making sure that the home is Staged to sell, and directing the marketing process so that the sale will go smoothly and quickly to bring the best price possible for the seller. That is why sellers hire you!

Control is necessary, but many of us lack it when we work with prospective sellers. We are afraid to control, mainly because we fear it will cost us the listing. We assume our potential sellers will react negatively and that we might therefore lose a listing. I know. I learned all this the hard way.

WHAT STAGING CAN DO FOR YOU!

Experience is the best teacher. There is therefore a lesson to be learned behind everything I'm going to share with you in this book. Those lessons have come from mistakes that I have made. Actually, I don't believe there is any such thing as a failure. Rather, I have learned from the mistakes I have made, and so I call them "experiences." I have worked hard to correct my mistakes and to put what I have learned from them to work in my business. Some of the experiences I am going to share with you come from the times I didn't do so well. At such times, I would say to myself, "I'm not going to let that happen again. I fell flat on my face." I learned it all the hard way most of the time, and yet the key was to persevere and to keep on going. The key was to say to myself, "What went well in this experience, what will I do differently next time, and how will I do it?" Specifically, I had to tune into the how and to keep at it until I came up with the ways that allowed me to serve sellers better and be more successful for them and with them. In sharing this information with you, I want to save you from those poor experiences, whether you are a seller, an Agent, or a Home Stager.

I am going to show you the ideas and techniques that I have developed over a long period. They are ideas that work, ideas that can save you a lot of learning time, and ideas that can definitely make you more money!

This book will teach you ways you can work and get the property sold and to do so in a way that the house should sell more quickly and/or for more money, no matter what the market is doing. And that should make you more money in any role you choose:

1. **Addressing objections before they come up.** If we head off an objection before it comes up, we're not going to face an objection. If we put the seller's mind to rest before the objections ever come up, then we are not going to have to deal with them! I do not believe that people have objections anyway; they have concerns. Treating objections as concerns places the professional and the seller in a more positive place, instead of a state of fear of—"Oh god, what will they bring up next?" Concerns it is, not objections. Say the two words yourself, and see which feels better to you depending on which role you are in.

2. **As professionals, developing your own *Career Book* and *Marketing Portfolio*.** These tools are priceless for Agents and Stagers when it comes to creating credibility, educating your seller, and answering concerns long before they are expressed. As a seller, you want and need to see what the Agent and Stager are going to do for you and what they bring to the table.

3. **Sharing many of my phrases or sayings that are absolutely dynamite in defusing concerns before they come up.** My Staging sayings have built an industry; I am told so all the time.

4. **Getting the seller to prepare the home for sale, that is, to get it Staged.** This can be a tough one for many Agents. It is important that sellers know that a lot of Agents don't know what to say or how to say

it because they are afraid they are going to hurt someone's feelings. Many Agents don't know what to tell sellers to get their property ready to sell. My contention is that when Agents list property, their *job* is to say, "Here is what we need to do, Mr. and Mrs. Seller, to get your property ready to sell." We are talking about marketing probably the most important product in your life: your home. Sellers look to Agents for guidance as to how to do that. I strongly believe that teaching the seller the benefits of Staging is crucial! The Agent's job is to teach sellers why they should Stage, and the Stager's job is to Stage the property. Stagers should always be part of the selling process. Remember, even used car dealers Stage their merchandise. The key is to teach the sellers why Staging is important and then get the house Staged to sell it. Don't worry: Whichever role you are in, by the time you finish this book you will know how to Stage a property inside and out!

5. **Pricing the property correctly.** Two things sell a home: Staging and price. Staging, I believe, is the greater of the two factors. However, a property that looks attractive also has to be priced right. If it is priced way, way too high for the price range of the neighborhood, how good it looks may not matter. Pricing in this market is no different than pricing in any market. People think that you price the property differently depending on whether the market is slow or fast. No, you price it in the same way; that is, you price it in the context of the surrounding market. Value is value, but it is not the appraised value or the seller's perceived value. It is the *market value*, the price that will sell the house in the current market. Every property will sell when it reaches the right price for the market it is in, and Staging helps immensely by presenting the property at its best. Although pricing is crucial, price the property according to the market value *and* in consideration of its being Staged. (I have seen homes sell for tens of thousands more than the neighbors'.) However, be aware that traditionally there still is a ceiling for each neighborhood. We have to have price and Staging working in balance for the current market. So, I have come up with some definite techniques and tools that will help you get that property priced right.

6. **Marketing the property to get it sold!** We can go through all the other goals, but if we don't do the marketing we should do, we may not get it sold. You can have the greatest house in the world, but if no one knows about it, then what good is it? One of my goals in this book is to give you a total marketing package, combining the strength of my many marketing techniques. And marketing in a slow market requires

some extra marketing ideas—not the same old put-the-sign-in-the-yard-and-sell-the-house routine. I don't believe in that approach anyway. It takes way more than that in a slow market, and sellers deserve more marketing than that even in a hot market.

An Agent once complained to me in a slow market that Agents were not even coming to her broker's open house; I recommended doing things that *would* get them there! I said to hire a belly dancer if she needed to—just get the Agents to her broker's open house. She said, "Oh, you must be kidding!" I said, "No, I am *not* kidding. I have done that myself, and that alone brought Agents to the house just to see the dancer. It worked, too, because one of the Agents who came later came back with buyers in hand and sold the house!" In slower markets creativity has to be the playing card used the most to get Agents and buyers there. As long as it is legal, moral, and ethical, be creative and think of ideas that will bring Agents and buyers to the house. Of course, have the house Staged. I assure you that the belly dancer house was Staged to the hilt, and the gimmick worked because the house *was* Staged. Belly dancer or not, if it had not been Staged, the Agents might have come to see the dancer, but the house would not have sold because it was a slow market and the Staging combined with the marketing got the house sold!

A LITTLE BIT ABOUT MYSELF

Now, before we go on, I would like to tell you a little about my background. After all, we are going to have a special relationship as you read my book, and I think it is important that you know a little bit about where I came from and my background. After I graduated from high school in Kansas, which is where I grew up, my family moved to Seattle, Washington. I earned a degree in education, with a major in music and a minor in design from the University of Washington, and went on to teach elementary school in the Bellevue, Washington, public school system.

What does all that have to do with real estate and listing residential property? More than you might think. Even though we don't usually associate teaching with real estate, a lot of the techniques and ideas that I am going to share with you in this book are adapted from skills I developed during my teaching days. When I left teaching, I ran my own interior design business. That was my minor in college. For about five years

I worked with single-family home owners, helping them design and decorate their homes. I also worked with builders and owners of commercial and multifamily housing. When we get to the section in this book on ways to improve the condition of a property, please don't say, "Well, Barb can do that because she has a design background." Actually, the things I am going to share with you have nothing to do with design. Design or decorating is *not* Staging. I will show you how to create more space and less clutter so that the buyers can mentally move into a potential home when they first see it.

After several years in design, the wonderful world of real estate came along for me. One day I happened to be calling on a real estate broker, and he said to me, "Why aren't you in real estate?" All I could say to him was, "Gosh, I love homes. I used to hold open houses for builders in Kansas when I was in high school. I've thought about getting into real estate but I've never done anything about it." He looked me square in the eye and said. "It sounds to me like you are procrastinating." When he said that, his words hit me like the proverbial ton of bricks! I headed out the door and didn't look back. I applied for my license, passed the test, started in this fantastic business, and have loved it ever since. It was one of those moments that can change your life forever, and that moment changed mine.

During my first 18 months in real estate—and this may shock you— I didn't get one of my listings sold. Not one! All the listings I had were overpriced and did not look very good. After a while I started to realize that the real money makers in the business were listing Agents and that if I were to become successful in the listing game I had to come up with a better way to get my listings priced right and prepared for sale to come on the market. I also really enjoyed working with sellers. I decided one of the reasons I enjoyed working with them was that they put their names on the dotted line. They made commitments to me, and they made them in writing. I knew if I worked hard, they were going to stick with me, and I, for sure, was going to stick with them!

Now, you may say to yourself, "This woman couldn't sell her own listings, how does she plan to tell me how to list and sell the property?" Remember what I said earlier: You are going to benefit from my mistakes. And I made a lot of mistakes in that first year and a half. I spent a lot of time hitting my head against the wall and saying to myself, "There's got to be a better way." What I am telling you is that I developed this program in the streets, that is, working with sellers. No matter what happened—or didn't happen—I was responsible to my sellers. I thought, "Hey, Barb, you haven't been very honest with these people. You didn't lie to them, but you also didn't tell them the truth. You listed at what they wanted for a price instead of at the price that would get the house sold in the current market." So the sellers' houses just stood there waiting, and as I know and say now, "Longevity on the market means one thing: reduction in price."

I also thought, "You didn't tell them what you thought they should do to prepare their house for sale. You didn't want to hurt their feelings. You were afraid you wouldn't get the listing." If you are an Agent or a Stager, does any of this sound familiar to you? So, I made a commitment to myself, to my sellers, and to all the people who would be my future sellers, which I have stuck by all these years: No matter what, I am going to tell all my sellers the truth.

You need to be honest. Whether you are a Stager or an Agent, you need to tell sellers the truth. As I said to my sellers as an Agent, "There are Agents out there who will tell you what they think you want to hear, and I really believe in sharing the truth that you deserve to know." You don't have to take a listing. As a Stager you don't have to take the Staging either. No matter what, don't be afraid to be honest with your sellers. Sellers will appreciate your honesty when you point out to them that you are being honest for their own sake.

So I started to be truly honest with people. Guess what happened? I came up with the idea of Home Staging based on my experiences in the theater productions I had been in. I began to appreciate that:

- Just as we set the Stage for each act in each play and musical, so, because each home is different and each room is different, we need to set the Stage for the buyers looking for their future home.
- The seller is the producer, the other Agents are the critics, the buyers are the audience, and I am the director.

It worked! Little did I know that I had invented an industry and would be now writing this book for you many, many years later. At that point I started to get my listings priced right and prepared for sale, coming up with the ideas I called Staging, and the houses sold! My sellers started to get their equities. With each listing I came up with even more effective techniques!

These same techniques are going to make you more money, and they are going to make your role as a seller easier or your career as a Real Estate Agent or Stager more enjoyable. Everything you learn in this book you can apply to your own business and life. People come up to me during my seminars and tell me how easily they have been able to work my program into their own careers. They say to me, "It works!" And it can work for you too.

AND NOW ON WITH THE SHOW

I want you to enjoy this book and to learn things you can use. But there is something else I ask you to do.

I am going to ask you to make some commitments and then hold yourself accountable. Commitment and accountability bring results. Make the commitment, hold yourself accountable, take the steps of action to bring you what you want, and get results. There is no way that it won't happen.

Have a positive attitude in all that you do, and the ideas I share with you here will work. You will also be making a difference by doing so in your life and in the lives of others.

Give it a go. Now, on with the show!

CHAPTER 2

THE LET-ME-TELL-YOU-HOW-I-WORK APPROACH

People don't know what you don't tell them.

BARB SCHWARZ

SELLER'S NOTE

As a seller, you want to know what people will do for you ahead of time! As simple as that sounds, many Agents do not tell people what they will do to sell their house. It is easy for Agents just to have sellers sign the listing papers without presenting a marketing program. First, you want to hear what is explained in this chapter from an Agent or Stager. If you don't hear it up front, good luck hearing it later on. So this chapter is about the right and the importance of your hearing what the Agent and Stager will do for you and for you to be educated in the beginning by the people who serve you. Without this initial communication, you can bet that there will be little later on. Both the Agent and the Stager should be sharing with you what steps they will do to serve you. From that point, seeing it in writing is the next step. But first let's talk about their educating you verbally; then we will get to the in-writing part in another chapter.

IN THIS CHAPTER

You will learn:

1. What the *let-me-tell-you-how-I-work* approach is, how to use it, and why it works.
2. How to use this method to find prospects.
3. That control equals education, that is, education will give you control!
4. My exclusive listing program, which you should do for all sellers!
5. How and why to develop your own professional policies.

People often ask me, "Barb, where do you find business? Where do you go to find prospects and the people who want to sell?" Well, the answer is easy. Prospects are everywhere! I'm serious. With the right approach, prospects will find you. They will practically fall out of the trees and hit you on the head if you know how to shake the branches a little.

I have a special technique for finding prospects everywhere I go. I call it the *let-me-tell-you-how-I-work* approach. It really is as simple as it sounds, and it really does work! You just tell people who you are, what you do, and how you do it. It is amazing how few people actually know what real estate Agents and Stagers do. Because most Agents don't tell clients what they do, it is even more important for you to learn and use the program I'm about to give you. Whether you are an Agent or a Stager, you must let people know who you are, what you do, and how you and your service are so different from all the rest. The more people you tell, the more business you will have. Remember, the public put real estate salespeople in the bottom five of trustworthy professions. By educating people about who you are and what you do, you open yourself up to an almost endless source of prospects by showing how professional you are. By taking just a few minutes to give them an overview of your service, people say, "Wow, you do all that?" They will tell other people about you, and they will remember you when they are ready to sell or buy their homes. And by telling this to everyone everywhere, you show that your sellers will also benefit because you will attract more buyers for your sellers' homes. So tell people up front, "Let me tell you how I work."

I use that exact phrase when I am on a call, meeting someone in an open house, or meeting anyone, anywhere, any time. If you don't share with your future clients up front how you work, all their assumptions about you will be based on the experience they had with the last person they worked with, and that may not have been a good experience. Don't take the chance of letting your reputation be based on that encounter.

Most Real Estate Agents or Stagers introduce themselves by saying their name and the name of their company: "Hello, my name is Barb Schwarz, and I work for Barb Schwarz Real Estate." From now on, please don't stop there. Instead, say your name, the name of your company, and follow that immediately with, "Let me tell you how I work." Then give them a quick oral outline of the services you'll be performing for them.

In fact you need a 60-second commercial that you have written and know by heart. You need to know it inside and out and be able to say it at a moment's notice. In fact you need a 30-second version, a 60-second version, and a 2-minute version, and you need to know them all so that you can share your important points in those different time frames as they arise. Sellers, when you talk with an Agent or Stager, make sure that you are hearing this commercial. If professionals don't tell you in the beginning how they work, they may never ever tell you in the end. That would not be a good thing at all. As a seller you want to hear, "Let me tell you how I work" from the Agent *and* the Stager you are talking to and may work with!

TIME UP FRONT VERSUS TROUBLE LATER

Some Agents actually believe it is a waste of time to educate sellers up front as they list homes. Yet investing more time with your sellers initially can save you a lot of problems later; your seller deserves to know. And as a seller you deserve and need to know. The time invested in up-front communication gives you the opportunity to educate your sellers about how you work and why they must trust you as a professional. This is crucial for working together, for setting the correct price, for Staging the home, and for marketing the property to get it sold. By getting to know each other you and the seller can learn whether you can work together as a team. Many benefits will show up, both early and later, if you invest more time up front with the sellers. For both of you, it is so much better to invest time up front than having to deal with problems later.

I know that, when you educate sellers up front, they will feel that they can give you the reins of leadership to get the job done. Remember, I've proved this fact by learning the hard way. In any relationship, one of the parties usually needs to have control to make the relationship work. This is true in a doctor–patient relationship, accountant–client relationship,

Stager–client relationship, and the Real Estate Agent–seller relationship. Remembering this phrase (let me tell you how I work) will help you with all aspects of your career. Also memorize one of my favorite sayings:

Education = Control and Control = Education.

Leadership is key, and the way to leadership is by educating the other party about the steps to be taken.

I'm talking about educating your sellers and doing it up front! If later in the listing process you have trouble getting the sellers to price the property right or getting them to Stage the home, either they really don't want to sell or you didn't educate them enough up front.

The let-me-tell-you-how-I-work approach is the key to education, and it can be done in a brief professional way. You can say it in any number of ways that are comfortable for you, such as, "I'd like to take a minute to explain how I list and sell homes," or "I work differently from a lot of other real estate Agents—let me briefly explain all of the services that I provide all my sellers." You can say it many different ways, but let-me-tell-you-how-I-work puts you ahead of most other Agents because you take the time to educate your sellers. Education equals control, and control will give you more power to help more sellers. It works! Do it!

As an Agent or as a Stager, I have at least two separate visits with my sellers, and I recommend you do the same. Now you may be saying, "Two visits as you list or Stage their property!" From my years of experience, it takes two visits (and in certain instances, even three) to get the job done and to do it right! There can be a lot of problems later if you go to the property only once, walk through the house, cross your arms, and say, "You have a nice home. I think we can get, oh, $425,000 for it. I'll put an ad in the paper. Sign here."

People deserve more than that. This is the old way of real estate that goes on every single day all over North America. How sad that is. How can you expect to establish a relationship, build rapport, share about your services, and make judgments right on the spot about crucial things such as pricing and Staging all in the few minutes that you see the house for the first time? I don't care how hot or slow your market might be, things change very quickly, and people deserve more attention. This quick approach also does not give you enough time to educate your sellers properly about you, about pricing or Staging, or about marketing as an Agent or as a Stager.

Remember, many of the points I am teaching are based on experiences from the beginning of my career, experiences that did not go well. When I first started listing homes, I tried to crowd everything into one visit, but I wasn't pricing each property correctly. I wasn't putting the property in proper showing condition. I was not educating the sellers and letting them know how I worked. And I also had a lot of problems. I soon discovered that one of the best ways to avoid the problems was to visit each of my sellers at least two times.

I therefore *invest* a lot of time up front with my sellers. The more time you invest with them in the beginning, the fewer problems you will have down the road. You will save yourself time in the end by investing more time in the beginning! I strongly recommend that you, as an Agent or Stager, *invest* time in the beginning, and you will not have to *spend* a lot of time later solving problems or explaining why or what you are doing. As a seller, you will benefit greatly by working with Agents and a Stagers who invest time in the beginning, sharing with you how they work and what they will do for you. It makes sense in any service-orientated business and for sure in the real estate industry, where it is needed so very, very much!

THREE STEPS TO LISTING OR STAGING REAL ESTATE SUCCESSFULLY: LET ME TELL YOU HOW I WORK

Here are the detailed components of the steps of service that I recommend you carry out when you work with a seller.

Step 1

Step 1 is the same for an Agent or Stager:

- Meet the sellers.
- See the house.
- Take detailed notes.
- Take photographs.
- Look inside and outside.
- Leave your *Career Book*®* with the seller.
- Leave my "How to Price Your Home to Sell for Top Dollar!" DVD with the sellers.
- Set the appointment for Step 2.
- Go back to your office and prepare your report/presentation for Step 2.

*The Career Book® is a Federally Registered Trademark of stagehomes.com.

Step 1 Details

This step is the same for both Agents and Stagers. Both professionals need to perform this step. And some Agents and Stagers do it together at the same time, as they team up to serve the seller in a great way.

Step 1 is for you as an Agent or Stager to meet the sellers and inspect the property. You need to see what kind of property you will be selling or Staging. You need to check comparables for that area after you see the home and before you return for Step 2. You have to see and check the condition and location as well. Just as important, you have to see whether you want to work with the sellers and whether they seem to want to work with you. Do they really want to sell? Are they willing to listen to you and your recommendations? These kinds of questions are very important! If the sellers aren't motivated to sell, don't continue to invest time with them. You don't have to work with anyone and everyone. It really is OK and important to say *no* sometimes. Experienced Agents or Stagers will tell you that they've had clients they wish they'd never worked with. In most cases they probably knew that in their gut from the first time they met, but they went ahead and worked with them anyway. Now is the time to bow out gracefully if things don't feel right. And the same is true from the seller's point of view as well.

Step 1 is also an important time for you to build rapport. Remember, all sellers are looking for someone they can like and trust, so invest time to build your credibility with them. Have them show you through their home, visit and ask questions, look for common ground, and take the time to present a more detailed version of your let-me-tell-you-how-I-work information so that they understand what you are going to do next and what they are going to do next. You'll also want to leave your *Career Book* (discussed in Chapter 4), so that sellers will find out all about you! This will help build more of a liking and a trust relationship for you in a powerful way that nothing else can.

Remember, this first step is something that both Agent and Stager should do. Each of you needs to follow the same step. Most of the time you will do so separately unless you do team up together to see the house together the first time.

Step 2

The Agent's Report

Step 2 for you as an Agent is for your listing presentation, which I would like you to call the "Exclusive Detailed Report." Why? Think about the words "listing presentation." Those words, which we have used in the real estate industry for years, have landed us among the bottom five in professional ratings. I have received greater respect from sellers over the years by using the words "Your Exclusive Detailed Report" when referring to their listing presentation. Many of the sellers you sit down with have to prepare reports for their employers, and they seem to appreciate us more if we refer to our presentation as a report.

And a report it better be. After you have met the sellers and seen their property (Step 1), you need to put together a detailed two-part report.

1. Part 1 describes how you are going to market and sell the property.
2. Part 2 is your pricing analysis.

I will explain both aspects of the Exclusive Detailed Report in greater depth in this book. If you do your Reports as I suggest, I know your potential sellers will say what sellers have said to me and to other Agents who use my program: "That was the best presentation I've ever seen! Now, I know what Agents should do. Thank you for educating us, and we want to list with you!"

The Stager's Report and Consultation

ASP Stagers must do the same! For you as an ASP Stager, Step 2 is for you to present your Home Staging Proposal, which explains what you will do for the Seller, or your Staging Consultation, which describes what the seller needs to do to Stage the home. Your Proposal should contain at least 7 to 15 pages of what you propose to do to Stage the property. The second part presents what the investment will be for the seller or Agent to make in Staging the property. I will explain these in more detail later in the book.

I believe that we will see more and more Agents pay for the Staging service and for the services of Stagers in the future. That trend is inevitable because Staging is a marketing tool. Why should Agents pay to run ads on messy houses when having the house Staged will sell the house? Paying for the Staging of the house gives Agents a big marketing edge because the seller will want to list with Agents who provide this service for them. And, because Agents seem to have to defend commissions all the time, this is a real opportunity to make a difference and to stand out in their marketplace to get the business. Providing an ASP Stager to do the Staging and paying for the service gives the Agent a much greater opportunity to receive the full commission that they want. Also, running ads on messy houses can in the end be even more expensive than paying to have the house Staged.

If you are doing a Home Staging Consultation for the seller as an ASP Stager, your report will be longer because the seller needs a detailed list of what to do in every room in the house to get the Staging done. Usually, an Exclusive Detailed Report runs from 35 to 55 pages in length, including the preceding pieces of the report. The consultation is longer because you must list everything that the Seller needs to do to Stage the house and you are writing up what needs to be done.

In a Home Staging Proposal, you do not need to list everything sellers need to do because they aren't going to be doing the Staging work; you're doing the creative service of Staging the home. And I want you paid for your creativity, not for decorating the house. You don't have to sell the seller more furniture, drapes, or other new items.

Sellers, I want you to pay our ASP Stagers for their creativity, not for selling you things. You will win in the end every time by having your house Staged instead of decorated! Pay your ASP Stager to be creative with what you have in your home now if you currently live in the house. Or, if your home is vacant, pay the ASP Stager to build the settings in each room with rented furniture or furniture from rental companies the Stager works with, in order to set the scene, and you won't have to buy anything. This is what a Home Staging Proposal or Home Staging Consultation is made up of. And what goes into the consultation or proposal depends on *who* is doing the Staging: the ASP Stager or the seller with the Stager's recommendations.

Step 3

Step 3 is the same for both the Agent and the Stager:

- Paperwork.
- Showing sellers my Staging DVD, "How to Stage Your Home to Sell for Top Dollar," which totally commits them to the process.
- Setting the deadline to get the Staging done by the ASP Stager and/or the seller.

Step 3 is actually doing the paperwork to work together as a team: either seller and Agent or seller and Stager. Then comes confirming the next steps for Staging the property. If the seller is going to do the Staging work, then the Agent needs to have the Stager come through and prepare a Home Staging Consultation for the seller to know what to do. This takes the Agent off the hot seat of being the bad guy because the Stager does the written consultation. If the ASP Stager is going to actually do the Staging work, which is usually the case, then the Agent needs to prepare a short list of what the seller needs to do to prepare for the Stager's coming, such as painting a room or taking large items to storage, that the Stager has asked to be done ahead of time.

Staging the home is crucial! In a buyer's market, Staging the house can help the property sell quicker. In a fast seller's market, it can help the house sell for more money. That means more dollars for the seller at closing and more commission for the Agent in any kind of market. Stage your listings so that they sell and sell for *top* dollar! As the person who has invented Staging and who's taught the concept in seminars all over North America to over one million Real Estate Agents, I will explain Staging in great detail later in this book. Also, as the inventor of the Home Staging industry, business, and career for those who want to Stage full-time for a living as a professional Stager, I will explain how to work with Accredited Staging Professional (ASP) Stagers later in the book.

So you can see that each step has a valid reason. Sometimes Agents or Stagers will say to me, "Barb, can't you combine steps two and three?" Well, of course you can. I didn't say "days", I said "steps"! If your sellers are ready to work with you, then everyone just needs to sign on the dotted line, and you are ready to go to work together . . . as a team!

But even if you combine the two steps, it takes time to do it right. So invest the necessary time to do it right. Staging could be the same day, the next day, or a week later. Presenting a professional Report like the one I will outline for you in later chapters is totally worth the time it may take. The paperwork can be signed then or as soon as you all are ready to go to work together. Then you only need to have the house Staged!

Service is the name of the game. It always has been, and I truly believe it always will be. Service is what you want when you go to your favorite department store or when you take your car in for repair. If you do not get service, you will start to shop somewhere else, won't you? Sellers are the same. Wouldn't you feel that way, too. They want and expect service, and if they don't get it, they will list or Stage with someone else. So, no matter how many trips or visits or steps you take to list or Stage a home, remember that service is the key. As the seller, the Agent, or the Stager, you can take the results to the bank.

I really believe in certain guidelines concerning this three-step program. Does the company you work for have guidelines or policies? Of course they do. Do they usually break them? I hope the answer is no. I believe that as individual businesspeople, we all need to have our own unbreakable guidelines as well. They are in place to give you added strength as the professional you are.

PROFESSIONAL POLICIES

Say these two words out loud right now: "professional policies." I want you to develop professional policies of your own, detailing how you will and will not work. Then I want you to stick to them. I owe it to you to explain some of my professional policies concerning the three-step program. They give extra strength to the program, to you, and to me as a professional. You can decide whether and how you will adapt them to your career, and I'm sure you will add some of your own as well. Some of my professional policies follow.

Policies for Step 1

One of my policies is never to see a property without at least one seller there to show it to me. No one knows the property like the sellers, and I might miss something if I just looked at it by myself.

Another reason for this policy is this: Not only do I want the sellers to show the property to me, but I also want to show it to the sellers. Let me explain. When you see the property for the first time, you see things that the sellers do not because they have lived there for so long. You and I see the property as a buyer will, and we need to point out some of these things to the sellers. An example might be, "Oh. Mr. Seller, tell me about that"—as we look up at a big spot on the ceiling. Many times the seller will look up, take a step back, and say, "Gosh, I didn't even know that was there." If the sellers are not there to show you the house so that you can also show it to them, you cannot do this. This also helps the sellers to start thinking about how important Staging their home will be.

Make it a policy to have at least one seller at the property the first time you see it.

There is one exception, but not really. That is when the house is vacant, and the sellers live out of town. If this is the case, take pictures or even a video, and send it to the seller, pointing out things that need to be done. Do this before you ever present your listing presentation, the Exclusive Detailed Report. This is a service ASP Stagers will gladly do for you as an Agent. Otherwise, it is tempting for sellers to think they live in an irreplaceable castle.

Remember, if the sellers tell you on the phone that they both work and the key is under the doormat, and they suggest you go look at the house by yourself, you want to share your policy with them. Use the let-me-tell-you-how-I-work approach in a nice way. "Mr. Seller, I understand what you are saying; however, no one knows your home like you do, and I have made this one of my professional policies to have one of you there to show your home to me." Stick to your policies. They work for you, and they work for your sellers. ASP Stagers, you can have the Agent show you the house, but because the client owns the house and not the Agent, it is also really, really important to meet the sellers at the house, too.

Policies for Step 2

One of my strongest policies, which I have never broken, is the following. If you sit down with just one of the owners in your presentation, then the other owner cannot know what you do and can innocently sabotage your efforts. You may not get the listing. You may not get the Staging. How do you educate someone who isn't there? You can't do it. I can't do it. No one can do it. If three people from a bank are on a committee and will pick the listing Agent to list the house or the ASP Stager to Stage the house, please do not sit down with just one member because the other committee members will not know what you do.

If you arrive at the sellers' home and the wife informs you that her husband just called to say he'd be late and to go ahead and give your presentation to her, what are you going to say? Acknowledge that he was trying to save you time, but that you have made it a professional policy to sit down with both of them as owners. "It is just too important, so let's reschedule," tell her and then reschedule. Either one of them is legally too important to miss it. Tell her that. It is true and it works. Remember, doctors have policies, and if they break them, the patient could die. Accountants have policies, and if they break them, the accountant could have big problems. We should have professional policies as well. So make yours and stick to them.

What if you are working with a family and the husband, let's say, has already moved to the new city to start working? I suggest giving the report to the wife in person and sending another original to the husband. Set a time to call him on the phone to go over it in detail; that way they are both educated about your marketing or Staging plan and about the pricing of the home or project. If you don't do that, the wife knows the program and the husband doesn't. The husband is in another city wondering what in the world you are doing to sell or Stage his house. This is because he wasn't educated, and without that education he will usually get out of control or upset because he will not know what you are doing—you didn't tell him. Remember,

Leadership = Education.

When you give your presentations, please take the proper amount of time. No one can educate a seller in 15 minutes. It takes time! Invest time up front and you won't have to spend time answering concerns from the sellers down the road. Any Agent who is giving sellers only 15-minute marketing presentations is not doing the job. Why? Because marketing today means more that just placing an ad and putting up the sign in the front yard. My presentations run, on the average, one and a half to two hours. I hope yours do, too. Sellers love being educated, and it is another reason you will walk out with the listing—because you took the time.

One more policy of mine, regarding my presentations as an Agent, is to always present my marketing plan to the sellers before I present pricing. If you present the pricing portion of your report first, their brains are on only one thing: the cost. They will never hear your marketing plan for their home. Present the marketing part of your report first, explaining that, because they will be paying you for marketing and selling their home, they owe it to themselves to know everything up front. Motivated sellers care. They will listen. Then after that, and only after that, go on to the pricing of the home. Make it a policy and stick to it.

For an ASP Stager, the ideas are the same. Make sure that you present your Home Staging Proposal from the front to the back. Don't skip parts. Don't just jump to the pricing. That is not a good idea. Educate, educate, educate sellers. They deserve it, and education will serve you and the seller well.

A quality Home Staging Proposal has parts to it, too. Page by page you need to educate the seller about the benefits of Home Staging. That includes statistics, graphs, before-and-after photos, letters, testimonials, and then the pricing page of the project. Stick to your policy of going through your Proposal in the way you put it together. Don't skip parts, and sellers will understand so much more what you are sharing with them and most importantly *why* they should Stage their homes with you! Stick to your policies because they work!

Policies for Step 3

I learned this policy the hard way. Do not Stage a home in total or in part until you have the sellers' names on the dotted line. Why would you Stage someone's home without their name on the dotted line? We may think that sellers will list with us if we give them tips or that they will Stage with us if we show them a few things. I know, because I made this mistake, once, and once was enough. I had called on an owner and, as we were looking through her home and I said, "I know some things we could do right now that might help you sell your home." I was thinking this might impress her and give me the edge. Remember, I had just met her and I hadn't even prepared or presented my presentation. She was eager to hear and learn everything I had to share about preparing her home for sale. So I spent (I choose the word "spent" on purpose) about two hours with her making changes throughout the home. About six o'clock she informed me they were going to have dinner guests at seven and could I come back the next day with my report. I said, "Well, ah, of course." I came back the next day and learned that they had actually sold the house overnight to the people who had come to dinner. Do you know who those people were? They were their very best friends. They said, "We've been in your home many times, but it has never looked so good. We'll buy it. It has more room than we realized."

I learned that lesson the hard way. Never Stage a home until a signature is on the bottom line. Staging works! It works over and over again. Staging is *the* S Factor! It is a secret whose power many people do not know about. It brings extra power and strength to your sellers and their properties. So that process needs to happen as you work together as a team with the seller. It is not fair to you any other way, and it is not fair for an Agent to list sellers' homes and not tell them about Home Staging! Agents need sellers' commitments in writing, and sellers need yours as well. A successful listing is all about commitment and teamwork. And this kind of commitment comes as sellers and Agents and Stagers make the commitment in writing. This is one of my policies, and it needs to be yours as well.

A great marketing idea for you as an Agent is that you tell your sellers that Staging their home with them is an extra, additional service that you provide to them at no extra cost. Then you bring the ASP Stager in to get the Staging done! This can help the seller get the most amount of equity in the shortest amount of time, and you as the Agent will win all the way around with a Staged listing that sold. But, again, no Staging gets done until the seller has signed the form.

By the way, something great did come out of the bad experience I had with that For Sale by Owner. It is one of my best sayings, and I hope you'll learn it and use it too. It is part of what I share with sellers when we Stage their homes to make sure that they will do it and keep it looking good.

Buyers know only what they see, not the way it's going to be.

That saying works! As a seller you need to know it, and as an Agent or ASP Stager you need to use it. This works when sellers aren't sure whether they should replace the carpet. It works for rooms that need painting. It works for homes that are very dirty or very cluttered. As you can see, in every unpleasant experience there is so much we can learn. I would probably have not developed that saying if I had not had that unpleasant experience and had seen firsthand that even best friends can't imagine what a house will look like after it's Staged.

●   ●   ●

Policies work. They are important. They will help you have more fun in this business. They will help you be better organized. And they will help sellers understand more of what you do and why. Always remember that sellers have policies in their line of work as well. They can't break them, because if they did, they probably would find themselves out of a job or career. Share your policies with your sellers. Ask for their respect for your policies, which benefit them as well. Let them know, "This is the way I work."

Learn to say to people, "This is one of my professional policies. This is the way that I work. And it really is to serve you."

CHAPTER 3

STEP 1: MEETING TOGETHER THE FIRST TIME

Teamwork is the key to success.

BARB SCHWARZ

SELLER'S NOTE

What do you think Agents or Stagers should do the first time they come to your home? In this chapter I go through this meeting in detail. Room by room, and inside and outside the house, the attention to detail is crucial. Would you want to work with a person who didn't write down what you said about your home? I think not. The visiting professionals should be taking photos of your home, and, as you show them your home, they can in a way show your home to you, too. This is relationship selling. This is about becoming a team and finding those who you feel you want to have on your team! Read this chapter with your third eye peeled because it will help you learn what to look for when an Agent or Stager comes to see you the first time.

IN THIS CHAPTER

You will learn:

1. How to build teamwork and rapport with your sellers.
2. The four key things you should be doing as you go through the property.
3. A detailed explanation of what to do and the objectives to have the first time you meet the sellers at their home (Step 1).

RAPPORT BUILDING WITH SELLERS

When you go to meet the sellers and view their home the first time, strive to arrive just a little bit early. As you drive into the neighborhood, you should be looking around the block. You have to spot things. Look for the homes that look terrific. Look for the homes that look like they have problems. You want to see where your sellers' house is in relation to these. Is their home next to the house that has a boat, a recreational vehicle, and six motorcycles parked in the front yard and weeds up to the windows? If it is, that is going to hurt the sellers' property when it goes on the market. Or is it sitting between two spotless, wonderful looking homes? That makes a difference, too.

So, as you drive to the prospective sellers' home, look around the entire block. When you get to the house, don't pull into the driveway and up to the garage door right away. View the house while sitting in your car across the street first, then pull into the driveway. You want to get the potential buyer's view. (Many of the top showing Agents park purchasers across the street so that they can get a good look at the property.) So just sit there a minute and look at the property. Take notes.

Use a notepad to make two lists: one for the things you like about the house, and the other for things you would like the sellers to change when you list the house and have it Staged. On the things-you-like list you might put "freshly painted, good color." (There's nothing worse than coming on a freshly painted house that is the wrong color.) Also, you might list "lovely rose garden in front yard." Beautiful! On the things-to-change list, you might list that "shrubbery is overgrown." Other problems might be that the "front door needs painting and shutter on second story is hanging loose and coming down." You'll have to get the sellers to take care of all these things when you list the house and have it Staged.

Now pull into the driveway, shut off your car, and go up to the front door. Be sure to have your note pad, your *Career Book*, the "How to

Price Your Home to Sell for Top Dollar" DVD (which I have prepared for Agents and Stagers to share with sellers and which shows the seller that, if you want top dollar you have to Stage Your Home), and your briefcase.

From the first time the sellers open the door until you say good-bye, you want to work on building rapport with your potential clients. Being sincere in your interest in the sellers' property makes a good initial impression, but you have to be real and mean what you say. Sincere enthusiasm for the sellers' property is irreplaceable. *I repeat: Sincere enthusiasm for the seller's property is irreplaceable!* At the front door get your hand right out there and make contact with the seller's. As you shake hands, be sure you have a nice, firm grip—not too loose and not too tight. There is nothing worse than shaking hands with a dead fish or with what I call "the killer crunch."

Once inside, ask the sellers if you can set your things down. Set them on a soft surface such as the sofa or on the carpeted floor. Never set them down on an end table or coffee table, because you could scratch the furniture with your briefcase or purse.

Now I'm going to let you in on a wonderful secret that really works! As soon I have met the sellers and put down my things, I keep my eyes open for something very important: the pets. I hope you're smiling. I know a lot of people laugh when I say this, but I have made thousands and thousands of dollars from the dogs! When you go to see the sellers' property, haven't you noticed that if they have a dog (or cat) they always introduce us? If the sellers have a dog, I reach right into my pocket and pull out—did you guess it?—a dog biscuit. I always ask the sellers first whether I can give the dog the biscuit, and they always say yes. Don't you dare give the dog a biscuit without asking; you wouldn't want to harm the animal. And, if you did, you definitely wouldn't get the business.

You know the saying: "Love me, love my dog." I can't tell you how many times I have gone to visit sellers who had a pet and was able to list or Stage the property because I paid attention to their animal. I also know how important this is because sellers sometimes tell me about others whom they didn't work with because they weren't nice to their pets. If you are not a pet person yourself, you need to understand that pets are part of the family or they wouldn't be there. So ignoring or mistreating a pet is, to some people, like ignoring or mistreating a bouncing new baby in the family. If you don't like pets, you better learn to.

Let me tell you how dog biscuits first became a tool in my listing career. One day, in the beginning of my career, I was supposed to show a successful businessman a high-priced property. I went to preview the property ahead of time by myself. I pulled into the driveway and started to get out of my car. All of a sudden a large Doberman Pinscher lunged at me, growling and snarling, with the biggest set of teeth I'd ever seen up close. I immediately jumped back into my car. I sat there shaking while he proceeded to jump at my window barking and growling with slobber streaming down the window. I tried rolling down the window just a little bit to baby-talk with him, which was the only thing I could think of at the time. That didn't work. I quickly rolled the window back up and tried to think.

"I've gotta see this house. No one seems to be home. What am I going to do?" All of a sudden it came to me. Go to the grocery store, buy dog treats, come back, and bribe him. I drove to the store, got the dog biscuits, and came back to the house. Killer was still there. I rolled down the window just a little, threw out the first biscuit to the dog, and said, "Please eat this bone." It worked! So I threw out another one. He ate that one, too. I then opened the car door just a little and stuck out one of my legs. It was still attached. So, holding the box of biscuits in my hand, I headed toward the front door throwing one after another until I unlocked the front door and jumped inside. After I saw the house, I went back out front, where now the dog was sitting, wagging his tall, waiting for me, and licking his chops for another treat. I still had the box in my hand, of course, so I threw biscuits all the way back to my car until I was safe inside and then drove away from the house. Later I put the box of biscuits in my trunk and promptly forgot about them.

One day I was sitting at the office working floor time. (You may call this "up time" in your office.) A call came in from a woman. She was very formal on the phone, and I worked hard to get an appointment to see her. When I went to see her for the first time, I'll never forget the fact that she never smiled as we went through her home together. Not once did she smile. Her name was Karla, and she was very stiff and formal as she showed me the property. We went through her home together, and she pointed at each room calling it by name and that is all she would say. "Barbara, this is the kitchen. This is the living room. This is our master bedroom."

Then, as we went into the guest room, I noticed the dust ruffle on the bed started to move. I said, "Karla, what's under the bed? Why is the dust ruffle moving like that?" Speaking in her stiffly accented voice, she said. "Oh, Barbara, that is my little dog, Fufu." I said, "Oh, I love dogs, I really do. Can I talk to him?" She said. "Oh, Barbara, he's hiding under there because he's afraid of you, and he will *not* talk to strangers." (Notice she called me a stranger.) I said. "Would you mind if I try? I really do love dogs." She said, "Be my guest. But it won't do any good. He won't *talk* to you." By this time I was thinking, "What have I got to lose?" So, I got down on my hands and knees, raised the dust ruffle, and said, "Hi, Fufu! How are you doing in there?" The dog, a little white poodle, just sat there, panted, and shook. Then I remembered I had the dog biscuits in the trunk of my car. I said, "Karla, I'll be right back." And I went to get the dog biscuits.

When I came back and Karla saw the box, she smiled for the very first time. She said in her own stiff way. "Oh, Barbara, that is very sweet, but he will not take that from you. He will not come to anyone but me." So I asked, "Well, would you mind if I try?" She answered curtly, "Oh, I suppose you can try, be my guest, but it won't do any good." I got back down on my hands and knees, raised the bedspread, and said, "Fufu, look here! I have this little bone for you. Would you come out and see me? Would you come out and say hi?" Guess what happened? Not only did the little dog come out—shaking all the way—but he actually started to eat the biscuit! Do you know what happened next?

Karla stood up straight, looked me square in the eye, and said, "You shall list my home!" I said, "Karla, I don't understand. You haven't even seen my presentation yet." She looked at me and said, "Anybody my little dog Fufu trusts, I trust! You shall list my house."

I made a lot of money from one dog biscuit because I listed her home, got it Staged, and sold it in two weeks for full price. Now you know why I say that I've made thousands of dollars from the dogs! Since that time, I've carried dog biscuits with me wherever I go. Never underestimate the sellers' pets. They can help take you to the bank! And pets are sellers, too!

The other thing I look for as soon I'm in the house is children. Let's do the same thing with the kids. No, I don't mean give them dog cookies, but do treat them with respect. You know, a lot of Agents don't pay any attention to the kids, and I think they are making a big mistake. Children are sellers, too! I've seen a little kid come up and say, "Daddy, that man that was here was mean. I didn't like him." Do you think that man will get the listing? No way. I've heard little girls or boys say, "Mommy, that lady that was here before was rude," and for that reason the Agent was not called back and didn't get the listing.

When you talk to small children, squat down to get to their eye level. Get on your knees if you have too. Get down at their level so that you face them eye to eye. Having giants walking around you all the time isn't any fun. Talk with them about their rooms and their toys, anything of interest to them. The kids can be fans of yours and really be a help in Staging their rooms. Try it. It works.

Throughout your first visit, continue to build rapport, even while you are accomplishing your other objectives. I always recommend that you do four other important things the first time you meet the sellers at their home.

1. **Make compliments in every room in the house.** Just pick out the things you like, as an Agent, and compliment them. This is easy to do and very natural. Try to compliment something about the house, but if the house is plain, then compliment a possession of the sellers. This is important too.

2. **Get used to using the words, "Seller-and-Agent team."** You will find that saying these words to the sellers several times during your first visit in their home will have a positive effect. They start to think of you as their Agent and part of their team.

3. **Mentally begin to think about how the house should be Staged.** This is really important. As an Agent, you don't want to have to figure out later what to suggest to the Stager. As the Stager, you want to be making mental notes as well as real ones for ideas that start to come to you right away. As you go through each room in the house, you recognize what needs to be put away or done when you see it. If there are stacks of magazines on the floor, you know it. If there is not one ashtray but four of them, you know it. If the sellers have too many collections, you know it. Never tell the sellers all the things you are thinking about at this point, because it is too soon in the educational process, and you don't want to hurt their feelings or offend them when you have just met. But it is very important to Stage the house mentally the first time you see it. Actually you couldn't shut off the voices in your head if you wanted to because they are talking to us all the time. As an Agent, when you return for Step 2 with the sellers, you will suggest a list price that reflects the home's value after being Staged.

4. **Agents and Stagers, if the sellers have collections, compliment them, talk about them, and learn about them.** They have the collections for a reason. You need to do this for several important reasons. Sellers have a collection in their home because they love it. If you draw attention to it and praise it, you are showing an interest in the sellers that will help in building rapport. That is the first reason to draw attention to the collection. When as an Agent you have actually listed the house or when as the Stager you have a Staging commitment in writing, you can refer to the first time you saw their collection. By sharing the following analogy with the sellers, you can get them to put it away entirely.

SELLER'S NOTE

Sellers, you need to be showing your home to the Agent and the Stager and sharing all you can about it. This is not the time for the Agent or Stager to start telling you everything to do, and most of you are not ready to hear it, or usually at least one of the sellers isn't ready to hear it. Also, these steps are for you too to receive the most service with quality time invested by the Agent and the Stager. To have an Agent whip a price off of the top of his or her head and tell you everything to do before you have even gotten acquainted can be unfair and alarming. It is like a doctor saying to someone at first glance, "Oh, you look sick. Lie down and I am going to take some of your parts out of you." How silly and sad that would be. So let the Stager and the Agent do their jobs in a time frame that works for you and for them, too. The work has to be done right, and the timing required makes sense and works for your benefit and for the professionals' benefit, too. Remember, this is a team effort aimed at the highest good of all.

Mr. and Mrs. Seller, do you remember the first time we met, how I was so attracted to your collection of [whatever the collection is]. Well, I am thinking we had better pack it up and put it away, because if you leave it out I'm afraid the buyers coming through your home will do what I did. And that is to buy your things instead of your house. We're not selling your things; we're selling your house. You better pack them up and put them away.

This approach works every time, but you must pay a lot of attention to the collection the first time you go to their home, or it may not work.

To illustrate the four important things to do the first time you see the sellers, as stated earlier, I will put them into a sample conversation to point out each idea.

I have just gone into the living room with the sellers and I [1] make a compliment about the large beautiful bay window. "Mr. and Mrs. Seller, I love your bay window. Look at all of the light it lets into the room and the spacious feeling it adds to your living room. Let me make a note of that, because as we work together as a [2] seller-and-Agent team that will really help me market and sell your home." (Mentally I am thinking, "Yes, the window is wonderful, but they have so many plants stuck in it that you can hardly see the window. When I list this home I'm going to get them to move every one of them." But I don't say anything about the plants to the sellers at this point. Instead I [3] mentally Stage the house.)

We go into the den, and the sellers have [4] a collection of stuffed ducks all over the den walls—a lot of stuffed ducks. I praise the ducks. "Mr. Seller. I love your ducks. Where do you shoot all of them? Have you named any of them? You have! Oh I really love this one. What is his name? Could I touch him? Oh, he is so beautiful. I always wanted my own stuffed duck." Praising the collection of ducks will make it so much easier to get the sellers to put them away as soon as we start to work together as a team!

I would continue through the entire house with the sellers this way in every room. Practice this method, and you will find these ideas really work, allowing you and the sellers to understand much more as a result.

Ask the sellers to take you through every single room, including the basement. Then ask them to show you around outside. (The only exception to this rule is if your seller is 105 years old, and it is pouring rain.) To prepare a report for Step 2 without having walked around the exterior of that property is, in my mind, a big mistake. You could miss big problems out there that would affect the Agent's pricing of the home or the Stager's work. So never prepare the report for the second visit until you have gone through the entire property both inside and outside.

As you tour the inside and outside of a home with the sellers, ask for permission to take pictures. You will be able to use them for a variety of reasons later, so do take them now. The quickest and easiest way is to quickly take photos from the doorway and from each of the corners of every room. Outside, simply take wide shots of the front and the back of the house. If there is a deck, pool, patio, or any other outside features, take more than one picture from different angles. With digital cameras it's easy to take a lot of photos, and you can decide later which ones to use.

Next, I suggest you ask the sellers to walk across the street with you. When you go over there, you might ask. "When was the last time you stood here and looked back at your home like a buyer?" The sellers will answer. "Gosh, not since the day I bought it." This is really the truth for almost every seller. Some will actually say "never." Then ask the sellers to think like a buyer and to tell you what they see. Doing this puts things into perspective for them, encouraging them to see the house from the purchaser's viewpoint. Turn to the sellers and say, "What do you see?" They might say, "Gee, I didn't know the roof had so many pine needles on it. Well, I can see we're going to have to get those cleaned off." They may also say, "I can't even see the left side of my house. All those bushes have grown way over the eaves. The front door doesn't look too good, either."

When you've taken the sellers across the street, they are now seeing it as the potential purchaser sees it, and that perspective can make a big difference. This also makes a positive impression with the sellers, demonstrating that you are someone extra special. Probably no other Agent or Stager took them across the street, and your approach as the guiding expert, who asked them to think like a buyer, really sticks in their minds. It also lets the sellers see their property as it really is. They get to be tough on themselves. I don't mention or point out anything until they have mentioned all the things they see. Then I will bring up anything that they didn't see that I saw when sitting across the street in my car. Taking your future sellers across the street also helps you bring back a suggested list price that they can accept more easily, because now they have seen their house from a different vantage point than from their own living room.

After you have looked over the entire inside and outside of the house with the sellers and you have taken them across the street, ask them to go back inside with you and sit down and visit for a few minutes. As you sit with the sellers back in the house or anytime before you leave, repeat your let-me-tell-you-how-I-work commercial. (Do this as an Agent or Stager whether you've already told them on the phone, in person, or not.) Telling them how you work does two things: First, you educate your sellers; second, it shows you know your stuff and it helps you be appreciated as the leader of this effort to list, Stage, and sell the house.

I hope you have already told them on the phone about how you work, but it is really important to repeat it now. Give them just an overview of the work you will be doing, not all the details. Leave the marketing and pricing to your Exclusive Detailed Report when you return as an Agent. And don't go into everything now as a Stager, either. You do things in three steps for good reasons, each of which is important and each of which, as I have proved, is needed by all parties.

Remember, by telling your sellers how you work, you are establishing control. If your sellers know what to expect of you from the beginning, they will be much less likely to resist your suggestions farther down the road. For example, if you wait until after the sellers have signed the listing to say, "Oh, by the way, I want to go through your house with you and tell you all the things that we need to change, fix, or clean," you could run into problems. Sellers don't like surprises. If you do that, their response might be, "Where did that come from?" So tell them the first time you meet them as an Agent or ASP Stager:

> I am here to serve you, and I work in steps. I want to help you sell your home for the most money in the quickest amount of time. And as an Agent one way I can help you do that is to bring in an ASP Stager to Stage the house with you [this can be a Home Staging Consultation or a complete Home Staging]. This will help you prepare your home for sale, which we call Staging. A Staged home usually can sell quicker and for even more money in any market.

As an ASP Stager, you would be sharing the same information without talking specifically about the actual list price. Never talk about the actual list price being to high or too low because that is not your role or job, and getting involved can get you into trouble. Not only will sellers want you to stage their home and expect you to do it, but they might fire you later if you don't do it because you taught them up front why Staging is so important.

So you see, in the first meeting you are not only selling yourself and establishing rapport, but you are also starting to educate your potential sellers about how you work. This approach is crucial for acquiring and maintaining professional leadership and control.

Before you leave, set up that appointment to return and present your Exclusive Detailed Report as an Agent or as an ASP Stager. This could be a day later or more. The timing depends entirely on your schedule and your sellers' schedule. Of course, you want to return as soon as possible. As an ASP Stager, I want to see you back with your report in 24 hours or less, and that is true for you an ASP Real Estate Agent, too. Set that time.

Now, here is where your magical tool, the *Career Book*, starts to work for you. Before you leave, always explain to your future sellers that you are actually the one who will be doing the work for them, and that you think it is important for them to know something about you. Tell them you have put something special together about your career in real estate. Your *Career Book* shows them your background, your credentials in the business, what you did before you got into real estate or Staging, and even some of the homes you've sold or Staged that sold for others, perhaps people in their own neighborhood. Leave the book and let it do the talking and bragging about you. Never show the book to them because it means more when they discover your assets for themselves. If you tried to show the book at this point you'd end up cheating yourself; you would never take as much time as they would on their own. I'll go into complete detail about the *Career Book* in the next chapter.

You should be thinking about something else, which brings me to my last point. Agents and Stagers, pay attention to qualifying potential sellers. As a Stager, you need to know what is going on, just as the Agent needs to know. When clients don't cooperate, it may be because they really do not want to sell or move at all. They may be just trying the market, and that doesn't work. Remember, I used the word "commitment" earlier, and this is where it really comes up.

QUALIFY THE POTENTIAL SELLERS: ARE THEY MOTIVATED TO SELL?

SELLER'S NOTE

Coming on the market isn't child's play. It is serious, and the public will be coming through your home. Do not come on the market unless you are serious. This is not, nor should it ever be, a market to just try it and see what happens. Trying it takes work on your part, too, and you need to be sure you want to put your house up for sale. You will have Agents, the Stager, and their teams moving things, giving you tasks to do, painting rooms, and sometimes more, and then the buyers come through. So be sure that you want to do what it takes. When you are ready, do all that your Agent and Stager tell you to do. They are the pros who know what it takes, and selling home takes an investment of time and sometimes dollars that will have a huge return on your investment for you in the Staging and selling of your house.

I know you are saying, "I've heard of qualifying buyers, but qualify a seller?" I have a philosophy about taking just any listing or Staging. There are a lot of people out there. Sometimes we take a listing or a Staging only because it's there. We think that if we don't take it, someone else will. If you have the time and that's the way you feel, then go ahead and take it. But listing and Staging the homes of sellers who just want to experiment with or test the market can sometimes end up being a waste of your time and money. As an Agent, the last thing you need is a bunch of overpriced properties and unmotivated sellers. All that does is wear you down and lead to a lot of frustration.

I'm not talking about the house that is a little overpriced and that you go ahead and list. I'm talking about the houses that are out of sight. You get the feeling from the sellers that they really do not want to sell. They are just not realistic or motivated. Stagers, the same is true for you. When sellers don't seem to want to get involved or do not want to do what you ask, perhaps they have other things items on their agenda that you do not know about. Perhaps they really are playing at selling and are not serious about cooperating and getting the job done! I have seen this in my career, and you have to address it by talking with the seller.

THE SELLERS' MOTIVATION IS KEY TO CONTROL

When you meet potential sellers, the first thing you want to gauge is their motivation. Asking questions is the best way to determine how motivated your sellers are. Don't stop asking questions until that sale down the road is closed. Their answers to your questions are going to tell you a lot. If they answer, "Well, we're not really sure. We just want to see if we can move," you might not put them high on your priority list. (When you are listing 10, 15, 25, or 50 homes, you should put your sellers in a certain order of priority.) But if they answer, "John is being transferred across the country in a couple of months, so we have to move and we can't afford to keep two houses," then you know they need to sell their house. They are very motivated, and they need their house Staged. So bring in the ASP Stagers now for sure!

When you come across sellers who do not want to let you do what you need to do to be effective and that little voice inside says. "I don't think these are sellers I should be working for," let them go. You'll be glad you did. Don't burden yourself with them, and don't burden your company with them. As soon as you sign up those impossible sellers, along comes Mr. and Mrs. Ready-to-Sell, who will listen to you, give you authority, and let you have the control you need to do your best for them. Why is having both listings a bad thing? Inevitably (and I hope you are smiling as Agents or Stagers as you read this because we've all experienced it), if we take both listings or Stagings, guess which sellers are going to be on the phone calling every day? Every day, you walk into your office and your secretary says, "Guess who called?" You know it is going to be the sellers whose house is way overpriced, in poor condition, and in a bad location. They are the ones who were not serious, who didn't listen to your advice and your expertise, and who now call and perhaps complain to you a lot.

So take time in that first visit to get to know the people and the property. What you learn about the sellers and the property in the first visit will help you in the second visit as you give your Exclusive Detailed Report listing presentation or Home Staging Consultation or Proposal. Invest time up front with your potential sellers. If you do, you are not going to have the problems that could come later. Remember two things:

1. **Education = Control.**
2. **Let me tell you how I work!**

Agents and Stagers, these points, together with your *Career Book*, will get you off to the right start with the sellers. You can literally take that assertion to the bank because everyone wins. In particular, sellers win by working with you as the professionals you are, who work the ways that I am teaching and explaining in this book.

CHAPTER 4

THE *CAREER BOOK:* THE KEY TO YOUR CREDIBILITY

Sellers deserve to know your background before they hire you.

BARB SCHWARZ

SELLER'S NOTE

How do you find out about the individual you are placing your trust with as an Agent or as an ASP Stager? It is a good question because in the industry of real estate, it is common for people to leave their business cards and perhaps a brochure with you. But what can you really learn from reading a business card? Not much! And just how much can they put on a brochure for you to learn about them? Usually the message in a brochure is what professionals want you to know about their services. They have written what they want you to read about the benefits of working with them. This is great, but how much do you know about them and how they will keep their commitments? A brochure doesn't speak to these questions. That is why a *Career Book*, presented to you by an Agent or a Stager, will really show you more

(Continued)

about who they are, what they have done for others, and what they can do for you. All this is what I suggest professionals put into their *Career Books*. As you read this chapter, you will see why this information is helpful. I want real estate professionals to share their background and experience with you in their *Career Book*, such as:

- Copies of their training certificates, so that you can see their qualifications.
- Their lists of clients, with their phone numbers so that you can check references.
- Pictures of homes they have listed and sold as an Agent and homes that they have Staged as an ASP Stager.

These are just some of the many things you need to see in order to know more about who these professionals are and what they have done.

I developed the *Career Book* so that my potential clients could learn more about why I was qualified to serve them. Read on and I think you will see why it is important that both an Agent and an ASP Stager share their *Career Books* with you. To trust people in the listing, selling and Staging of your home, the more you know about them, usually the more you can trust them and be assured that they will serve you.

IN THIS CHAPTER

You will learn:

1. Exactly what the *Career Book* is and how it was developed.
2. How the *Career Book* will give you more credibility than you've ever had before, regardless of your experience in real estate.
3. How you can build a *Career Book*.
4. Why, as a seller, it is important to be given a *Career Book* so that you can learn more up front.

CREDIBILITY

The greatest challenge you face is establishing credibility, that is, convincing homeowners that you are the right person to list and sell their homes or to Stage their homes. In this chapter, I want to tell you about an exciting tool I've created and developed, called the *Career Book*. I honestly tell you that the

Career Book works! It is literally revolutionizing the way professionals work with sellers because it helps build credibility for you. If I could, right now I would hold the *Career Book* in front of you and say, "The *Career Book* could make you twenty-five thousand to fifty thousand dollars more in income this year." Those numbers are really impressive, aren't they? Just think about it. If you could earn $25,000 to $50,000 more in income, wouldn't that make building your own *Career Book* worthwhile? It really can happen for you! I've seen Agents and ASP Stagers all over the country boost their income by at least that much—the very first year—using this exciting tool.

The Birth of a Bright Idea

As I began my career in real estate, I was virtually unknown. As I set out listing residential properties, no one knew who Barb Schwarz was in real estate or what I could do. I observed that sellers had little information to guide them in making decisions about whom they would hire to be their real estate salesperson. When sellers look for an Agent to list the property, they often look in the *Yellow Pages*, call a real estate office from an ad in the newspaper or on TV, or ask a friend for help and advice. Finding the right Agent can be just a matter of luck. If the sellers do not care for the Agent who comes to see them, they don't call the manager of that company and say, "I didn't like Mary. Do you have another one down there you could send me?" Instead, they call the competition.

I started to think seriously about how little time we have to make the right impression the first time we go to see potential sellers. Maybe we make the right impression and maybe we don't. People are judgmental. Maybe they like our appearance and maybe they don't. They make judgments based on how we handle ourselves in about 30 minutes of time, not really knowing anything at all about us except what they see. And, as the saying goes, people buy people.

"But how then can they decide whether I'm the right Agent based on just what they see," I asked myself? "If I brag, they will think I have a big head and not hire me for that reason. What do I have that could let them know about me?" The answer became the *Career Book.*

I now want to ask you five questions, and I want you to be very honest with yourself about the answers.

1. **Who does the work in representing a listing and marketing the property: you or your company?** That's right, it's you! Your company knows that. And the same is true for Stagers. You may have your own company, but they still pick you as the person to do the work.

2. **Whom does the seller really pick: you or the company?** Right again. It's you. (Now, managers, I don't want to lose you here. The company's job is to find the best Agents it can for that very reason. But if the sellers don't like an Agent or Stager for one reason or another, you know that they call the competition. In most cases the Agent makes the reputation for the company in the minds of the sellers.)

3. **Does your company have credibility?** Yes! That's one of the main reasons you are with the firm. Remember, your company does a lot of marketing and may invest a lot of money to build that credibility. Usually, companies do a great job of marketing the company as a whole.

4. **Do you have credibility?** Yes, you do! Of course, you do!

Here is the biggest question of all! Again, be honest with yourself.

5. **Do the sellers you go to see usually know as much about your credibility as they do about your company's?** The answer is no!

Let's summarize. You are the one who does the work. You are the one the seller picks. Your company has credibility. You have credibility. But then notice that, when you go to see the sellers, they usually do not know as much about your credibility as they do about your company's. Yet we expect them to pick us when they don't know much about us. This is a little like Russian roulette. No thank you! You can't afford to leave the choice to chance.

Now think about what we take with us when we go to see potential sellers. Most of us take our business card and a company brochure. If you work with a large company, then the firm has probably done a great job of marketing already because it appreciates the need. It understands and realizes the need for marketing information about the company.

But what about us? Oh yes, we have our card. It is time for individual Real Estate Agents and ASP Stagers to also get into marketing, in addition to what our companies already do. This is the age of marketing. Are you in public relations? Are you in sales? And are you in real estate? The answers are all obvious. So, if you don't sell yourself, who will?

No one; that's who.

As I continued my thought process about how sellers pick Agents, I asked myself, "Who is my employer in real estate?" In listing property, it is the seller every time. And as a Stager it is the seller, too! If I went out to look for a new employer other than in real estate, what would I take with me? I would have to prepare a resume and take it with me everywhere I went.

A resume helps an employer make decisions about whom to hire. In real estate, I realized that my employer is the seller. That's who is paying me. So I decided to apply the resume idea and take it a little further. I also remembered that as an interior designer (my former career) I had carried a notebook with pictures of my work. I said to myself, "I need to do something like that but add more to it to let people know more about me and my work, too."

I got a notebook and clear plastic sheet protectors. In addition to my resume, I asked myself, what else could I put in it? I went back to my office and sat down at my desk. As I looked up on my walls, I saw my five company awards. I saw the accreditation certificates for classes I had taken in the business; I had framed them and put on the wall. I asked myself—as I want you to ask yourself—"What are those doing on your walls? Whoever sees your walls, anyway?" Sellers sure don't see your walls. Only your fellow Agents see them—and they are not paying you! I took my certificates off the walls and put them in my *Career Book*. I took pictures of the plaques, blew them up to 8 × 10 prints, and then put them in my book. I put in other information about myself: my background, work record, education, and so forth. I also decided to put in pictures of the homes I had listed and sold during my career in real estate.

I started leaving my book with every seller I met, whether the contact came from a phone call, a referral, or knocking on doors. Guess what happened? When I started leaving my *Career Book* with sellers, I started to get more listings. My listings sold, and my income started climbing. "I've really struck gold!" I thought. And you can too.

CREATING YOUR OWN *CAREER BOOK*

By preparing a *Career Book,* you are way ahead of most other salespeople. This is true of you as Stagers, too! You have to build the credibility just as much as Agents do.

With your *Career Book,* sellers have something positive by which to judge you. Remember, people are judgmental. Now, however, they can make rational decisions, and most of those decisions I find are positive. With a *Career Book*, your image will soar! Try to imagine yourself as a skyscraper because your image goes up about that high. You will stand out from the rest. Most salespeople either haven't heard of the idea or are just too lazy to put one together. Even if it were a perfect world and every

Agent or Stager had a *Career Book,* please remember competition is good! It's good for you and for me, and it's really good for sellers. If the people who were competing for listings all had their own *Career Book*s, the decision for sellers would be much easier. No longer would sellers throw a dart at the biggest ad in town. Please don't get me wrong: There is nothing wrong with having the biggest ad, but the sellers have the right to find the person who meets their needs the best. The *Career Book* really helps to make that happen. Besides, I truly have never left my *Career Book* and had another Agent or Stager leave his or hers at the same time. Even if that happened, you wouldn't go to a job interview in another industry looking for a job and say, "Well, I don't think I'll take my resume because everyone else will be bringing one, too." You would say, "I'd better bring mine because others *will* be bringing theirs." Think about it. It makes sense.

Common Ground and Credibility

Before taking you through my *Career Book,* I need to discuss two concepts. These concepts are powerful, and you have heard them all of your life. They are the reasons you like your friends and they like you. The *Career Book* shows these concepts off as nothing else can. They are the concepts of common ground and credibility. Common ground can take you to the bank over and over again. There is no way that sellers can tell by looking at you that the two (or three) of you probably share common ground. There is definitely more to you than meets the eye.

Where did you grow up? Do you know how many listings as an Agent and how many Stagings as a Stager I have gotten because my *Career Book* shows I was born and raised in Kansas? If the prospective sellers used to live in Kansas and they see I used to live in Kansas, we have common ground.

Never—I mean *never*—underestimate the power of common ground. It works. Most of us have something in common with other people we meet that would help us earn their trust. Some of these things are not immediately obvious, and that is where judgment comes into play. People tend to screen us out rather than in, based solely on what they see. People know only what they see, usually. You cannot get your background, all the accomplishments you may have in real estate or Staging, all of your credentials, and the other areas of common ground all on your business card. It's impossible. This is why the *Career Book* works so well. It helps you establish common ground as nothing else can. I'll give you more examples soon.

(handwritten note in margin, rotated)
What will I do for Seller?
As an agent a Stager for seller
1) Who am I?
2) What do I do.
3) How do I do it?

...rd I mentioned was "credibility." Remember, the public ...e Agents in the bottom five of 25 professions. People ...not as honest as other professionals. They think Agents ...ards. Many times sellers know the credibility and reputa-...ny that you work for, but they do not know about your ...lity. They cannot tell that by looking at you, either. No ...tage their property with a person whom they do not like ...g to potential clients that you are the right Agent to list ...e right Stager to Stage their home is the first step in work-...The *Career Book* is one of the most powerful tools for ...will help you bridge the credibility gap by showing off ...lism. The *Career Book* definitely helps you establish the ...and credibility you need to help you get more listings.

...a take toward building your *Career Book* is to mark a date ...and write, "I'm going to put my *Career Book* together." ...wer in your desk and start collecting items that can go into ...ok. When the day comes for you to put your book together, ...time and the materials to do it! There is no perfect *Career Book*. The size of it does not matter. It's what is inside that counts. If you are new to real estate or Staging, you can develop just as good a *Career Book* for yourself as a person who has been in the industry for years.

Let me share with you in detail the ideas and information that I think you should put in the *Career* Book. For information on ordering a professional "Career Book Marketing System," please see the Appendix of this book.

Ideas and Information to Include in the *Career Book*

Here are some guidelines and ideas, plus a variety of things you can use to build your *Career Book*.

Photos, Certificates, and Awards

You are going to be selling you. That is the key. You want to impress the sellers right away with who you are and what you have been doing. The beginning of the book is the perfect place for you to include such things as the announcement of when you started working for the company, your background, and your resume. If you just started working in the real estate or Staging industry, it is even more important to include what else you have been doing.

Remember, sellers have backgrounds, too. You may really find common ground with them in this area. Most people don't get into Staging or real estate as their first job out of school. The other jobs that you have had can help build credibility and common ground, and they can help sell you to potential sellers. If you used to be a top salesperson for a Fortune 500 company, that will give you credibility. If you used to be a U.S. Marine, you will build rapport with those who are or have been in the military. If you used to be a teacher, that background can build credibility or common ground, too. You never know what in your background can create a favorable impression with the many buyers and sellers you will meet in this wonderful business. So don't be afraid to include lots of information about yourself. Whatever you are comfortable sharing can benefit you.

Put your resume in, and talk about your background in depth. List any schools you have attended and extra courses you have taken. When you have secured those educational clock hours, where does the certificate go? If it goes into your desk drawer, it is not working for you. If you put it up on the wall, very few people will come to your desk to see it. You now know where it should go: inside your *Career Book* where sellers can see any and all certificates you have earned. Whether your certificates are for accomplishments in real estate or in Staging or a former career, put them in the book: Awards are crucial. They can definitely take you to the bank. Take your awards to your future employers so that they can see what you've done. Winning awards in anything shows that you excel, that you are better than most. Even an award for selling widgets will be appreciated by sellers thinking of hiring you to be their Agent or Stager. Just take pictures or copies of your awards and certificates, whether they are real estate related or not, and put them into your *Career Book*. You don't have to brag at all because the sellers will see them in your book; the book does the bragging for you.

Don't forget anything about your background. Screen yourself in, not out! The smallest item may be just the thing that strikes a familiar chord of common ground with your potential sellers. Be proud of your background. If you are not proud of yourself, no one else will be either. This is really a brag book. So brag. People love finding out and reading about someone else. And now that someone is you.

Be sure to include photos in your *Career Book*. If you were ever in the newspaper, put in the articles. Show off the personal side of your life.

Put in pictures of your family. People love seeing your family. That can be spouse, children, parents, even brothers, sisters, or close friends. Yes, that may sound corny at first, but remember that corn can make you rich!

You should even put in photos of your pets. Remember my dog bone story. Sellers have pets don't they? And they love their pets. Sellers love their pets so show off your pets too!

Show off your hobbies. Golfers love to talk to golfers. Fishermen love to talk to fishermen. Skiers love to talk to skiers. Common ground in these areas can really break down the walls and get you more listings or Stagings.

I know some of you might be doubting me. But I can't tell you how many letters and emails I have received from Agents and Stagers over the years telling me how they got a listing or a Staging because of something they shared in their *Career Book* that uncovered some common ground. Sometimes the most obscure item was the key. Many times these stories have come from brand-new Agents or Stagers who beat out the office's "old pro" because of their *Career Book*. The common ground had nothing to do with real estate or Staging; it always had to do with where people worked in the past, where they grew up or went to school, or what pets or hobbies they had. Trust me, as you put a *Career Book* together, it will bring you more business.

Letters of Recommendation

As you work with people, ask them for letters of recommendation. If you don't ask, they may not write one. You can do the most wonderful job in the world, but many times sellers just never get around to writing you a letter unless you ask for it. What's more, most people will write you a better letter if you ask for it than if they think of it themselves. Don't be afraid to ask. Letters really work. You can also contact past clients, which, of course, is a great way to prospect for new business. Ask them for a letter as well.

Keep adding letters to your book. This section can grow and grow, which greatly helps you sell yourself. When you've left your *Career Book* with home owners and they are reading all these wonderful letters about you, the effect is fantastic! Every letter written about you is like an ad about you. The more letters you have, the better the advertising is.

Now, if you are new in the business you might ask me, "Well, gee, Barb, I just started my career. I don't have any letters of recommendation yet." Then put in letters from your other careers. They will fit well in this section, too. They might help you strike a common bond with someone. Besides, they show that you are a reliable person. I assure you, a future seller will not read a letter written by IBM saying how great you are and think to themselves, "He was great at IBM, but he'll stink in real estate" or "She won't be good at Staging." People do not think that way. They assume you made the change to your new career for the better, not the worse, and they transfer the credibility you had in your last career to your new career in real estate as an Agent or in Staging as an ASP Stager.

Photos of Listed, Staged, and Sold Homes

This section is powerful! Everyone knows a picture is worth a thousand words. Let me tell you how this section came about in the first place. I had been using the other sections of my *Career Book* as described for quite a while, and the book worked every time. One day when I came back to give a particular seller the Detailed Report, however, he made a comment that changed my book (and now yours) forever. The seller said, "Barb, my wife and I think you're great. We trust you more than anybody else who has come through our home, because frankly we now know more about you than we do about any other Agent. We've already decided to have you list our home because of that. But there is something missing in your book that you really ought to add." I said, "Please tell me what that is. I really would like to know." He looked me square in the eye and asked, "Lady, what have you ever sold, anyway?" At that moment I realized that sellers are also very interested, of course, in production. And the same is true for us as Stagers. In other words, the seller was saying, "Show me what you have done!"

So I went out with my camera and took pictures of every home that I had listed and sold, and I put the photos into my book. No matter who sold the homes, they were my listings, so in my book they went. I also included any home that someone else had listed that I had sold. Now sellers could see my production. As a Stager, you should do the same thing, too!

Every home you list and sell goes into this section. You've told them about your background. You've shown them your resume. You've shown them pictures of your family. They've seen your awards and credentials in real estate in addition to ones you earned in other careers. But you also want them to say to themselves, "This person knows what she is talking about when she talks to us about Staging or real estate. I can see that she really knows what she is doing. Here are some of the listings she has actually sold or houses she has Staged."

Highlight the neighborhoods and the price ranges in which you specialize. When I put in the homes that I have listed and sold, or that I have Staged as a Stager, I put in individual information sheets on each property. In my own book, I also put the price for which a house listed or sold. I suggest that you put in one or the other: for example, "Listed for $395,000. Sold to an out-of-town purchaser." On another home, I would just say. "Sold for $585,000."

This is truly a powerful section! Sellers love seeing all the pictures of the homes you've sold. If you have been in business for 15 years and sold the same home three times, then take three pictures of it and write under each picture about each sale. Dynamite! And I have also Staged the same house through the years for different sellers, and you bet I have that house in my book as an ASP Stager! If your focus is on a particular market, be sure to represent only that market. If you work in the high end only, don't put in the one low-end sale you had. If you work in the low end, don't put in the one high-end sale you had. But if you focus on people rather than on properties, then represent all market ranges in your book. I have sales in my book from $35,000 for land all the way into the millions of dollars for homes. I have many resale homes in my book, new construction, town houses, condominiums, vacant lots and acreage, and horse ranches and farms. I want it all covered. Put in the commercial sales you've had, too. You never know when the person you leave it with may be an investor or may know someone else who is.

As your book grows, you eventually won't have room for all of your sold listings sold and personal sales. As an ASP Stager, you won't have room for all of the houses you have Staged. You also don't want to overwhelm the reader. Therefore, I keep the most recent sales I have had or homes I have Staged, as well as a representation at all times of the various markets and price ranges in which I work.

Take photos. Fill your *Career Book* with them, and they will take you to the bank!

A Winning Idea for Those New to Real Estate

If you are brand-new, you may not have any listings or sales, or very few of them. How do you achieve credibility? When I first went into real estate, I didn't have any sales to go into my book, either. I came up with the idea of a title page that talked about the company listings. I asked other Agents in my office if I could take pictures of their listings. I put the pictures in this section of my book with my card on each page. I said to the Agents, "Who knows, maybe I can sell one of your listings and then we will both make money." Meanwhile, this section helped me gain credibility. It worked. I sold several of the other Agents' listings. As I got my sales and they closed, I added the sold section to my book. As I got my own listings, I added them as well.

Again, the same is true for ASP Stagers. Ask other ASPs with whom you do projects whether it's OK with them to put pictures of the rooms you team-Staged into your *Career Book*. You did the work on that team, and you deserve to have it in your book, thus helping you build credibility too. ASP Stagers are such wonderful people that "sharing" is their middle name. Most ASP Stagers feel that one of the greatest benefits is the community of ASPs who share together every day. Staging is all about the network of ASPs, so it will be easy for you to put a *Career Book* together from the many pictures that I have placed on the StagedHomes.com university and that you will have from other ASP Stagers, showing projects you have been involved with. Do it! It works!

Ending the Book

One of the best ways I know to end your *Career Book* is to put in a photo of yourself with a *sold* sign. Here's how to do it. The next time you go out on a open house tour, have an associate take your picture standing in front of a house alongside the for-sale sign with "SOLD" attached. It's easy! Don't show the whole house. In fact, it doesn't even have to be for sale. This photo is for public relations, and the important things to show are you and the sign. The house will become a blurred background, and that's just fine.

Take several shots so that you can choose the best one. Once you pick the one you like, blow it up to 8×10 and put it into your *Career Book*. It will make a powerful statement about you at end the book. "I sell homes" is the message, and a picture like this will get it across loud and clear. I have done this as an Agent and as an ASP Stager. Either way, it works.

A SIMPLE BUT CRUCIAL PROCEDURE: STARTING AND BUILDING YOUR *CAREER BOOK*

Preparing a *Career Book* about yourself is as simple as collecting the material and following the order I've outlined, although you may want to rearrange it a little to suit your needs. There is no right or wrong way to do it. Anything that you feel comfortable sharing about yourself is great. Do what fits you, but do it! Don't wait until your book is perfect; I really believe that you are perfect in your own way right now. Even a partially finished book will bring you great rewards. Just get your book together, and get it out there so that it can go to work for you now. Sometimes I will meet someone who got a *Career Book* from me, and they will say to me. "I'm not using my book yet because it isn't quite good enough" or "It isn't quite finished yet." Think of the business they are missing while they are trying to make it perfect or while they are procrastinating. Procrastination is the biggest killer of sales. Don't put off what you can do today. Get going and put your book together.

Once started, your *Career Book,* like you, should constantly be growing and changing. You should always be adding new listings, new Stagings, and new pictures of those that have sold. Continue to collect new information all the time, and keep it in a drawer in your desk at work. Then, one night each quarter take everything and update your *Career Book*. It's easy! So get started now. You will be amazed at how much the *Career Book* will help you educate the client, will help you sell yourself, and will really help you build your career.

Who should build a *Career Book?* Anyone can.

Let me share a true story with you that happened at one of my seminars. The day was over, and everybody was gone by about half past five in the evening. I was packing up to leave, and I didn't realize anyone else was still in the room. Then this slender, blonde woman approached me. She said, "Can I talk to you a minute?" I said, "Sure. What would you like to talk about?" The large ballroom was completely empty, but she didn't want to talk with me out in the open. She literally took my hand and said, "Let's talk over here behind this partition, if you don't mind." I didn't know what she was going to do. As we walked behind the partition, she said, "I loved your program today, but there is one thing I have a real problem with. There is one thing I just can't do." I asked, "Are you new in the business?" She said. "Yes, I am new." I continued, "Are you a little worried about having your listing Staged? Is that it?" She said, "No, I think I can really have my listing Staged after spending today with you. That's not it. The problem is that I am the only one here today who can't put together a *Career Book*." I said, "Oh, sure you can. Anybody can put a *Career Book* together. Everybody should! What you want to do is put in a lot of pictures. Pictures are great. Then list the clients that you had in your last career. They are great names for references. Oh, and get letters of recommendation and fill your book."

She repeated, "No. I can't. You just don't understand. I just can't do it." Now by this time she was getting red in the face, and her voice was getting a little louder and a little shaky. "Well," I said, "I guess I don't understand. Help me." What came out of her mouth next no one has ever said to me before. This woman stood up straight, put her shoulders back, looked me square in the eye, and said, "Well, you see Barb, this is kind of hard for me to say, but for the last eight years . . . ah . . . ah . . . for the last eight years I've been a prostitute."

You could have knocked me over with a toothpick. But think of the courage it took for her to say this to me. I stood there thinking of what to say. Then all of a sudden I looked her right back in the eye and said, "Wel-l-l-l, listen, you have may have better people skills than anyone else who was here today." It was all I could think to say. Then I added, "You told me you learned a lot today. So go home and write up what you learned and put it in your book. You have certificates of clock hours, so put those in. You got a certificate from me today, too. Do you have children?" She did. "Well, put your kids in your book. And your pets, too. You can get company listings and company ads, and before you know it, your book will be full. You can put a book together!"

By the time this woman left, she really felt she could put a *Career Book* together and was on her way home to start it. The beautiful thing, I thought, was that this woman was changing her whole life, which really took a lot of courage and guts. I give her all the credit in the world. Even though I haven't seen her since that day, I did receive a letter about a year later thanking me and telling me she had just been awarded the top production award in her office. She had married and was taking her new husband and children to Bermuda, which was the prize for the top producer that year. How wonderful!

What do you want to happen this year in your life? I believe that you can make whatever you want happen. I truly believe that God has given us the greatest gifts in the world: our mind, our ability to have great passion, and our spirit.

You have the power inside you to make things happen. It is already there. The key is that you have to want to do it. You have to want to do whatever it takes to make it happen.

Now I want to give you a challenge from the true story I have just shared with you: If the woman in the preceding story can put together a *Career Book*, I *know* you can do it too! Just do it and do it now!

GUARANTEED SUCCESS

I can't urge you enough to put a book together. You can go www.stagingshop-pingcenter.com to invest in the official *Career Book* kit. This kit comes with a CD containing PDF files for divider pages already professionally designed and prepared for you to print out. It also includes a DVD to show you how to put the book together and use it. The kit also gives you directions in writing and sheet protectors to place your papers in to protect them.

If you have a *Career Book* already, you know how powerful it is and the great things it does for you and your career!

If you have not yet started a *Career Book*, get to work and get it done! I promise you, when you use your book correctly, you will serve your clients and yourself much more successfully than you ever imagined possible.

Proving to potential clients that you are the right Agent to list their homes or the right Stager to Stage them is the first step in working with sellers. The *Career Book* is one of the most powerful tools for doing just that.

Do it *now*!

CHAPTER 5

PROSPECTING AND USES OF THE *CAREER BOOK*

There is a world of business just waiting for you *to show up.*

BARB SCHWARZ

SELLER'S NOTE

The *Career Book* is a wonderful tool for professionals to use. As a seller, you should note which Agents and Stagers use them. The book helps you learn more about them, helps you to get to know them in an easy way, and hopefully helps to build more trust in your relationship with them. And it shows that these professionals have invested time in wanting you to know more about them and what they can do for you. Many, many sellers have said to me, "Well, if you will take the time to put this book together, then I know that you will take the time to market my property and do what is needed to sell it [as an Agent] or Stage it [as an ASP Stager]." And other people who see it will feel that way, too, such as buyers and appraisers and title representatives, who also know buyers and who need to make referrals to Agents or Stagers. In the last chapter, I explained why the *Career Book* works. This chapter is about how strong the *Career Book* is when used with people other than sellers and how it can benefit the professional *and* the clients whom they serve!

IN THIS CHAPTER

You will learn:

1. The six major uses of the *Career Book*.
2. How to prospect using the *Career Book* to bring more business to you *and* to your clients too!
3. How to knock on one door and reach thousands of people at a time using your *Career Book*. It all starts with someone you already know!

MARKETING YOURSELF

Marketing is the name of the game. This principle is true in real estate, Staging, or any sales field. If you work for a company right now, most likely it knows how to market. The firm splashes its name anywhere and everywhere it can. It spends or invests thousands—even millions in some cases—on name familiarity, public relations, and marketing. This is undoubtedly one of the reasons you are with that company.

But how about you? What kind of marketing do you do regularly? Most of us would not or could not afford to take out a full-page ad in the Sunday newspaper about ourselves—and you just wouldn't do it. Nevertheless, we typically leave too much of our marketing up to the company. We cannot sit in our home offices or cooperate offices anymore and say to an associate, "Do you see they gave another referral to Mary Jane! What has she got going with the manager anyway?" It is time we start to market ourselves in addition to what our company is or is not doing already.

As explained in the last chapter, the sellers you meet pick you, not the company. So you need to market *yourself*. I think that the *Career Book* is the best marketing idea and tool in the industry today. It sells and markets you wherever and whenever you leave it. Your *Career Book* is a silent talker that speaks for you. It is a hardback definition of who you are and how you work. You can take it with you everywhere, and you can lend it to everyone you know. Once you start circulating your *Career Book*, believe me, prospects will find you! Your *Career Book* tells people exactly who you are and how you have sold homes for other people, and it shows all the reasons people should hire you to list, Stage, or sell them a property. And that property could be the seller that you work with right now!

How many places can you be in at once? Your answer is only one. There is only one of you. But by using your *Career Book*, you will see how many places you can be at the same time. The more books you put together and leave with clients, the more places you can be at the same time.

The *Career Book* does so much more than your business card could ever do. There is no way you can put all the information we talked about in the last chapter on your business card or even in a personal brochure. The *Career Book* is now the marketing tool that will bring you countless clients and customers. The number one thing you are selling is yourself. And, if you don't do it, who else will?

How can you use your *Career Book* to prospect, and who are your prospects? Finding prospects is mostly a matter of recognizing them. You may not know this, but you are surrounded by prospects. They might be people you have never considered as potential clients. Even the people who aren't prospects right now can probably lead you to someone who is. Many times it starts with someone you know, which makes prospecting less scary. If you study networking principles, which I certainly recommend—they are the same as prospecting—you only have to prospect to those around you who know you or whom you come in contact with.

I want to share my list of solid sources for prospects that can keep you productive until you are ready to retire. I have developed these over the years using my *Career Book*, and, believe me, they are solid prospect sources that can take you and your clients to the bank over and over again. You can do all your prospecting without a *Career Book*, but it's definitely not going to be as powerful or the same!

FINDING BUSINESS

Source 1: Sellers

Sellers! Sellers! Sellers!

I would never go to see potential sellers without my *Career Book*. Period.

Other Agents will go to see the seller and leave their business card, and when they go, they are gone. You leave your *Career Book*, and you remain in their homes! I have never had potential sellers list or Stage with someone else as my book lay in their home. Never! One seller even said to me. "Barb, we got to know you so well, we took you to bed with us last night." (They had looked at my *Career Book* together in bed as they watched TV before they went to sleep!) How can you beat that? Of course, you are going to list their home, now that they know all about you. Having gone through your book, they like and trust you much more than the competing Agents.

They always find some common ground with you from looking through your book, and common ground puts the humanness back into selling yourself!

Imagine that I left my *Career Book* and you didn't. Who do you think will get the listing or the Staging? You decide. I will leave my book, you don't leave one, and we will see who gets the business!

Source 2: Buyers

Of course, show your *Career Book* to buyers. We need them to "buy" into us, too, don't we? Buyers know only what they see when they look at us, just like sellers. Yet we need credibility when we work with buyers as well.

Getting Out-of-Town Buyers to Know You

Think about it: You send a relocation packet to out-of-town buyers; then they come to town to buy a home, and they know more about the town and your company than they do about you. You know all about them ahead of time, but they know nothing about you. Then we wonder why we have trouble getting and keeping the loyalty of our buyers. Credibility, again, is the key. As an ASP Stager, you want people who are buying homes, too, because you can refer them, in addition to sellers, to the Agents you are working with. Also, buyers usually have homes that need Staging, so that they can sell their house and buy the next one.

As an Agent, ask the out-of-town purchasers to look at your book overnight when you drop them off at their hotel. Ask them to look through it and then return it to you in the morning when you pick them up to look at homes. Simply explain to the purchasers:

> You know, Mr. and Mrs. Purchaser, I know a lot about you. I know your wants and needs and all about your family. But you really don't know much about me, do you? I want you to trust my ability to find, show, and sell you your new home, so I have put together a book about who I am and what I have done in real estate, including some of the homes I have sold, my background, and even my family. I'd really appreciate your taking it up to your hotel room this evening and looking through it. It will help you get to know me so much better. I also show it to sellers that I work with.

I've never had a buyer refuse to look at my *Career Book*. Why should they? You show me a buyer who says no, and I'll show you someone who is not a serious buyer!

Now some ASP Stagers may say or think, "Well, I can see how this works for Agents in this case, but what about us?" Please see the big picture! What works for one works for the other, and that is *you* too! Give the Agents whom you work with and who have and use a *Career Book* information about yourself, so that they can put *you* into their *Career Books* too! Think about it. Then the buyers can learn about you, and they or the Agent may hire you to Stage their new home when they buy it. They probably have a house to sell, too, and even if it is out of your area, you can do a Home Staging Consultation based on pictures that the buyers send of their home for sale, no matter where it is. Think *big picture*. Too many people, in my view, think small, think about limitations, and lack a big vision. Look for how you fit into the picture, not outside it. It is a *big picture*! And you are there all the way as an Agent or ASP Stager!

You can also send your *Career Book* to out-of-state buyers and include a prepaid box to send it back to you. It's worth the investment!

Getting Local Buyers to Know You

Local purchasers need to know about you, too. Don't just put them in your conference room and give them an advertising magazine. All they'll do is find 25 more houses they want to see. Instead, give them your *Career Book*. As an Agent, ask them to look through it while you set up a couple more appointments for homes you are going to show them. Give them at least 15 minutes alone with your book so that they have time to go through it before you come back. It works every time to help you sell yourself to the buyers.

ASP Stagers, as you look at the home of a client, you can have them look through your book, too, when you are doing a Home Staging Consultation. You should always have them look at it if they stay at the house while you are going through their home. How can you do the consultation in writing if they are asking you questions in each room as you write? No, you need to have them look at your *Career Book* and my "How to Price Your Home to Sell for Top Dollar!" DVD while you write up the Consultation, and everyone wins and learns more, all at the same time.

Source 3: For Sale by Owners

For Sale by Owners are wonderful! They need you. They are a great source of listings. I built part of my listing and Staging careers on For Sale by Owners. I used to knock on their doors and think to myself, "I have to list this house [as an Agent] or Stage this house [as an ASP Stager], or I'll die." Have you ever had that thought at one time or another? Why do that to yourself when you haven't even met the sellers or seen the house.

So I decided to work on one goal at a time, and it worked. As I knock on someone's door, my only goal is to get inside the house. When I first talk to the owners, I express my interest in their neighborhood. I tell them that I have sold or Staged homes in the area and would love to see their home to keep up with the neighborhood. Almost all sellers will let me inside their homes. They just say, "Fine, you can look at my home, but I'm not listing it." I acknowledge their right to sell their home themselves and that I know how much work it is. I *never* say the word "list" the first time I visit a For Sale by Owner. It's a dirty word to them at this point.

I have my *Career Book* in my arms, and I carry it with me as I look through the home with them. I am thinking to myself, "Is this a seller I would like to work with and a home that I would like to list or Stage?" Remember, we are the executives. The sellers not only pick us, but we also pick them. If this is a home I would want to list or Stage, then I want to leave my book with them. This is my next goal.

Now, when it comes to For Sale by Owners, I do not use the name *Career Book*. I call it "a book that has secrets of tips on selling in it." When you say "secrets" and "tips on selling" to an owner, you definitely will get their attention. They usually say, "You have a book with 'secrets' and 'tips' on selling in it?" I then tell them that I have left my book with many other For Sale by Owners, because it helps people know more about showing and selling their homes. I say that I don't have to show them the book at that exact moment, but rather I'll just leave it so that they can look through it on their own. This really takes the pressure off, and I have never had a For Sale by Owner turn me down. They like the idea of looking through it on their own. The book doesn't pressure them as you and I might, anyway, because books can't talk back. I always tell them that there are pictures and information about other homes that I have sold or Staged in my book and that I think they will enjoy looking at it. Some of the For Sale by Owners have almost torn it out of my hands. Once I give it to them, I also inform the owners that the book contains information about me that will also help them to know me better.

Now, as you use this idea with For Sale by Owners, you will learn what I have learned. Your *Career Book* is now "living" in the house. Both sellers look at it. Their children look at it. I have even had them lend it to neighbors because they were so impressed. The beautiful part is that other Agents or Stagers may come and go. They leave their business cards with the sellers, and when they go, they are gone. Meanwhile, you will have the definite overall advantage because you are "living" in the house. I have never had a For Sale by Owner list or Stage with anyone else when my book was in their home.

The key, once again, is building credibility. These owners always find some kind of common ground in your *Career Book*, without fail. They also tend to look on you as someone they now know. How can someone else's business card compete with your book? Impossible. It can't even get close. Now, when you return to pick up your book, the negatives they may have thought or expressed before are gone.

This brings me to another important point. You have a perfectly logical reason to return: to pick up your book. It is so easy and simple, and it really works. This gets you back in the house for the second time without the sellers' saying, as they open the front door, "What are you doing here?" Not only do they not say this, but they welcome you with open arms. Again, the common ground in your book bridges the credibility gap. Only then do I ask the For Sale by Owner for an appointment to return and present my marketing program or Home Staging Proposal. I don't believe they realize my credibility is above many of the other Agents or Stagers in the area until I have left my *Career Book*. Now I am on the offense, not the defense. Why? Because I have shown them my credibility through my book, and I have built trust and found a common ground. It makes all the difference in the world. I then return at the agreed time to present my Detailed Report as an Agent or to show my Home Staging Proposal or do a Home Staging Consultation as an ASP Stager. I always tell these owners that I do not pressure people into listing with me. I don't need to because most of the sellers in my area are already pressuring *me* to list or Stage their homes. I go back to the office, put together the report with their permission, and return at that appointed time to present it.

This, then, almost always leads to listing as the Agent or to Staging as the Stager. I cannot stress too much that the reason I have been so successful in this area of listing is because of the credibility I have built with the *Career Book*. You can do it too!

Source 4: Open Houses

I had my *Career Book*s in my car for almost a year before I ever thought of taking them into my open houses. How could I have been so slow to realize how great it would work there?

The potential dawned on me one day. I asked myself, "What am I taking into the open house to market myself? I have my company sign out front showing the open house. I have the company brochure and my business cards." But they might throw my cards out the car window as they drive down the freeway, or they might lose them between the seats in the car. Any way you look at it, I needed something more to market myself at the open houses, and the answer was sitting in my car! I started to bring at least two of my books to open houses. (Once I built one *Career Book*, I then saw that I needed four of them to call on multiple clients.) I gave them to people I really clicked with—you know the ones. These are the people who give you their name, address, and phone number at the open house. You really are getting along well with them. They seem to like you and you like them. But now they are going to leave. Sending a *Career Book* with them made so much sense, and it worked. Because they had already given me their name, address, and phone number, they did not hesitate to take my *Career Book* with them. I would simply tell them that I would love the chance to work with them. I had something to show that would help them to know me better. Then I would give them my *Career Book*.

Remember, many of the people who are looking at open houses are also looking for a salesperson they like and trust to help them find a property or list theirs. Your *Career Book* will make that decision a snap.

I used to call all the people I met over the weekend in my open houses on the following Monday morning. You know what I was thinking when I called them: "Are they still interested? Are they still motivated?" Now I didn't have to call them anymore, nor will you, because I got to go over to their home on Tuesday or Wednesday evening for a perfectly logical reason: I had to pick up my book. They expected me. Next thing you know, I was sitting in their living room, perhaps meeting the spouse I did not meet at the open house. I could then see their home in person and say, "Why don't you let me do a workup on the amount of equity you really have to see whether you can make the move?" That is exactly what I would end up doing. The next thing you know, I was listing their home and selling them another one. Try your *Career Book* at open houses. Once again, it works!

ASP Stagers, the same advice goes for you! You need to be at the open houses with the Agents you work with to answer Staging questions while you and the Agent and the sellers or buyers are coming through the open houses. What a great place for you to be with your ASP Stager *Career Book*! The Agent will introduce you and back you up by saying how great Staging is, and the next thing you know, you have a client as well. Think about being at open houses. This is a perfect situation, whether you are dealing with a buyer or a seller. Either way, that is a new client for you to Stage to sell or Stage to live!

Teaming up with an Agent is a great way to work open houses. (When we come to the marketing the house portion of this book I will share a great idea with you about how you can help market the house and the Agent in a very productive way, which both Agents and Sellers will love!) There is no greater topic to talk about at open houses than Staging homes. This I know because I have proved it to myself through all my many years over and over again. The open house is a great place to be with the Agent who has the listing, and you are meeting the clients coming through at the same time, too. Any of those people could be the new buyers for the house, and they may have a home to sell—and you are there to talk about Staging their home so that they can buy the one you and the Agent are in. That kind of interaction benefits the seller of this home, too, of course! Everyone benefits.

By the way, my recommendation is that no one should accept a contingency in the sale of their home that is subject to the sale of another home *unless* the house is Staged. That should be a professional policy of all Agents, so sellers reading this book remember that, please. As soon as an Agent agrees to accept a contingency on the sale of another home to sell your home, you are in essence saying that the other house will sell before your house does. If you feel that way, then take the contingency, but you better be sure that the other house is Staged too. Otherwise, the chances of its selling before yours are much lower than the chances of your selling your home. Sellers and Agents, I remind you once again, it is so crucial that you work with a Certified ASP Accredited Staging Professional!

Source 5: Builders

Builders love the *Career Book*, because they are always looking for an Agent or a Stager who knows about marketing. They realize that the *Career Book* is a marketing tool about you. They will respect you more than the other people in your area if you put one together and show it to builders. That is how I attracted the builders whose homes I have listed and the many builders' homes that I have Staged.

Actually, the first builder I ever listed gave me the idea of showing him the book. A man in jeans and a T-shirt walked into my open house and said, "Are you Barb Schwarz?" I said, "I sure am." He then said, "Well, you don't know me, but I build a lot of houses in this area. One of my friends said I was supposed to look you up and ask for some darn book you've got. Where is it?" I was chuckling inside because I realized one of my other sellers must have told him about my *Career Book*. I gave it to him, and I went on to list for one of the best and most productive builders in my area. In fact, he called me in two days after taking my book with him. This was even before I called him.

As I worked with more and more builders, I got to thinking that, if the *Career Book* works for me, why wouldn't it work for builders, too? So I got my builders to give me their backgrounds in resume form, all their credentials, their family pictures, and letters from subcontractors they used in building their houses. (If the subs want to get paid, they will write the letter, I promise you!) In addition, I took pictures of every house they had ever built in town (with the purchasing family in the front of the house) and included letters from families naming my builder as the best in the area. I put all of this in what I called the *Company Career Book*. Each builder had his own book, but I didn't let my builders keep the individual books I had put together for them. Rather, I kept them with me at all times. I would show them at any time to anyone, and I especially used them whenever I was holding a builder's open house on the weekends. As with my own book, my goal was to send the builder's book home with buyers who might be interested in having my builder build them a home—either as a presale or as a custom home. Do you know what started to happen? The buyers would literally start to fall in love with the builder's work, and I'd get a call that went something like this: "Barb, we met you in a builder's open house last week, and you gave us his *Career Book*. Well, we have looked through it several times and would like you to come over to our present home and talk to us about your builder doing a custom or presale home for us!"

It was like taking candy from a baby—in a nice way—because the book had done almost all of the selling for me. For any builder whose homes you currently list *or* have Staged as an ASP Stager, I strongly urge you to do these two things: Show them your *Career Book*, and put together a *Company Career Book* for your builder. It makes so much sense, and it works.

ASP Stagers, I expect you to use your *Career Book*s with builders, and after builders read this book, they will expect that, too. And a Stager, of all people, can sure make a great builder's *Career Book*! Stage it! Everything needs to be Staged: your *Career Book*, their *Career Book*, your car, how you look, your presentations for Proposals and for Consultations. Everything you do should be Staged, and working with builders is a great place to Stage property. Builders are finally finding and seeing that having model homes doesn't make sales. Why? Many models are the crowded, overdecorated homes that people sometimes visit just to get decorating ideas, not to buy the builder's house. Builders are finally finding that Staging their new homes is the way to go, too, just as in the resale market, so that they can sell the house and not the decorating. And I am saying it here and I will say it again and again from this point on: "Decorating is *not* Staging!"

Decorating Versus ASP Staging

Decorating is personalizing a home way, way too much. Staging is showing the space and selling the house. Staging doesn't have all the decorating stuff that interior designers use and bring into the house. Staging is about selling the house, not the stuff and not all the goodies that decorators have and put into homes, which is usually way over the top. Decorating is not Staging. It never has been and it never will be. Remember, I used to be a decorator, and when I went into real estate and invented Staging, I saw the difference big time because many homes were decorated and the buyers were not buying. By the way, back in the 1970s, I told my decorator friends about my home Staging ideas, saying, "You should look at what I am doing and look at this too to be able to help people." I will never forget what several decorators in Seattle said to me: "Oh, gosh, we wouldn't be caught dead in those dirty messy houses that people live in!" My, how times change, with some decorators now calling themselves Stagers because this means extra cash flow for their decorating business. But Staging it isn't decorating, and some feel that to train as an ASP Stager is beneath them.

We sometimes see the difference between those who want to help people and those who want to have more cash flow by charging way too much as a decorator to Stage. In Seattle, I just saw a decorator charge $50,000 to Stage a home. That is not Staging. That is taking advantage of people and selling people things that they do not need to sell a house. Doing that is all about the things instead of the house. It is about the decorator, not the seller. We went head to head with a decorator recently in the same neighborhood, we Staged a house as an ASP team, and the house sold in three days at full price. The house the decorator says she Staged was still sitting there three months later; so you be the judge. And the fee she charged was 10 times more than what we charged our seller, who sold in three days at full price.

Sellers, make sure that you work with a trained ASP Stager who really Stages for a living to help sell your home, instead of decorating your home with extra unneeded stuff. That is where seeing the ASP Stager's *Career Book* can really help you see whom you are working with and why Staging is the right way to go. I have story after story of home owners who have called me after bringing in a decorator and then realizing their mistake; they wanted me to fix the decorating by Staging the home the ASP way!

Source 6: Anyone!

This source is my favorite. You can knock on one door and reach thousands at a time. It all starts with someone you know, so it is not scary.

In your area, to whom do you give business? You give out people's names because we are asked for them all the time in our business. "Do you know a good doctor?" "Do you know a reliable CPA in this area?" "Barb, I need a new dentist, one I could really trust that my kids would like." I got to thinking about all the business I hand out and how I never really ask for any of it back. Now is the time to change all that. I made a list of people: my accountant, doctor, dentist, hairdresser, stockbroker, insurance agent, banker, directors of major companies in town, and so forth. I then decided to do the following, which I strongly recommend to you because it works:

1. Call them up and ask each to lunch, one at a time.
2. As you take each to lunch, make the point, over lunch, that you are so much different from most of the other Agents or Stagers they have ever worked with before. In other words, "Let me tell you how I work."
3. Ask for their business. If you don't ask, you may not get it. Remember, the Bible says, "Ask and you shall receive." But you have to ask. Even though we are in sales, many of us simply forget to do that.
4. Give the person your *Career Book*. Ask him or her to take it back to their workplace and pass it around. For example, I did this with my accountant and obtained his company's entire account of referral business. The key is that if you give them business, they will give you business; it only makes good business sense. But, again, you have to ask. The key is your *Career Book* because of the extra credibility it will build with these people.

Professional people want to refer their clients to an Agent or Stager who is likable and trustworthy and will make them look good, not someone who will embarrass them. Do you know that some of these people I asked to give me their business actually asked me to put an extra book together for them to keep at their office to show their clients? Then future clients seeing my book ahead of time builds trust before they ever meet me. Terrific!

Invest the small amount of time it takes to put your own list together. Whom can you take to lunch and ask to send you business? You know many more people than you think you do. Networking works!

How about your accountant? I knew that mine did taxes for about 15 other real estate Agents. But I wondered if he really knew how differently I worked. So I took him to lunch one day to tell him and left my *Career Book* with him. When I talked to him later, he said, "I didn't know you did all of this production. Our clients are always looking for investments, buying and selling houses and property. I'm going to start sending them to you." This is true for listing and selling homes and for Staging homes too! You can do the same thing, so don't wait!

Let your attorney know what you do. Many times in divorce cases or other types of settlements, people need to Stage and sell their houses. If your attorney knows what you do, he or she will be more likely to spread your name around to clients. So take your attorney to lunch, explain how you work, and leave your *Career Book*.

Leave your *Career Book* where you have your hair cut, where you bank, where you work out—everywhere! The more people who know how you work, the more leads you'll generate. People are usually happy to refer you, but they forget. Your job is to help them keep you in their minds at all times when thinking about real estate. They say that everyone on the face of the earth knows at least 250 other people. Think of the numbers you can reach by this method. Your *Career Book is* a crucial tool as you do this because it takes away any doubt that you are the right person to receive their referrals and replaces it with credibility.

By the way, there is only one best place to keep your *Career Book*s as you go about the business of real estate—in someone else's hands! Between loans, however, I have found the best place to keep them is in the back seat of my car. I got a box from the grocery store, put it in the back seat of my car, and put my *Career Book*s there. Why? Because our cars are really our offices, aren't they? (By the way, don't keep your books in your trunk because out of sight means out of mind.) I wanted them with me at all times so that I could hand them out at a moment's notice. If you leave them at your office, you'll forget about them. I know because that's what I did. The same is true for leaving them at home. Keep them in your car.

One more tip is to put each book in an old pillow case, in the box in the back seat. The pillow case helps prevent scratches and having them stick together in hot weather.

Show your *Career Book* to your spouse or significant other and to other family members. Ask them to take it to work and pass it around at the office. If you take the time to prepare your book professionally, your friends and family will be proud of your book, too. I decided to call my husband's secretary at work and ask her to be sure that my *Career Book* went all throughout the company, to every department and floor. She wants to do anything extra to please her boss, right? It worked. I can't even begin to tell you all of the extra referrals I began to receive and those referrals turned into many sales.

Let your neighbors know what you do. Think about it. Do your neighbors really know what you do? Tell them what you do; better yet, show them what you do in real estate or in Staging by leaving your *Career Book* with them, one neighbor at a time. Chances are that they will want to Stage or sell someday. Wouldn't you rather have them come to someone they know—you—instead of turning to strangers?

Remember, everyone knows at least 250 other people, including your neighbors. They know many other people in other neighborhoods whom you don't know. Why not put the people you don't know into your hands as referrals from the neighbors by showing them your *Career Book*? I can't say this enough: Prospects are everywhere because everyone is a prospect—if you let them know how you work. If you educate people and let them know what you can do for them, you can have as many prospects as you can handle.

The *Career Book* is one of the best ways I know to let other people know what you do, and it's one of the most exciting parts of my listing and Staging program. Real Estate Agents and ASP Stagers who use it tell me that it is changing their business and helping them individually; they also say that this book is changing and helping our industry. At long last sellers have a proven way to find the Agent and Stager who meets their needs. The day is really coming when the ASP Stager or Agent who does not have a *Career Book* will not get the business because the business card is simply no match.

The *Career Book* is your walking resume. It is a hardback definition of who you are and how you work. Take it with you everywhere. Lend it to everyone you know. Once you start circulating your *Career Book*, believe me, prospects will find you! Because your *Career Book* tells people exactly who you are and how you have sold or Staged homes for other people. In other words, your *Career Book* shows all the reasons, in a simple and professional way, why sellers should hire you to list or Stage their property.

Get your *Career Book* together and then out there prospecting for you. It is now possible to be in more than one place at the same time through the use of your *Career Book*. It works.

CHAPTER 6

STEP 2: THE EXCLUSIVE DETAILED REPORT

The education of everyone leads to success for everyone.

BARB SCHWARZ

SELLER'S NOTE

Communication is everything. The Agent sends a message to the seller, and the Stager sends a message to the seller as well. Even the house communicates a message to a buyer. What message does your house send to buyers? Dirty, clean, messy, neat, Staged, or not Staged? What messages do Agents and Stagers send to you as a seller? I have a saying about communication: The quality of your communication determines the quality of your business and of your life. Too many Agents do not know how to communicate as effectively as they should. Some do, and many do not. Agents assume way, way too much. Agents assume that sellers know everything about what it takes to sell real estate today. That is a huge and wrong assumption. Real estate isn't usually sellers' area of expertise, not unless they are Agents as well.

(Continued)

That is why you, the seller, hire an Agent to tell you what to do to sell the house and to tell you what the *Agent* should do to sell the house. ASP Stagers, I find, many times communicate better than Agents. Of course, this is not always true, but because ASP Stagers study how rooms and things communicate, they practice communication skills more than some Agents. However, everyone needs to improve communication skills because they can always be improved.

So in this chapter, sellers, I want to you read and learn how your Agent and Stager should be presenting their presentation to you. Then in the next couple of chapters I will tell you what they should be saying and promising you they will do in their presentations. So take note and please realize that I share the information in this chapter with you so that you will better understand how the Agent and Stager should perform during their presentations. I have tested this thousands of times myself, and it is for the good of all.

IN THIS CHAPTER

You will learn:

1. How to set the stage for your presentation.
2. The two crucial parts of the Exclusive Detailed Report (listing presentation).
3. Why you, as an ASP Stager, need to know what is in the Agent's Exclusive Detailed Report and why!
4. The benefits to you as a seller of working with an Agent who does what I share in this chapter to sell your home.
5. The benefits to you as a seller of working with an ASP Stager who does what I share in this chapter to Stage your house so that it sells!

Agents and Stagers, educating your sellers is the key to getting a "yes!" from your seller. In addition to your *Career Book*, the greatest opportunity for educating your sellers is during your presentation, which I call the Exclusive Detailed Report. An Exclusive Detailed Report as an Agent is when you present your marketing program and the market pricing to the seller. And for Stagers your presentation is a Home Staging Proposal or Consultation to your seller.

The best presentation is one that explains the listing process to sellers as well as informing them of your skills as a listing Agent. To be able to accomplish both these objectives, you must be willing to spend time preparing and practicing your listing presentation, in addition to spending at least an hour and a half giving a presentation to your sellers.

The Report (or listing presentation) contains two important parts: Part one is your Exclusive Marketing Program and part two is your Comparative Market Analysis (CMA). Each part is crucial to educating the seller about how you work and all the services you provide.

Many times we say more than we think we do. We make statements with our bodies. So it is a good idea to be aware of what signals you are sending with your body language and what others' movements are telling you.

Knowing where to sit and where to have your sellers sit is very important for maintaining professional control during your listing presentation.

What do you include in your report (or presentation)? There are definite facts and pieces of information that you need to share with your sellers. Now is when education of the sellers is crucial. Here is where you can end objections before sellers ever think of them. What you teach your sellers during your presentation can literally determine whether you become the listing Agent for those sellers.

SETTING THE STAGE FOR PRESENTATION

Notice I used the word "Stage." You can Stage anything. Stage your car, Stage your appearance, Stage the sellers' home, and Stage your presentation. It is very important.

The Right Touch

I want to explain some ways you can add more power to your listing presentation—small but important details. Do you ever think about how you actually conduct your presentation? Do you pay attention to body language, where you sit, where the sellers sit, and so forth? You might think these are all items of very little importance, but they can make a big difference.

The Greeting

Let's say it's time to go to the sellers' home for your listing presentation (Exclusive Detailed Report). You have your complete presentation, which is your Exclusive Marketing Program, Comparative Market Analysis, and *Marketing Portfolio* as you approach the door and ring the doorbell. (In the next chapter we will cover the *Marketing Portfolio in* detail.) When the sellers come to the door, extend your hand, and say something like, "Oh, it's great to see you again." Of course, they invite you inside the house. You probably sat in the living room for the first visit, but I recommend that you *not* sit in the living room again until the sale is closed and they have the proceeds from the sale of their home in their hands.

The Meeting Location

Always say to your potential sellers, "Could we sit at the kitchen table?" Then go into the kitchen to sit down. Sometimes they might say, "Let's sit at the dining room table." Explain to the sellers that that is fine, but that you don't want to scratch it. Tell them that unless they have a table cloth or table pad, you would rather give your presentation in the kitchen. The important thing is that you are all comfortable and that you don't have to stretch out your presentation materials from a sofa to an easy chair in the living room. No one can give a professional presentation and maintain the necessary control sprawling from a wingback chair to the living room sofa across a coffee table. You just can't do it. From now on, use the kitchen table or a covered dining room table as your workstation with your sellers. All the work you do in the future should be conducted at the same table. You are setting the stage for work. It doesn't really matter where the table is as long as there are as few distractions as possible. Round tables are better than ones with corners.

Placement and Body Language

Body language is crucial. I believe in placing people where I can be most effective with them and for them. For example, let's say you go to make a presentation and think that the wife is more dominant and outgoing than the husband. Sit closer to her. If you think the husband is the decision maker, sit by him. By sitting closer to the person who seems to have the most authority, you can use that power to control the flow and mood of your presentation. To do this when the woman is the dominant one, ask her where she usually sits at the table. Like most of us, she probably has her own seat. Then, have her husband sit on one side of her, and you sit on the other. That way, she is in the middle.

Why does it matter whether you sit beside the wife? If she is the decision maker and she starts to get out of control because of pricing or anything you talk about, she is much easier to control because you are beside her. You can even pat her elbow a little and talk her through the problem. If she is across from you, there is no way you can calm her down as easily or keep the situation under control. If the husband is the decision maker, you simply reverse the placement.

A quick tip: I believe in touching, and I believe it can really help you in real estate sales if you do it the right way. I believe you can touch people in a professional, nonthreatening way to help you get your message across. A touch on the elbow or a light hand on the shoulder can have a calming effect and can help build rapport. I have also found that in the beginning, as I work with sellers and touch them on the shoulder or elbow, I do not look them in the eyes. I simply look toward the object I am talking about (such as a mantel on the fireplace or comparable homes in the market analysis) and reach out for their elbow or shoulder at the same time. Contact with the eyes is more intimate than touch, and I don't combine the two when I first work with sellers.

Of course, you want to be careful not to invade a seller's personal space. We all have a certain amount of space around us, and if someone breaks that barrier, we put up our defenses. For example, think of how you would feel if you were in line at the grocery store and the person behind you kept looking over your shoulder as you wrote a check to pay your bill.

You don't want to put your sellers on the defensive. So be very subtle when touching them. If you feel comfortable doing this, just offer a reassuring pat now and then. If you don't feel comfortable doing this, then don't do it. For touching to work, it has to feel natural; otherwise, forget it. I would never want you to do anything that you did not feel comfortable with because your discomfort will come across loud and clear to sellers.

When setting the stage, you have to be careful not to evoke jealousy. For example, it does not matter whether I am 20, 40, or 79 years old. It does not matter how I look. As a female, I must be very careful not to pay too much attention to the husband. If he is sitting beside me and I don't pay any attention to her, guess what is going to happen? She may become jealous. When I leave, she may say to him, "There is no way that woman is listing our house!" I do not want female sellers saying that because they felt I was too attentive to their husbands. Male Agents have to be aware of the same thing if they are working with a woman. Be attuned to how your actions are being perceived. Pay equal attention to both partners.

Place people where you want them, but do be aware of your body language and what it is saying about you. Listen to what their actions tell you, and be careful that your actions don't say the wrong things. You don't want to inadvertently insult a potential seller. No matter what company you work for, you are still representing yourself and your company. Talk as a professional and behave as a professional.

CONTROL OF FLOW

Although your sellers are ultimately your employers, you have to control the presentation if you are to do your best job. In the end, control is in their best interest. It is your show. You worked hard, you did extra research to be sure your price recommendation is accurate, and you stayed late at the office to prepare your report for the sellers. Perhaps you didn't get to go to the movies with your family. So why give a presentation unless you set the stage, give the introduction, and be the keynote speaker? It only makes good business sense.

Also, as you give your report, you need to be the one turning the pages. I once had a seller (the only one like this I've had in all my years of selling) who just didn't want to wait. I was in the middle of my presentation, and I could just tell he was really excited. He loved everything, but he just couldn't wait. So he leaned over and started to turn my pages to peek at what was coming next. I thought, "He's going to see the price, and he is going to be shocked." So I just put my hand down on the page very calmly and said, "Joe, you know, there are special things I want to share with you on every page and don't you worry, we're going to get there. So hang in there with me. OK?" He said, "OK, Barb" and put his hands back in his lap, and I went on with the presentation. So, if things start to get out of control a little, you have to get that control right back. The flow and timing of your presentation are very important.

If the kids come in and interrupt the flow of your presentation, stop. Let them talk to the parents. Let the parents handle that situation. Whatever the interruption, let the sellers take care of it before you go on. If one seller leaves the table to take care of a child or a phone call, don't go on. Wait until he or she returns to go on with your presentation. Talk to the remaining seller about the weather, sports, anything but the presentation. It doesn't do you any good to make a presentation if you don't have all your sellers' undivided attention. Remember, they don't know what you don't tell them!

LANGUAGE

The words you use when talking to sellers can have a profound effect on whether they accept or reject what you are telling them. I believe you can tell sellers anything. But it isn't what you say, it's how you say it. No matter what you are sharing with the sellers, always represent yourself in the most professional way possible. Otherwise, things we say that are not professional may come back to haunt us later. We must always be personable but professional. For example, I love the word "transaction." In my mind that is the most effective word we can use. The word—I almost hate to say it—"deal" does not belong in the world of real estate. Also, use "professional fee" or "brokerage" instead of "commission," which sounds hard on a seller's ears.

When you put a document in front of someone, always say, "Will you please authorize this for me?" or "Will you please approve this agreement?" That sounds so much softer than, "Sign here." And the word "agreement" is so much more pleasant than "contract." That's what you do: come to an agreement.

By all means, share stories with sellers. I call them war stories. We've all gone through challenging and interesting situations. Funny things happen. Sad things happen. Stories about these situations lend credibility to your character, add strength to your presentation, and help you illustrate your point.

Last, but very important is to *not* use industry jargon without explaining it. I don't know how many times I have witnessed Agents talking to sellers about CMAs, GRI, MLS, brokers opens, comps, industry legal terms, or any number of words that most sellers have no knowledge of. Most people don't want to embarrass themselves by admitting they don't understand certain terms. Therefore, you are not only talking down to them in a way, but you are failing to properly educate them when they don't understand part of the presentation. Use layman's terms as much as possible and if you need to use industry jargon, make sure you define it for them so that the sellers understand. It makes you look like a true professional, not a confusing name-dropping salesperson. Stagers can easily fall into the same situation by talking about colors, types of furniture, styles, even terms such as "vignette" or "consultation." What does all that mean?

PRACTICE MAKES PERFECT—AND INCREASES INCOME!

What is your average Staging fee? What is your average individual brokerage commission per listing or sale? Have you ever taken the time to figure that out for yourself? In most areas of the United States, the average sales commission you earn can be approximately $5,000 per listing sold. Some areas are higher, and others are lower, but let's use $5,000 as an example. Every time you give an Exclusive Detailed Report, you could be earning that $5,000 if you are successful. If you were asked to give an hour-and-a-half talk for $5,000, it would be safe to assume you would practice that speech, right? Not only would you practice it once, you would probably practice it over and over again. Why do we tend never to practice in real estate? Actually, we do practice, but we practice on the very person who is going to be our employer: our future sellers. Practice does make perfect. So practice your presentation and then practice it again and again. Make sure it is perfect *before* you try it on sellers. It will get you more listings and sellers that are properly educated.

Think of your presentation as a $5,000 speech (or insert your average commission or Staging fee). If the seller is motivated by your speech, you will get the listing or the Staging project. With that kind of income at stake, doesn't it make sense to practice your presentation?

If you want to get more listings and sales, heed this advice: Take what you learn from this book, develop your own presentation in your own style, and practice it. Practice it until your presentation is natural and smooth. Practice alone. Practice with people in your family. Know your material so well that you can be flexible enough to handle interruptions and answer questions and relaxed enough to put the sellers at ease. The individual with the strongest and most educational presentation for the sellers will usually get the listing.

THE PRESENTATION

Remember, with every Exclusive Detailed Report you give, you are marketing yourself and your service. By using a professionally prepared marketing program, a visual aid such as the *Marketing Portfolio,* and a well rehearsed verbal presentation, you decrease the chance of misunderstandings and capitalize on your professionalism as a licensed Real Estate Agent or as a Stager. If you use these presentation ideas, you will be Staging more houses or listing more houses than ever—and making more money! Remember, it is your show and your income. I want you to make money and stay in this wonderful business!

Two Parts of the Exclusive Detailed Report

At the end of this section, you will see a list of the different parts of the Report. These are my suggestions to you. I know that you probably already have a presentation or are forming one for yourself at this time. Look at what I have in my report to the sellers and compare it with yours; see what you might add to make your presentation even stronger. I have also found that the order of items you see on my suggested list really works. By giving a Exclusive Detailed Report in this order, your presentation logically unfolds before the sellers. They love it, and, more important, they are totally educated on both marketing and pricing. The two parts of the listing presentation follow.

PART ONE FOR AGENTS AND STAGERS

- A cover page for your Exclusive Marketing Program.
- Letter of introduction from you thanking them for the opportunity to work together.
- Information sheet or sheets about your company.
- Pictures of the home you took during your first visit.
- The Exclusive Marketing Program for the sale of the home (use with the *Marketing Portfolio*).
- *Marketing Portfolio* (use with the Exclusive Marketing Program).
- Tips for selling and/or Staging ideas from you or your company.
- Property records from the county.

PART TWO FOR REAL ESTATE AGENTS

- Comparative Market Analysis cover page.
- Estimate of the sellers' net proceeds form. (I like to leave this form blank and fill it in with the sellers as we zero in on their list price at the end of my presentation.)
- Multiple listing service statistics.
- Solds, expireds, and off-the-market comparables; Staged comparables and non-Staged comparables.
- On-market comparables; Staged and non-Staged on-market comparables.
- Recipe for a sale.

- Pricing your home using the market position triangle.
- Paperwork to list the house.

THE PARTS OF STEP 2 FOR AN ASP STAGER: THE HOME STAGING CONSULTA-
TION OR HOME STAGING PROPOSAL TO STAGE

- Cover.
- Letter of introduction.
- Staging statistics.
- A page of testimonials from other sellers.
- Pictures of other homes before and after ASP Staging.
- Pictures of the seller's home before ASP Staging that you took on Step 1.
- The Consultation pages of what the seller should do to Stage the home or the Proposal to Stage by the ASP Stager.
- Your creative service Staging fee page.
- Return on Staging investment page.
- What is an ASP Stager page.
- Reservation Staging page.
- Paperwork to work together.
- List of things the seller needs to do before you can Stage the house.
- Back cover.

Look at these lists of what I would like you to have in your report, and compare them with what you are doing already. See what you might add to make your presentation stronger. Think about what could be missing from what I have shared with you and that you aren't doing or don't have in your presentation now. I have also found that the order of items you see on my suggested list really works. By giving a Report in this order, your presentation logically unfolds. Sellers love it, and, more important, they are totally educated on both marketing and pricing the house or on Staging and the Staging fee.

In the chapters to come, we will take a detailed look at all of these materials. As I come to see the sellers for Step 2, the Exclusive Detailed Report, all of the preceding information is in the listing packet I bring with me. I also bring my listing presentation book, or *Marketing Portfolio*, to show the sellers samples of the work I promise them that I will do. You will soon learn why and how this is so powerful. Notice that in the two parts of the report the price is the next-to-the-very-last piece of paper I show the sellers (the very last piece of paper is the actual listing agreement, which I have already shown them earlier in the presentation to remove some of the fear of the paperwork). I leave the price to the last because I want to thoroughly educate sellers on how and why I arrived at the suggested list price before I show it to them. In more than 30 years in this business, I have never had a seller want to skip the presentation and say, "Just give me the price." I think this is because I have taught them up front in let-me-tell-you-how-I-work that they deserve to know everything. They owe it to themselves. This approach works, and they not only remember it but expect it from me. It also gives you the edge to get the listing because most other Agents won't take the time to educate the sellers up front and show this type of Exclusive Detailed Report.

Take the time to educate your sellers. No one on the face of the earth can educate sellers on the marketing they will do in 15 minutes because Agents who are doing only 15 minutes of marketing in this day and age will not get the listing any more. Sellers deserve the time and the education. We owe it to them. You will benefit by getting the listing, having the control you need to price it right, getting the house Staged for sale, and then taking it to the bank.

CHAPTER 7

THE *MARKETING PORTFOLIO*

Let me show you how I work.

BARB SCHWARZ

SELLER'S NOTE

How do you know what an Agent is going to do for you? How do you know what an ASP Stager is going to do for you? One of the easiest ways is to see examples of their work, which you have the right to see. Telling you what they will do is very important, but seeing examples of their work is even more important. The world is really all about show-and-tell. We tell people things, but, to make sure what we are saying is true, we use this well-known phrase: "I will believe it when I see it!" In other words, show me!

Sellers, you have the right to see—and you need to really make sure that you do see—samples and examples of what Agents and Stagers say they will do for you. In

(Continued)

my training classes, I train our ASP Agents and ASP Stagers to do this for you. It is important also that you make sure it happens on your end. How can you tell the quality of the ads the Agents will do? How do you know what the Agent's flyers or brochure will do for your property? How can you know the latest statistics that show how Home Staging works in today's market? How can you make sure that the quality of the Staging is what you expect? The list of questions goes on and on for both Agents and Stagers alike. You have to be shown.

Too many times sellers are not shown enough of what will be done for them. Too many times presentations are dropped off because the Agent or Stager doesn't take the time to go through it in person with the seller. How can you ask questions that way? Surveys show that many Agents don't share enough time, don't share enough information, and do not let people know what they are going to do for them. This is one of the reasons that Real Estate Agents rate in the bottom five among professionals at large. Therefore, you need to ask questions as a seller. You need to ask what you are paying for. And, you need to be shown, by means of examples and samples of work, what will be done for you. This should be easy for an ASP Agent or ASP Stager to do.

IN THIS CHAPTER

You will learn:

1. Why you need to have and use a *Marketing Portfolio* as an Agent.
2. Why you need to have and use a *Marketing Portfolio* as a Stager.
3. Why you should care as a homeowner/seller that an Agent and Stager uses a *Marketing Portfolio* to show you how they work.
4. How and why I developed the *Marketing Portfolio*.
5. How to develop and use your own *Marketing Portfolio*.
6. Why your presentation must be an educational show-and-tell presentation for the seller, whether you are an Agent or an ASP Stager.

Stagers and Agents, to be able to show your sellers what you will do for them, as you work together with them, there is no doubt in my mind that the *Marketing Portfolio* is the easiest and best way to do this.

THE *MARKETING PORTFOLIO*

If you were excited about the *Career Book*, hold onto your hat. What I am going to tell you about now is just as powerful as the *Career Book,* yet it is used for an entirely different purpose. I'm talking about the *Marketing Portfolio*, which is a special, personalized presentation book. By the time you finish reading this chapter, every time you see or hear the words "*Marketing Portfolio*," you're going to think dollar signs because of the listings it will bring you!

Seed of a Sample Book

In the beginning, it was very simple. I wrote out my marketing program—all the things I would do to market a property. I would type up the list and sign my name to it. This was my commitment to the sellers in writing. Then I started to bring samples of my work with me to my presentation because I could see that sellers did not always really understand my marketing techniques if I just listed them. They wanted to see samples of my work. How did I know that? They asked me to bring samples of my work with me. I just called it "my sample book." It was actually in a small folder containing a few papers: a copy of a flyer, maybe a bulletin or two, a copy of an ad, and even a letter I had written to another Agent about someone's property. I had just a few simple things to show potential sellers what I would do to market their properties as an Agent. Or I would bring before-and-after pictures of homes I had Staged. And showing the sellers samples really worked—even at that point. It began to help sellers see what I was talking about and helped them understand the importance of my many marketing techniques. So I made it a permanent part of my presentation. It added weight to my marketing program, and I listed more and more homes. And as a Stager I Staged more and more homes. That little folder grew into the *Marketing Portfolio*, and I know that the concept can help you give a more powerful presentation and get more listings and Stagings.

Over the years, as I refined the *Marketing Portfolio* and started to include more samples of my marketing techniques, the book naturally evolved into sections, so I designed divider pages to cover each technique. The more I educated my future sellers with examples of the work I would do for them, the more they liked my presentation and the more professional control I had. I wouldn't give a presentation without it now, because the *Marketing Portfolio* is so powerful. I know that once you fully understand its merits, you won't give a presentation without it either.

As I go from city to city, I see different companies and Agents all over our great country and all the different materials they use. Many real estate companies have a company listing presentation book or recommended things to use in a listing presentation. That's great, but they invariably talk about the company, how great it is, and what the company will do for the seller. The real power of the *Marketing Portfolio* is that it is something *you* personalize to show off *your* ideas, the techniques *you* use, and the work *you* do. That's the beauty of it! It is the work you do as the Agent or the Stager working for an individual seller. It is the best way to educate sellers. It shows off what you as an individual will do for the seller as you decide to work together as a seller–Agent team or a seller–Stager team.

Do not ever leave your *Marketing Portfolio* with the sellers as you do with your *Career Book*. I have four *Career Book*s that I drop off and leave for different sellers to look through, but I have only one *Marketing Portfolio* because I never leave it, ever, with anyone. You don't need additional *Marketing Portfolio*s at all because your one copy stays with you always; it has your marketing secrets in it. The *Career Book* is about you, and the *Marketing Portfolio* is about what you will do for sellers. Don't confuse the uses. One is for sharing your qualifications, and the other is for showing what you will do to sell or Stage a home. They are two separate tools with two separate purposes, yet both are to be used to educate the seller visually, each in its own way. One is about you and the other is about the services you will perform.

Why can't you just tell people instead of having a presentation book? You have heard of show-and-tell, and you can tell people what you will do for them all you want, but when you show them what you will do, the world opens up to you, because sellers really get it and understand what you are trying to tell them. Studies show that when you combine verbal and visual presentations, your audience will remember and retain three to four times more information than if you have just visual or verbal by itself. How can you really educate the seller about your brochures or your Staging if you don't show samples of what you do? You start with let-me-*tell*-you-how-I-work, and then this takes you to the next step of let-me-*show*-you-how-I-work! First you tell people, then you better show them.

Bring your *Marketing Portfolio* with you for Step 2, and use it as a part of your presentation. In the next chapter I will show you exactly where the *Marketing Portfolio* fits into your presentation and ways to use it to showcase your work. It is an excellent tool for educating your sellers—and selling your services!

Show-and-tell = Success.

The *Marketing Portfolio* needs to be put together in the same order as your marketing plan as an Agent or your Staging proposal as a Stager. Your marketing program or your Staging Proposal *tells* sellers what you are going to do, and your *Marketing Portfolio shows* them what you are going to do.

THE *MARKETING PORTFOLIO* CONCEPT

Now, let's go through the concept of the *Marketing Portfolio*, and I'll give you ideas on what you can show your sellers to make your presentations the most powerful they can be. You can make your own sample book and use all the ideas in this chapter, or you can use my *Marketing Portfolio*.

Start with Your Company

Your company is important to you, or you wouldn't be with them. It's important to your sellers, too, because they want to be reassured that you feel you are with the best company. The rest of the *Marketing Portfolio* is primarily about you and your individual ideas and techniques for them, but I think it's good to start your book by including information about your company. Include things such as company pamphlets, newspaper articles, awards, pictures, and so forth. Show off your company. Your *Career Book* is all about you, so you should have some company information in the front of your *Marketing Portfolio* to educate sellers about the things that you feel are the most important for them to learn about your company. This is true whether your company is large or small or whether you are an independent sole proprietor and own your own company. Either way, you need to share information about the company with sellers.

Preview the Listing Process or the Staging Process

As the Agent, start out by showing your sellers the process you will go through with them together to actually bring their property on the market. In the beginning of your *Marketing Portfolio*, show a copy of the listing agreement and the forms needed to come on the market that your company and the multiple listing service use in your area.

As the ASP Stager, you need to put in the forms that you and your client will sign to work together as a team. You show them without yet filling them in so that they get used to seeing them. Remember, I have all these pieces of paper in my *Marketing Portfolio* in plastic sheet protectors, so I just turn the pages as I talk about the different pieces of information. I find that by having a copy of the agreement at this point in the presentation takes some of the fear out of the paperwork later. Simply let your future sellers know that this is the paperwork you will complete together in the future.

Educate Future Sellers About Staging Homes

As soon as the paperwork is filled out, the next thing is to have the sellers' house Staged. So this is the next section you need as an Agent in your presentation book. You are showing them the steps you are going to be taking, step by step. The seller deserves to know this ahead of time!

As an Agent, you must share with sellers the importance of Home Staging and the many benefits it brings to the sellers and to their property. If you do not, then I sincerely believe that you are not keeping your fiduciary responsibility to the seller to educate them about what they can do to receive top dollar in *any* market!

Even though I have been speaking about Home Staging since I invented it for over 30 years, I shared it first with all my sellers. Then, since 1985 I have spoken in live seminars to over one million Real Estate Agents about the benefits of Home Staging. I have shared ideas with the same number of people and others about how important it is. That said, though, many, many Agents still don't know how to share the whys of Home Staging with sellers. They also seem to have trouble sharing why sellers should work with Home Stagers to Stage their homes. This reluctance is for the same reasons that it always has been. The Agent doesn't really understand what true Staging is (and therefore doesn't support it), the Agent is afraid of hurting someone's feelings, or the Agent doesn't know what to say when the seller raises a concern about something. What *is* happening is that more Agents are saying that Staging is more important in today's market, but many, many Agents still don't know what to say to motivate sellers to get the job done. Otherwise, we wouldn't see so many houses *not* Staged in today's market.

But one step at a time: After more than 30 years and counting, I am seeing more Agents at least wake up to the fact that Staging *is* important. In a 2008 study by Home Gain, 91 percent of today's Agents see Home Staging as being important to the sale of the home. That figure moved up from 72 percent last year, so we are making advances in the overall view of Agents seeing the importance of Home Staging in today's market. You can see this study and also our Stagedhomes.com weekly study of Home Staging Stats on our site's home page.

Now, ASP Stagers, it is crucial that you do two things:

1. **Give Agents information about Home Staging to put into their Marketing Portfolios.** This information should be about the benefits of Home Staging, about you and your services, and about statistics on homes selling more quickly and for more money in your own market. You should be keeping stats of your business and of the market where you are, and you need to get those stats into the hands of the Agent you work with.

2. **In your Marketing Portfolio as an ASP Stager, you need to have visuals in written documents and pictures of your materials for the steps that you and the seller will go through together in the Home Staging process.** You need pictures of your work, before-and-after pictures, pictures of your inventory, pictures of your team of the ASP Stagers who work with you, and other pictures. Pictures are crucial for telling the seller what you will do for them. At the same time, using your *Marketing Portfolio*, you are showing them what you are talking about. Again, your presentation needs to be a show-and-tell, especially because Staging is essentially show-and-tell. First we set the stage to show the buyer the space in its very best way. Staging itself tells the story of the house by showing it off in the best way possible, room by room, inside and outside.

Agents and Stagers, you need to put Staging articles in your presentation books as well because the press gives additional credibility to you and Home Staging.

Stagers, you need to have before-and-after pictures of homes prepared for sale, and you can provide these to Agents, too. You also need to assist the Agent in educating the seller. It is crucial that you see, in the big picture, if you don't educate Agents on how you can help them help sellers, then you are leaving business on the doorstep.

As the Stager, you, not the Agent, need to be doing the Staging of the house, and by helping the Agent with materials that they can put into their presentation books you make it much easier for them to sell Staging and sell you too as the ASP Stager to work with. This measure can seem obvious, but I talk with many, many Stagers who still haven't done it. They hear it, but they don't do it. Be the visual partner of the Agent. I say that tongue in cheek, but it is true. You can provide the impact and the force of the Agents *Marketing Portfolio* by providing them with information to educate sellers. And that way you are also maximizing the potential of helping both (Agent and seller) at the same time. Also, in this way, the Agent is introducing you as the ASP Stager and selling you to the seller. This is, of course, in cases where the seller called the Agent first. Later in the book I will share with you more on the future of the seller's calling the Stager first.

In the process of educating sellers, a picture is really worth a thousand words, and it can actually be worth thousands of dollars for you. One sure way to get sellers to Stage their homes is to show them pictures of other homes that have been Staged. Before-and-after ASP pictures work! Remember, sellers just need to be shown how and why Staging is so powerful and necessary. People are smart, and they just need to be shown the why and the how. Money motivates most people, including sellers. That is why they are selling the house: They want the money to do something else, to buy a new house, or to spend it in some other way. Teach them that a home that is prepared for sale, or Staged, will often sell more quickly and in certain markets even for more money. Either way, the sellers will be able to get their equity faster if they prepare their home for sale. Don't take it for granted, ever, that the seller understands the process of Home Staging.

Now you may be asking, "Barb, where am I going to get the before-and-after photos of homes?" This is easy! Just ask the sellers if you can take photos before you Stage the house. You should always do this. If you don't, you are missing a great opportunity. I have never had a seller say no. Then, after it is Staged, ask whether you can take a second set of photos. Again, I have never had a seller say no. Then, I ask whether I may show the photos to future sellers in our area after they have moved away or to another house. There is no reason for them to object because they will not live in *this* house anymore; some may not even live in the same city anymore. Take photos before and after of at least the following primary rooms: living room, kitchen, family room, master bedroom and bath, and the front of the home from across the street. These photos are the most powerful way to teach future sellers about preparing their home for sale.

Also, as an ASP Stager or an ASP Agent, you should know that I have placed thousands of before-and-after pictures on the Stagedhomes.com *Staging University* for you to use and select from to show your sellers to educate them about many rooms and ideas of Home Staging.

In addition to before-and-after pictures, I also use pictures of rooms that are *not* Staged, and I ask the sellers what these people should have done to prepare their home for sale so that the house would have sold. This is a really, really great idea. I thought of it one day when the regular before-and-after pictures were not doing the job that they normally do. I went out to my car and got pictures of a home that was for sale and that I was going to show to a buyer from out of town. The house was not Staged and had not sold, so I showed the rooms to the seller I was sitting with and asked what he thought should be done. Although the regular pictures had not worked, which was rare, these did. Once the seller took the pictures in his hands, he could not resist saying what he thought was wrong with each room. That day I realized that people cannot resist becoming the expert when given the opportunity. So from that day forward I have always used, and strongly suggest you do too, before-and-after pictures of homes *and* pictures of rooms that have not been Staged. As long as you do not show or say the legal address, the actual address, or the sellers' names, then I am told by attorneys that it is OK to show pictures of rooms and homes.

You also need to take photos of your own home. That's right. Don't misunderstand; I'm not suggesting that your home is messy. If it isn't messy, then just mess it up to make it look very lived-in and take your before photos. Then get it Staged and take your after shots. The difference will be amazing, and your photos will really help to get your points across. When you show your photos to sellers, tell them that you have even Staged your own home and ask them to look at the difference it made for you. I have done this for years and that is how I actually got my very first set of pictures to show a seller more than 30 years ago. I still take before-and-after pictures of my home because it is in a way my Staging laboratory. I take pictures weekly and monthly for new Staging ideas and vignettes that I come up with.

If you have sellers right now that will not prepare their home for sale, I would bet you haven't shown them photos. Try it. It really does work. Put these photos in your *Marketing Portfolio* so that you don't forget to educate each and every one of your future sellers. The pictures allow you to educate the sellers so much easier than without them.

Prepare Professional Brochures for Sellers

Sellers deserve to be represented in the most professional way possible, including the brochures, the information sheets, or the flyers about the property that are left inside or outside your listings for buyers and especially that are posted to the Internet! Do your future sellers really know the quality of work you do in this area? Place samples of the professional information sheets you have written for past sellers' homes in your *Marketing Portfolio.*

I have come up with my own format for an information sheet that I know can help many Agents. I do not simply use the standard information sheet from a multiple listing book. At the top of the information sheets are pertinent information and facts that purchasers can look at right away upon coming to view the property. Below that is a list of the unique features and special aspects of the property. Remember, good information sheets also help sell other Agents as well as buyers. I promise the sellers, at the presentation, that this will be the type and quality of the work that I am committing to them. I show them that they will be represented in the most professional way possible. Educate. Educate. Educate.

As a Stager, I started asking the Agents that I Staged for whether I could help them make their listing information sheets and put myself on the back side of them. Agents loved the fact that I saved them time by making the sheets, but also they were very happy to have me on the back side to verify that the house had been Staged. ASP Stagers, you need to do this, too, because the Agents who understand how this will help them save time *and* promote the house as Staged will be happy to cooperate.

I also keep the brochure box filled. This helps the Agent avoid having an empty box outside the sellers' home. Everyone wins, most of all the seller. I cannot believe in this day and age just how many houses I see for sale that have empty brochure boxes on a post or sign outside the sellers' home. The seller should raise a stink because buyers are driving by and are not able to take any information about the house with them. How sad! Sellers, an empty brochure box is not acceptable, as I am sure you will agree. With both the Agent and the Stager working together as a team, when Stagers come every week to fine-tune the Staging (especially for vacant houses), they can bring the brochures or flyers with them to fill the box.

Prepare a Separate Marketing Booklet for Each Listing

After the listing agreement is signed, I make a separate home marketing booklet for every one of my sellers. It is designed to be left in their home at all times. I therefore show a sample of one in this section of the

Marketing Portfolio so that sellers will fully understand its power. On the cover page it says, "Do Not Remove." The booklet has all kinds of facts and features about the particular sellers' property. It includes things such as the taxes, plat map, lender information, any disclosures, and a master copy of the information sheet, which I have prepared. Use your creativity, because anything that can encourage the buyer to buy can be included. Consider including information about schools, churches, recreation, shopping, heating or air conditioning costs, copies of blueprints, landscaping plans, and so forth. Also, Stagers, you can help the seller and the Agent by giving the Agent pictures of the Staged property. I am amazed at the poor pictures that many Agents take for the seller. These should be dynamic pictures, with professional lighting, showing off the features of the house. Just whipping out a camera and clicking a few photos in a house is not what it is about. So ASP Stagers, get on with it and have great Staged pictures taken of the house and provide them to the Agent and to the seller alike. The Agent can put them into the marketing booklet about the house, as well as in the flyers and brochures. The whole idea of the marketing booklet is to provide as much information about the property as possible. This is not only for potential buyers, but also for the showing Agents who are working with the buyers. In the small space you are usually given through your multiple listing association, you may not be able to give Agents all the information they want. As an Agent I have always relied a great deal on other Agents showing and selling my listings, and I don't want them embarrassed by not knowing many of the answers to purchasers' questions. When they came to show one of Barb's houses, I wanted it to look terrific, but I also wanted the Agent to be able to find the answers to questions a purchaser might ask.

The marketing booklet sample also gives you a marketing edge because you are promising the sellers something that many other Agents haven't thought about doing. Sellers love it.

Teach How the Multiple Listing Works

As an Agent, you need to educate sellers about how the multiple listing service (MLS) works. Without the sellers, there would be no multiple. Let's not keep everything we do such a secret. In this section of the *Marketing Portfolio*, you need to include printouts from the multiple's web site, maps that show the sellers the areas where most potential purchasers are looking today, along with a sample of one of your listings, to show how they will look as you represent them in the multiple. Make sure that you show sellers that Staging their house will be included in the remarks section so that other Agents know that it is Staged to show. You can also note the name of the ASP Stager in the remarks. Many of you Stagers haven't thought of this. As you work more together as Agents and Stagers and as ASPs, getting your name in the listings can be a kind of branding for you and the Agent, and that can help you both in many ways. For some of us it is all about working together and helping each other to bring the best for the seller—first, last and always!

Make Brokers' Open Houses Work

I believe in brokers' open houses because you can reach so many other purchasers by holding them. Through brokers' open houses, you reach other Agents in the multiple and therefore their purchasers. And Stagers, you need to be involved in these, too!

In your *Marketing Portfolio*, show a sample of the bulletin you get each week from the MLS and show the seller the list of brokers' open houses for a sample week. Include examples of tour sheets or whatever method you use in your area to coordinate and advertise brokers' open houses. You can also use photos or flyers to show samples of activities promoting your own brokers' open houses. It is important that sellers understand how brokers' open houses work and how powerful they are in the marketing process.

If other Agents in your area do not hold brokers' open houses, then this is something you can promise to your sellers that goes a step beyond. I did this in my own area, and then slowly other Agents started holding more and more open houses. Eventually, it became almost a standard. Agents who would not commit to holding open houses wouldn't get the listing. Brokers' open houses work.

ASP Stagers, you may want to cater the brokers' open house for every one of the listings you Stage for an Agent. This helps the listing Agent who gave you the business, but it also enables you to share information about Staging with other Agents. Catering the brokers' open house really helps the Agent save time and dollars. You may not do this for every Agent, but I would recommend that you did. Also, when you work with a seller giving a Staging presentation, you can offer to do this for them and their Agent no matter who the Agent is. As you will experience more and more, the public will be calling you before the Agent as the ASP Stager to come Stage their home, and as they do, you can share how you will help their Agent by catering the open house.

Agents, as you work with an ASP Stager on a regular basis, which you should do, then you can count on the ASP Stager doing this for you. Remember, your job as an Agent at a brokers' open house is to sell the house to the other Agents. And ASP Stagers, your job is to support the Agent; when you go to see Agents in open houses that you are not a part of, always give the Agents space when you come in. That way, you do not distract them from talking with other Agents. Wait until the other Agents are gone, then introduce yourself to the Agent holding the open house. If you interrupt them, they will think you are a buyer, and then they'll be disappointed that you interrupted their selling the house to the other Agents when they find out you are there to talk with them about Staging. Use your manners, Stagers, and feel the situation when you visit Agents at open houses.

Hopefully you will be holding open houses *with* an Agent for the houses you have Staged. When you hold the open house together, it is a double win for sellers, and you should point out that fact to them when you give your presentations, whether you are an ASP Agent or an ASP Stager.

Use Quality Flyers

Flyers are wonderful! Agents, show off examples of your best flyers in this section of your *Marketing Portfolio* to educate your sellers on the quality of the work you do. Also explain how flyers work, how many Agents or offices you market to, and so forth. Take time to prepare your flyers for other Agents because you are representing your sellers and yourself. Make it quality work—the best that you can do each and every time. Then you can offer sellers your highest level of marketing service, which they deserve.

KEEP A TOP-SELLING AGENT LIST

Years ago I got the idea to come up with a mailing list of other top Agents to whom I could market my listings as an Agent or my Stagings as a Stager. My mailing list to other Agents has been an extremely effective marketing tool for me, so I hope you will use this idea to be even more successful.

First, I want to tell you a little about how it started. One day I thought to myself, "Where are today's purchasers?" I was working as an Agent with a number of purchasers and a number of sellers, but they didn't match. The buyers were looking for other kinds of houses than the sellers were selling.

This type of mismatch is quite common in the industry. "Well," I answered my own question, "I know where most of the purchasers are—they're working with Agents. But which Agents?" I didn't know, so I decided to check. I got on the telephone and called every major broker or manager in town. "Who are your top three selling Agents?" I asked them. "Which Agents working with you primarily like to work with buyers?" They could hardly wait to tell me. (Stagers, you can do the same thing, too.) So I compiled what I called a list of the top 50 Agents for that time in my area, and I started calling them. I asked them whether I could put them on a list and let them know about my listings because they were priced right and prepared for sale (Staged). They were flattered that I had called and were glad to be on the list.

I started running off copies of my listings and mailed them to the top 50 Agents on a biweekly basis. (Later I emailed them the information instead of mailing.) That list grew to over 450 Agents, and I'm really proud of the list. These people work hard to sell my listings for several reasons:

1. They know my listings are Staged and look great.
2. They know my listings are priced with the market.
3. They know my sales close.

As I tell sellers about my list, I point out all those reasons while I explain my exclusive Agent mailing list to them. A mailing goes out to the top 450 Agents in the multiple every three to four weeks, and they watch for the mailings. They show my listings from the mailings, and they sell my listings from the mailings. Each seller I show this technique to thinks it is dynamite! They know that listing with me means they will be in the next mailing to those top Agents. In my mailings I use a copy of an information sheet on the home plus any extra information and a photo. This will work for you too! And ASP Stagers, you can do the same thing. You can mail to other Agents flyers about homes you have Staged for the listing Agent you are working with, and doing that will help your listing Agent, too. Either way, the seller is served!

I also started the policy of sending Agents a gift when they sell one of my listings. On the day of closing, the female Agent who sells one of my listings might get roses or a fruit basket, whereas the male Agent might receive a bottle or two of his favorite beverages, flowers, or a fruit basket. This policy has built camaraderie among these Agents and helped sell more homes for my sellers! It is such a small thing to do, and yet many of us never really stop to thank the selling Agent for bringing that buyer to our listing. Where would we be without each other? We really need each other. So the first person I am going to give a small gift to is not the buyer or the seller, but rather the other Agent. You should see the stack of thank-you notes I have gotten over the years from other Agents who worked for other companies in my area! You better believe I show some of those to my sellers as well.

At the beginning of each year, I contact each of the Agents on my exclusive mailing list. An example of what I send follows. I find it is a great way to get the year off to a positive start and to remind them of our relationship in the past and how I hope we will have the chance to work together this year.

Dear Fellow Agents,

Happy New Year!

This past year was an exciting one in real estate in our area, and I hope it was a very successful one for you.

During the year I have been sending you information on the properties I have listed. I'm proud of the quality of listings that I always strive to obtain, and I want you to know that my listings will be easy for you to sell because I work hard to price them right, Stage each listing, and help you close each and every transaction.

Thank you for showing and selling my listings. I'm going to continue to keep you informed this year so that you can show and sell my listings with confidence. I've enjoyed working with you, so please look for my listings so that we will have the opportunity of working together soon.

I wish you a happy and prosperous New Year!

Sincerely,

Barb Schwarz

Have a copy of an email like this one in your *Marketing Portfolio,* and show it to your sellers. Not only will they be impressed with your professionalism, but you are educating them on the importance of their property looking good and being priced right!

I've built a tremendous network of Agents in the area where I work. In a way it is like having my own real estate company. It works because I have dozens of other Agents constantly showing my listings. So start to build a network of Agents in the area where you work. They can be with all types and sizes of companies—not just the company where you work. I'm talking about all the other companies around you. Strike up friendships. Meet other Agents in the area where you live. Tell them, "I'll show your homes, if you'll show mine. Together we can make more money, and we can help out a lot more sellers that way." This really works.

In most multiples there are thousands of Agents, and, of course, we can't get to know them all. However, you can build a strong network, and once you start it, it will grow. Once you get your sellers to prepare their homes for sale and agree to a reasonable price and terms, Agents will love to show your properties. They can count on you to help them with the work.

So, in this section, put some of the letters or emails you have written to other Agents with other companies. Include a list of the names of Agents you do business with in other companies. Display copies of the email list, mailing labels, or business cards to impress your potential sellers with the quantity of names you have on your marketing list. Then show examples and printouts of some of the mailings you have done to market your listings to these Agents.

Stagers, everything I just shared is for you too. Whether we are Agents, Stagers, or Stagers and Agents, this kind of list will work for you. You want to build a team of Agents and Stagers who are fun to work with, who are easy to work with, and who get the fact that it takes all of us to make the world of real estate go round! Agents, mail to other Agents and to Stagers, too. Stagers, mail to other Agents and to other Stagers, and let the sellers know in your presentation that you will be doing this for them.

COMPANY ADVERTISEMENTS

Agents, insert your company's ads from as many different kinds of media as possible. If you do individual ads on your own, be sure to include samples of them as well. Put in the best advertisements you can find: black-and-white ads from the newspaper and color ads from magazines. Take the space to show off the quality of your advertising program, and explain how it works. If you send a newsletter to your centers of influence, be sure to add that as well.

Also, if you have had articles in the newspaper about any of the homes you have listed, be sure that you include them in this section. Public relations and advertising let sellers know about what you and your company do. As an ASP Agent or ASP Stager, you have the right to use the logos and marketing materials I have for you on the *Staging University* as long as you are an active, current ASP in good standing. And those logos are fabulous for bringing more visibility and recognition to your houses.

RELOCATION

In the relocation section of your *Marketing Portfolio,* put information regarding the various relocation companies with which your company may be associated. It is crucial that sellers realize how relocation works and how buyers reach you through different relocation companies. Also, be sure you ask where your sellers are moving. You should always know where they are going. If they are moving out of the area or out of state, it is a great way for you also to make additional income from referring them to an Agent or firm outside your area. Too many Agents simply let dollars slip through their hands by not even asking the sellers about their out-of-town move.

Another important reason to help sellers in this fashion is that you can put them in touch with a top Agent in another area who can serve them. Don't leave sellers to their own luck in trying to find a top Agent. As you know, that is not always the easiest thing to do in a new area. One resource that can help is to search for Agents and Stagers on the Stagedhomes.com web site by city, state, zip, or name. It is a very useful tool!

THE BEST IDEA FOR SUSTAINING COMMUNICATION WITH SELLERS

Several years ago I thought to myself, "I do a lot of work for my sellers, and I am really proud of what I do. Sometimes, however, they forget what I do, especially if their property hasn't sold yet, such as in a tough market. So how can I let all of them know in a concrete way, consistently, what is being done to market their property?" I concluded that regular reports were the answer, so I decided to keep a log. All the marketing that I do for each property goes into the log—and I mean everything. I recommend you do the same thing. Just keep a spiral notebook in your car. Label every other page for each of the sellers you list, and then write down everything you do. Or you can have a separate Word document on your laptop or in your handheld that you continue to add to. It's easy to forget all the little things that you do, so if you use this idea you have to commit to sitting down *every* day and updating your logs. It's the only way to be sure you are being consistent. For example, let's say it's January 23.

> January 23—Met with Jane at her house to look at the property. I was there from 11 to 12:15.

(Now, you see, I've just posted in two short sentences the work I just did. Let's say the next date is January 28)

> January 28—Met with Jane in my office from 9:30 to 11:00 to present my marketing program and my comparative market analysis. Agreed to meet on February 3 to list her home.

All I'm doing is listing everything I do. If it is a newspaper ad, I record it. If I hold a brokers' open house, I note it. If it's shopping for groceries for that brokers' open house, I include that on the log. Each seller's log just keeps growing and growing.

As you go through your marketing program and your *Marketing Portfolio* with your sellers, commit to giving them an update report, expanded from that log, every two to six weeks, depending on the length of selling time in your area. If the market is hot, promise a report every week or two. If it's slow, promise a report every four to six weeks. It's just good business. Too many Agents will list a property today and never really talk to the sellers again. Sellers deserve a lot more than that, and they really appreciate receiving a written report on the work you have done. This is one way I keep all my listings. The market could be good or poor, but I can still keep my sellers happy. It is difficult for them to refute the work that has been done when they see a typed, detailed report. Be sure to take it to them when you present it. Do not go over it on the phone. Take it to them and go over it in person. It's the best kind of professional communication there is. (We will look at the actual form I use in the next chapter.)

Show sellers samples of your log and the reports you do for your sellers. This way they will fully understand the importance of the concept, and they will really appreciate the professional service.

Also, these reports can be used—and should be used—to show sellers what you have been doing when you ask them for a price reduction. Going in empty-handed as an Agent causes a seller most likely to say no when you ask for a reduction. If you go in to see the seller without a report, you are going in on the defense. Report to people what you do in writing, and you will see that you receive so much more appreciation from the seller. It puts the P into Professionalism.

As a Stager, I found the same to be so true. I always keep a list and report all that I do for the seller and the Agent. The key is to keep this in Word for each seller and Agent so that you can report to them the work you have done, hour by hour and day by day in the shopping, selecting of items, loading of the furniture and accessories, talking with the other people involved such as painters and landscapers, and the time on the phone with the seller and Agents and others for the Staging of the house. I found that my sellers were very appreciative of my keeping a log for them. I gave this to them during the project at intervals of a long project or at the end of a short one. People don't know all that it takes to Stage a house and how much work it really can be and is. And the prep work is often what takes a lot of time. So keep a log for your sellers and Agents as ASP Stagers, and tell them ahead of time you will be doing this and show them sample logs in your *Marketing Portfolio* ahead of time. People will appreciate this, and you need to tell them about it ahead of time in your presentation and have a copy of it in your *Marketing Portfolio*. Sellers and Agents alike will regard you as being very professional, and it really lets people know more of what you will do and also what they will be paying for.

FORMS THAT ARE USED IN THE SALE AND CLOSING

In this section of your listing presentation book, show copies of the purchase and sale agreement that the multiple listing service in your area uses. If your company uses its own form, display it instead. Here, you can take the time to talk about the paperwork for the purchase and sale agreement. This takes care of some of the sellers' fears ahead of time. Remember, the time you spend now can head off problems later.

You can also include copies of a local lender's financing rate sheet, title insurance information, a sample inspection report, sample appraisal report, or a blank deed form. Let them hold and touch these forms. Let them look at the small print on the front and back to get used to seeing it. This is a good time to share your experience and expertise in these areas.

I've also written down the steps of what it takes to close a transaction. I call this section "steps to close a sale." I always take all the time needed to go over this with my sellers so that they know how I will be involved every step of the way on their behalf until the successful culmination of their sale. I also always go with every seller to the closing. In some areas this is not a standard practice, but I believe it is an important last contact—both professionally and for future referral business. Why miss the closing when this is the moment we all have been working for? In my opinion it is like missing the birthday of the sale. Go to the closing; it is also a great time to ask that seller or buyer to write you a letter of recommendation about the great job you have just completed, which gives you another addition for your *Career Book*.

A powerful way to end your *Marketing Portfolio* is just as you did your *Career Book*: with a photo of you with a "SOLD" sign. I recommend that you have a photo taken of you in front of a home holding your company's sold sign. Remember, we are selling you, and if you don't sell yourself, then who will? Sellers are looking for an Agent who knows how to market. They also know that the first thing you should market is yourself—to them. Have someone in your office take a photo of you, and then put it into your *Marketing Portfolio* as a great close to your marketing program.

THE EDUCATION OF SELLERS TODAY!

The preceding points are all key things to share with your sellers ahead of time and to put into your *Marketing Portfolio*. Certainly, as an Agent or a Stager, you can include other things in your *Marketing Portfolio*. As a Stager, you can put in additional pictures of Staging ideas, pictures of your inventory, your forms of permission to Stage a house, your professional policies, the main commitments you ask of the seller, such as having the house professionally cleaned before you Stage it, your agreement to Stage their home, and so on.

As an Agent or a Stager, a powerful way to end your *Marketing Portfolio* is to have a picture of you with the seller in front of their home. Everyone is smiling, they are shaking hands with you, and one of them is holding a "SOLD" sign. Remember, we are selling you, and if you don't sell yourself, then who will?

Using a marketing presentation book makes it so much easier for you to show your sellers what you do. Not only do they hear what you're talking about, they also *see* the fantastic work you do. Once you've used it, you won't want to give a presentation without it.

Now you have the information you need to build one of the most powerful selling tools you will ever use. Put your *Marketing Portfolio* together now! Yours can be just the way you like it, tailored to your own style. Put your own Agent marketing techniques or Stager Staging ideas in it. Make it your own working tool. Use, enjoy, and be proud of your *Marketing Portfolio*. It will help you educate your sellers and get more business. Do it now, because it really works and your sellers will say, *"That was the best presentation I've ever seen!"*

CHAPTER 8

RECIPE FOR A SALE: PRICING THE PROPERTY RIGHT

The right ingredients make the sale, and they work every time.

BARB SCHWARZ

SELLER'S NOTE

Pricing your home is usually what is uppermost in your mind as you come on the market. I understand that as an Agent, as the inventor of Home Staging, as a trainer, *and* as a seller myself. I have purchased a number of my homes during my lifetime, and I have sold a number of them, too. Pricing *my* home has always been one of the top priorities to me, of course, too.

This chapter is about pricing *your* home. Pricing a home, in a way, is an art and a science. To me, Staging is at the heart of pricing. Having sold thousands and thousands of homes for people as an Agent, I always see the house Staged in my mind even when it is not yet Staged. As all of my sellers will tell you, I price the house Staged. They will tell you that I had them get the house Staged regardless of its price range.

(Continued)

It is and was my professional policy that they had to Stage the house with me or I could not serve them. I truly know that this served every single seller for their highest good. My sellers knew that once I educated them about Home Staging, they took to it as if it were money growing on a tree because they knew that is exactly what Staging would give them, no matter what the market conditions were. You, as a seller, and the public at large are very smart. The key to pricing today is that the Agent and/or the ASP Stager educate you, as I did my sellers, about the many benefits of Home Staging. In this book I also want to educate you myself, offering the lessons of the many, many years of experience I have as a Broker and as the creator of Home Staging. I do hope that one day all Agents will feel this way and also carry out the same policy that I have.

ASP Stagers also fill a very important void and need to educate any sellers who will listen to them because many Agents do not do a good job of educating sellers about Home Staging. There are, of course, those who do, but too many still shy away from talking about Staging because they either don't know what to say or are afraid to say it. Look always for an ASP Real Estate Agent to list your house with and an ASP Stager to Stage it! They have the training to educate you and the knowledge to do what it takes to get the job done and done right. The Stager's role is *not* to price the property, nor should they give you advice, ever, about the listing price or the selling price. What ASP Stagers can do is show you the statistics regarding pricing and how Staging affects the selling prices of homes everywhere. The statistics are amazing, they are real, and they are *not* too good to be true. We collect and keep the Staging statistics on our home page of Stagedhomes.com. To get top dollar, you need to Stage your home! Don't even consider not doing so. Of the two things that sell a home—price and Staging—the greater is Staging, in my opinion, because Staged homes sell more quickly and for more money in any market. And it doesn't get any better than that in any market. Pricing your home to sell for top dollar and Staging it go hand in hand.

What this means to you is that you can price your home to sell for top dollar, but if it isn't Staged, it won't sell for a top dollar price. How could it? My experience has shown me that when you Stage your home, it will sell for top dollar. So let's look at pricing in this chapter, and we will get to more on the Staging your home in upcoming chapters, in more detail, of course.

IN THIS CHAPTER

You will learn:

1. The ingredients of a sale.
2. How the ingredients of a sale can help sellers understand the current market and the pricing for their homes.
3. The importance of Stagers' knowing how Agents price homes.
4. The crucial importance for sellers to know the art and science of pricing their home.

What is a Comparative (or Competitive) Market Analysis (CMA)? A CMA is a pricing analysis of a property that includes a summary of the homes sold in the area that are similar to the size of your home, that have a similar number of bedrooms and bathrooms, and that are of the same approximate age, amenities, and lot size. For as close a comparison as possible, the Agent should show you homes that have sold and those that are for sale. Whether you call it a Comparative Market Analysis or a Competitive Market Analysis, it is basically the same thing.

A CMA is easier to do in a housing development, where many homes are similar, and harder to do when dealing with one-of-a-kind custom homes where no houses seem similar at all. Still, it comes down to size of lot, size of house, age of property, and whether it is Staged or not! The phrase "Staged or not" is a new thought to many Agents. They have not looked at that as much as I would suggest that they do. This is something that I am also working hard to teach members of the real estate industry to do, because Staging makes the biggest difference of all in comparing similar homes.

Your Agent needs to explain to you what is honestly happening in the market area. In a down market this is critical! That has to do with many things really. I wrote "The Ingredients of a Sale" to help explain to my sellers how a price is built and the components of setting a price. In the next section, I go through this process with you as a seller, as an Agent, or as a Stager. The information I write is based in my years of experience and what I know really takes place in any market at any time.

SETTING THE LIST PRICE: THE INGREDIENTS OF A SALE

One of my best sayings is:

Just like the product on the shelf at the store, the purchaser of today buys the best available product, for the best price, in the best package, to meet his or her needs.

Throughout the Comparative Market Analysis that you as an Agent have prepared and brought to your sellers, you must show them what is happening in the marketplace in their area. You need to show them comparable properties in their area and what houses are selling for. And Staging also needs to be at the heart of pricing the home that you talk about with your future sellers, too. Agents, I will now share a way to show comparable homes that you may have been aware of.

Once you educate your sellers, you can talk about the price you feel is most suitable for the sellers' home. Sellers don't want a figure thrown at them, pulled out of the air. That is also why the steps I have shared with you in this book are so important. Therefore, with every seller, before we look at the pricing-a-home triangle, I always go through what I call the "ingredients of a sale."

Six main ingredients must work together before you can sell a home. After sitting down with thousands of sellers to talk about the elements and ingredients of a sale, I started to refer to it as a "recipe for a sale." That is a good description because the ingredients make up the successful recipe for pricing a home. It is a recipe with ingredients that are proven to work again and again over time.

I found out quickly that my sellers could relate better to this than to a sea of figures that seem to circle round and round. Before you zero in with your sellers on the price for the house, it is far better to go over each of the ingredients of the sale. When you educate your sellers on the importance of each of these six ingredients, your properties should be priced right and Staged every single time. The ingredients are as follows:

1. Location
2. Condition
3. Price
4. Terms
5. The market
6. Staging the property

Ingredient 1: Location

We have all heard it before: location, location, and location.

It is a truth that some homes are simply in better locations than others and that the location will be reflected in home's price. Agents, you need to be honest and talk to sellers about their home's location. For example, if a home is on a great spot on a cul-de-sac where there isn't a lot of traffic, point that out as a plus to the sellers. If it is on a busy street, don't let your sellers shut their eyes to that fact. It is your job to be honest with your sellers and to tell them when you feel their location may be working for or against them and affect the pricing of their property. It is your job to help the sellers price their property correctly, and you can't do that if you don't help them look at it objectively. Remember, you are the expert, and you have done the work to arrive at the suggested list price range. Doctors, lawyers, and accountants all stick to their professional opinions because they are the professionals. You must do the same when it comes to your role and profession. It is in the best interest of your sellers as well to do so. There is a buyer for every house, even if it's on a very busy street; however, to get it sold, it has to be in a price range that is less than the houses on quiet streets because they are not in the same comparison range.

Location has to be reflected in price because the public will put it there anyway when the offers come in. Staging will often surely help the house on the busy street sell more quickly and even for more money, as I have seen, but it has to be in the correct price range to start with, as reflected by the location. Comparable home sales will always support this, and Staging the house will give it a much better chance to sell rather than just sit because of location.

Carrying a grossly overpriced listing is not in anyone's interest at all. It doesn't help the seller, it doesn't help the economy, it doesn't help the neighborhood, and it doesn't help the Agent. Statistics always show that houses that sit on the market overpriced invariably end up selling for less than if they had been priced right from the beginning.

Ingredient 2: Condition

Staging has nothing to do with condition. That is the first thing I must share with you. Condition has to do with whether the property has a bad roof, whether it has dry rot, whether the furnace works properly, or whether the carpet needs replacing. These things have to do with the condition of the property, and that is not about Staging the house. However, a house can and has to be Staged even if the condition is poor. It can still be clean and have the clutter put away, and the seller can buy a can of paint for the front door. So even properties that are in poor condition can and should be Staged to sell for top dollar.

However, the upkeep of the condition of a property is also crucial to obtaining the highest value for it. Agents, you cannot stress this enough when talking with your sellers. This is necessary in any market at any time. Sometimes the things you and I see as Agents are just unbelievable. Some people do not take care of their homes while they live there. For example, while they have been there 10 years, the roof is leaking and there are holes in the carpets, and all of a sudden they want to bring it on the market. In such cases, they have some catching up to do on what is called "deferred maintenance."

If sellers are unwilling to improve the condition of that property, the price has to reflect that decision, especially in a down market. When you come across sellers who fit this description, point out to them how important condition is. They will have to do the repairs for the home or settle for a lower price. This is especially true in today's market. Most buyers today expect homes to be turnkey, that is, ready to move into without having to repair things. This is because most families are very busy, with both spouses or partners working, and there just isn't time to repair things all over the house after they buy it. Nor do people expect to buy houses that need fixing in today's market unless they are buying the house as an investment. If that is the case, most investors are looking for a good buy and a discounted price to take on the condition of the house.

Staging, which I will discuss at length in later chapters, is different from condition. If the roof leaks, you have to price the house accordingly and, of course, disclose the flaw (disclosure, disclosure, disclosure). Sellers in all states have a huge legal responsibility to disclose any known defects. Sellers, if the furnace is broken, you have to price your home accordingly and, of course, disclose it. It is far better to replace it and disclose that you replaced it, but if you don't replace it you have to disclose it for sure! When you replace the furnace, you need to disclose that you have a new furnace, too, which is a very good thing.

The key is to have all of the ingredients in balance, and one of the big ones is condition. It is just like a car. You want good tires on the car, fenders that are not bent, no rust underneath the car, and upholstery that is not torn. And if the car has bad tires, bent fenders, rust, and torn upholstery you will not pay what you would for a car in good condition. The same thing is true for the sale of a house. Condition is one of the major ingredients for pricing a home and for a sale to take place. Agents, you cannot turn your head the other way when it comes to condition; when you see it and/or find out about it, you have to call it out, too.

ASP Stagers, when you are working with the Agent and the seller Staging the property, it is crucial to mention things you see to both the seller and the Agent because they may have missed them. Also, we *never* cover up any poor condition when Staging a home. If there is a hole in the carpet, do not ever cover it up. It there is a hole in the wall, do not ever cover it by hanging a picture over it. You could cause a challenge for everyone, including yourself, by covering up any challenge on the condition of the house. I would recommend to the ASP Stager to get the property disclosure statements from the seller or the Agent. You need a copy of those in your records, too, and with you as you work in the house Staging it. And when you do a Home Staging Consultation you want to also call out things as you see them and put them on a to-do list for the seller to fix—things like a hole in the wall or in the carpet or things like fixing the backyard broken fence or a broken step, which the seller should put white tape on at the very least.

Part of your Home Staging Consultation, where you list all the things that a seller should do to Stage a property, is also a good place to put a to-do list of things that the sellers should fix because they are paying you a fee to give them your recommendations. It is up to the seller, of course, to fix them, but when the Stager sees things the sellers don't see that need fixing, the sellers also need to disclose the flaws to the buyer as the Stager points them out. As a seller, you must do that whether you fix them or not. And ASP Stagers, always give a copy of your Home Staging Consultation to the Agent so that everyone is on the same page and knows your recommendations for the Staging of the property and anything you see about the condition of the property. To my knowledge you are not legally bound at this time to tell an Agent or seller what you see about condition, but I always want you to err on the side of caution rather than silence. A Home Staging Consultation is a plan—room by room, inside and out—for what the seller needs to do to Stage the property. Listing things to fix is as important for a seller and/or Agent to do as it is for the Stager. Although you are not a home inspector and do not need to get into all the things that an inspector does, it is still good service to tell the seller and Agent when you see an obvious thing that needs fixing. Just add it to your suggested list of things that the sellers need to do to Stage their home, and it may also help the home's condition at the same time.

Ingredient 3: Price

As I stated more than once, the two things in today's market that sell property are Staging and price. Of the two factors, price is a big one. A property is worth only what one person is willing to pay another in order to gain ownership, and price must also reflect the other five ingredients. Any property, anywhere, in any condition eventually will sell—if it has the right market price on it. This is a good place in your presentation to share this with your sellers.

Here, also, is a good place to explain to sellers that the appraised value of a home and its selling price can be two different things. How a home appraises for replacement costs and what the market will bear—what someone will pay for a house as a buyer in any market—are often two different things. Sometimes you come across someone who has never sold a house and who has already hired a fee appraiser to come in and determine what the house is worth. Then, all of a sudden, as an Agent you come in with your Comparative Market Analysis and a completely different price. In this case, it is time to say, "Remember, Mr. and Mrs. Seller, a home is only worth what buyers are willing to pay for it and that price can be different in a buyer's market." When you are working in a buyer's market, it is especially crucial for you to share this with your sellers and to show them the comparable houses that sold under the appraised value because of market conditions.

Stagers, you are never, never to talk pricing with a seller. That is not your area of expertise unless you have a real estate license, and even if you do, do not talk with the seller about pricing their home—period! Sellers, I know it is so tempting to ask your ASP Stager, "What do you think about our price? Are we too high? Are we too low? Should we raise the price now that we have Staged the house?" Whatever the questions are, Stagers, do not answer in any way except, "You need to talk with your real estate Agent!" No matter how many times a seller asks you, that is the *only* acceptable answer. If you open your mouth in any other way, you have crossed the line into an area that is not in your expertise area. And, sellers, Stagers are not trained to price properties and your Agent is; so although Staging is a huge part of the pricing, it is not acceptable to ask your Stager, as tempting as it is, and it is not acceptable for the Stager to answer you in any other way than to refer you to the Agent.

In summary, in pricing a home remember that a house that is priced right *and* Staged has a great opportunity to sell for more and more quickly, too. Time is important because time on the market is generally not good. Houses don't stay on the market and have their price go up. The prices of houses that stay on the market have to be reduced to get the buyers and the Agents back to see them. It is a fact. As I often say, "Longevity on the market means one thing: reduction in price." So sellers and Agents, price the house right to begin with and get it Staged. It will sell for so much more than pricing it too high, not Staging it, and playing the non-Staged, overpriced game. That game doesn't pay at all, and sellers lose almost every time.

It's also important to remember that, in today's difficult market, Staged homes sell faster than comparable non-Staged homes and that really does equal more money for the seller. How much does it cost the seller every month to continue to own a home? Mortgage payments, home owner's dues, utilities, taxes, insurance, maintenance, and other expenses all add up very quickly. The total can easily be $2,000 to $3,000 a month—or much more, depending on the price range. So a home that is Staged and sells in 30 days saves the seller many thousands of dollars compared to selling in six months or more, a common length of time in today's market.

Ingredient 4: Terms

The more attractive the terms are on a property, the more potential purchasers you can reach. The seller who is able to offer FHA and VA loans or a seller deed of trust, in addition to conventional financing, leaves the door wide open for more potential purchasers. Every additional term offered by sellers opens the door a little wider. (Of course, remind your future sellers that the converse is also true.) The more terms offered, the more buyers you will reach. In most markets, conventional financing is the way that most houses sell. In tight markets offering FHA and VA loans on your house will open the door to more people. I remember markets when sellers offered paying points for the buyer or paying the closing costs and offering bonuses for a buyer to buy their houses. So far we haven't seen that in today's market, but we very well may.

If one thing is true, it is that markets change all the time. I am always surprised when people seem surprised that market conditions change. That is what life is: change. Markets come and markets go, but in the long term they go up. The first house I ever bought was actually $18,000, and you can't even buy a bathroom for that these days. So even when the market goes up and down, it is still going up over the long term. Real estate is still the best investment in the world. Also in the United States, we still get to write off the interest we pay on the loan that most of us have on our houses, all while building equity. In tight markets, see if the seller can offer several kinds of terms for the sale of the house. But in most markets it is not urgent to do that.

Ingredient 5: The Market

The market includes several things: interest rates, the competition, and the economy. All these factors influence the state of the market when you sell a home. And, once again, the price of a home must reflect the current status of the market. If there is one thing we cannot control, it is the market. You can control the Staging of the house, you can control the condition of the house, you can decide on the terms you offer, and you can set the price, but you cannot set the market. As sellers, we have to take what we get when we decide to sell a property, and you just cannot control the market conditions at that time you set the price.

In a down market, do not come on the market just to try it, as some sellers say. As a Real Estate Broker, I advise you as a seller not to do that. As funny as this sounds, I love to quote Yoda from *Star Wars:* "There is not try . . . only do." Don't leave money on the table by not Staging your house, no matter what the market is doing. And in a buyer's market, it is not the time just to try it to see what happens. Be serious about coming on the market, based on what is happening in your life and when you decide to come on the market. Do it for real, not just for trying. As an Agent, you should take plenty of time to discuss the market you are in right now with your sellers. No matter whether it is hot or not, it is really worth the time to educate your future sellers. Do it now, because this is serious business in any market, and you are bound by your fiduciary responsibility to do so. And it will really pay off down the road for your seller and for you.

Ingredient 6: Staging the Property

This is one of the big two!

When it comes to the ingredients of a sale, Staging is at the top, and that is why I have it at the end. Staging really is the beginning and the end—it is so crucial. It is the difference between selling and not selling. It is the difference between getting all that you can for a property and just letting it sell. It is being smart, product wise, and proactive. Remember, your home becomes a house and your house becomes a product on the market for sale. It is your product. Buyers have no affinity for your home until they make the decision to buy. And how they look at properties is with an eye to eliminate houses. They only buy one, so they thin out properties as they look at houses. As buyers look at properties, it is all about comparison.

Staging, conversely, has to do with how the property shows. Houses that have clutter and that are not as clean as they can be simply cannot compare to the homes that are Staged! Staging influences the price in any market. In a seller's market, houses really sell for more. And in a buyer's market, Staging helps homes sell much faster than those that are not Staged. So, no matter what the market is doing, always Stage the house because it pays off every time in every market.

Agents. always price the sellers' house as Staged and have the professional policy that your sellers do so, too, by getting it Staged. I always price a home with sellers knowing that it will be Staged. I recommend that you do, too. You will ask, "Well, how much more would you price them for?" The answer to that is, "You know your market and you should know what Staged houses have sold for in your own area, so you are the judge in your own market." I would have to do the market analysis in your area to know just how much more it would be. The statistics run from selling for the exact list price to 7 percent to even 50 percent more. I have worked with sellers in all kinds of markets, and price is all over the place. The most important fact is that Staged homes sell for more money in any market and in a shorter amount of time. Timing and price depend on the market you are in, on the houses that have sold, and on what they sold for.

I wouldn't sell a car without detailing it. Would you? I wouldn't sell a house that wasn't Staged. Would you? I hope and think not. With Staging your home, the odds are on your side, and that is the side you want to be on when pricing and selling your home.

SUCCESSFULLY COMBINE THE INGREDIENTS, AND YOU HAVE A SALE

When all of the preceding ingredients are in harmony, you have a sale. If just one of them is out of line, it may take longer to sell the property. The more the ingredients are out of line, the longer the sale will probably take. Sellers, please understand this. For example, let's say a home is in a good location, but its condition is questionable. Because those two ingredients are not in balance, the sellers will have to wait possibly a long time before they sell and settle for a lower price. To balance them out, they need to bring the condition up to where it should be.

Agents, you must explain to your future sellers how important it is to have all of the ingredients in balance. You cannot (usually) move a house and you cannot change the market, but most sellers, when it really comes down to it, can balance price, terms, and condition. And they can add the power of Home Staging. They have to realize this, or they will simply sit there and not sell. It is all about balancing everything for the best price possible. And the top of that list is Home Staging.

CHAPTER 9

THE PRICING-YOUR-HOME TRIANGLE

The investment of Staging in *your home is far less than a price reduction* on *your home.*

BARB SCHWARZ

SELLER'S NOTE

A Pricing-Your-Home Triangle will really help you see the art and science of pricing your home, and you should know what I want to see your Agent do. There are no secrets, and I certainly have shared what I share with my sellers: the reality of the market and where their properties need to be priced to come on the market to sell for top dollar. The fact is that if you come on the market too high in price, you end up sitting and not selling, whether you like to hear this or not, and selling for less than if you had come on right in the beginning. You really do not get another chance to price your house again. Homes don't sit on the market, and their prices go up. They sit on the market, and the prices go down. The one exception is when a seller has sat on the market, didn't Stage the home, and decides to Stage it, and then the property

(Continued)

sells for top dollar. So it is never too late to Stage, and it is certainly better to Stage at any point than not to Stage at all!

I ask you, as a seller, to take to heart what I share and hold your Agent accountable. The homes that the Agent shows you on paper as comparable need to be seen in a special way that Agents haven't done before: Staged and non-Staged. You will see this in more detail in this chapter. The Pricing-Your-Home Triangle I came up with for my own sellers, I believe, will benefit you as well. Pricing is pricing, and it is a balance of the ingredients. Also, the market falls into thirds that I share with you, too.

Also, you have to consider two other factors: time and buyers. A house doesn't sell without a buyer. Otherwise—and this is quite a statement I am making—"You are buying the house back yourself." Think about it: If someone else doesn't buy the house from you at the price you are asking, then in effect you are buying it back at the price you are asking! And do you really want to do that? Most sellers wouldn't buy their house back at the price they are asking. It is quite a concept, isn't it? So you need to price your home to sell to the most buyers in the fairest and quickest amount of time. And The S Factor for you is Staging! That is the wonderful secret—the wild card, the ace in the hole, however you want to put it—that gives you the most room to set your price for. Staging works! Again and again and again. So read this chapter, make your Agent accountable, hold yourself accountable, and get the ASP Stager in your home to do the Staging now!

IN THIS CHAPTER

You will learn:

1. How to fill out and use a Pricing-Your-Home Triangle to help you establish the list price with your sellers.
2. How to do a market analysis using Staging as the main ingredient of the sale.

Agents, as I have said, your job is to teach your sellers where you feel they fit in today's market in price and terms. So the last page in the pricing your home presentation should be the Pricing-Your-Home Triangle. I recommend that you fill it out ahead of time. Don't meet with your sellers for your listing presentation without a written statement of the price range you believe is suitable for the sale of their home. And it should be a Staged list price range. Show the comparable homes that you are feel are correct, and then as go through them one by one, summarize each section. Most Agents have not taken the presentation approach I am going to teach you in this chapter.

Stagers, you can help Agents, too, by sharing information about homes you have Staged when the houses close and the information becomes public record. (After the closing, anyone can obtain the information about a given property regarding what it listed for *and* what it sold for.) As a Stager, I always provide that information once it is public to other Agents I work with, so that I can help them all to my very best. Agents like that kind of information, and they don't mind my sharing information about their listing when it is sold and closed because they know that they will benefit from other Agents' information as well.

THE WAY TO PRESENT COMPARABLE HOME SALES AND LISTINGS WITH YOUR SELLERS

Agents, I ask you to provide the comparable homes in four ways:

1. Sold homes that were *Staged*.
2. Sold homes that were *not Staged*.
3. For-sale homes that are *Staged*.
4. For-sale homes that are *not Staged*.

Although this may make sense to you as a Stager, I promise you that most Agents have never thought of this. It seems obvious perhaps to us as Stagers, but Agents have not been taught to do a market analysis this way. I assure you sellers and Stagers that this is different. As an Agent, you probably have just sorted the houses by size and location. And although that arrangement shows those aspects, real estate is a whole new world with Staging in it. From now on, as an Agent, you need to do a market analysis to show the effects of Home Staging on pricing, as well as the other elements. So now, as an Agent, I am asking you to sort the houses by square footage, location, *and* Staging. After you have grouped them according to the way I am sharing with you, then summarize each group with a summary sheet. When you do that, you will have four summary sheets, each showing the average time on the market and the average price for:

1. Sold homes that were *Staged*.
2. Sold homes that were *not Staged*.
3. For-sale homes that are *Staged*.
4. For-sale homes that are *not Staged*.

Agents, that again gives four groups of comparables to show the sellers.

The flow of a pricing presentation is very important. Doctors don't say to someone they just met, "Oh, you look like you have pneumonia." They do tests and meet with the patient several times. And you as an Agent shouldn't say, "Oh, your home looks like it could sell for *x* dollars." This, too, is why I ask you as Agents and Stagers to meet with people in steps, with pricing the very last thing you go into in the last step: not the first, but the very last step. Step 1, remember, is to build rapport, take notes, take pictures, and share your credentials and the pricing DVD. Step 2, then, is your Detailed Report, with the first part being marketing as an Agent or the Proposal as a Stager; and then the second part dealing with the pricing of the property as an Agent and the pricing of the Staging project as a Stager. So, as an Agent, you must do the pricing of the property in the second half of Step 2. Go through the ingredients of a sale I have shared with you, and then show the homes you have chosen as comparables. As you summarize each group its the summary sheet, then and only then move that information onto the Pricing-Your-Home Triangle. (See Figure 9.1.)

Always point out that the facts and figures on the Triangle came right from the comparable homes you just looked at together in the Comparative Market Analysis and that all you did was to group the facts and showed them. That may seem obvious, but sellers have said to me, "Where did you get these figures from," even though we had just looked at them on the summary sheets. So, again, point out the source of the figures on the Pricing-Your-Home Triangle so sellers see the transition from the summary sheets to the Triangle. I always state that just to make sure that everyone is on the same plane headed in the same direction.

Pricing Your Home

There are _____ homes for sale in your area
priced between _____ and _____ .
The total number of homes on the market is _____ .

$ _____

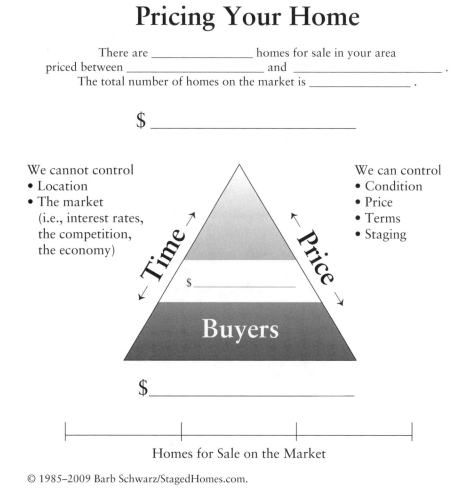

© 1985–2009 Barb Schwarz/StagedHomes.com.

Figure 9.1   Pricing-Your-Home Triangle

HOW TO USE THE PRICING TRIANGLE

As you can see in Figure 9.1, at the top of the page you can include some information on the number of comparable homes in the sellers' area. For example, you might point to the top of the page and say to the sellers, "I've counted all the homes in your area that fit in the price range of the comparable active homes we have just looked at and summarized. There are twenty-two homes for sale in your area priced between four hundred and eighty and four hundred and ninety-five thousand. That's a lot of competition!"

Count all of the homes in their area for sale whether or not they are the same size. Why? You and I both know how many times a buyer will say to us, "Only show me one-level homes," and the buyer ends up buying a two-story house. I rest my case. Count all of the homes for sale in their area as competition, and put that in the top area of the Triangle!

Then for the actual price range, do two Pricing-Your-Home Triangles! Do one Triangle for competing homes that are Staged and another for competing homes that are *not* Staged. Then fill in both the price ranges that appeared in those two different groups: one for Staged homes and one for homes that are *not* Staged. Of course, the price ranges are going to be different, and, of course, the Staged Triangle is going to be higher because it should be higher! All you have to do is to ask the seller, "Which Triangle or price range do you want to be in?" Well, I have never met a seller yet who wanted to be in the lower price range, Triangle of Homes that are not Staged. It doesn't happen. What I developed and found by doing so is that this is a very good visual of why Staging makes the difference on the sellers' bottom line that it does! For sellers who like facts and figures, this sure puts the dot on the *i* and the cross on the *t* to get the house Staged and priced right.

CONTROLLABLE VERSUS UNCONTROLLABLE INGREDIENTS

You will see that I have divided my pricing discussion in the last chapter into two groups on the Triangle: what can be controlled and what cannot be controlled. To explain these elements, I recommend that you say the following:

> In addition to these figures, Mr. and Mrs. Seller, I have divided the list of ingredients for a sale into two categories: ingredients you cannot control and those you can. As a seller of a resale home, you cannot control the location of a property. You cannot control the market, which includes interest rates, the competition, and the economy. It would be nice if you could keep the prime rate at *x* percent, but you cannot control the market. These are variables beyond your control or mine. But you can usually control the very important other ingredients: condition, price, terms, *and* Staging.

Most sellers can control the condition of their property, or at least they can do something about it. And even though sometimes sellers don't want to admit it, they can control the price of their property. You see this in properties that have been on the market for a long time. Some of them have dropped their asking price $50,000 to $100,000 in order to sell. Others in a lower price range have dropped $5,000 or $10,000. They had to drop because they started out significantly overpriced or they were not Staged and sat, and the market moved underneath them. Even though they felt when they came on the market that they couldn't control the price, they *had* to control the price in the end to sell the property. Again, this is where the statistics about Staged homes really come into play. These sellers probably wouldn't have had to drop their price and would have sold if they had just Staged it to start out with. Explain all this to your sellers. They need to understand the impact that price and Staging have on the sale of their home.

LEARN ABOUT PRICE REDUCTIONS VERSUS STAGING FROM THE BEGINNING

It is very important that you as a seller know that the average price reduction is 5 percent to 10 percent off the list price of the home, and in a down market it could even be more. To get Agents back to show a home that has sat on the market a long time, it takes a good price reduction—or getting the house Staged. So my question to you is this: "With the average Staged home investment at approximately $2,800 in the United States and the average price reduction at 5 to 10 percent, which costs you less: reducing your price or getting your house Staged? The answer is clear. You pay out of your pocket one way or the other. And with these statistics for price reductions it becomes really clear that, when you own a $500,000 house, a price deduction will be $25,000 to $50,000 off the list price. So Staging is the far better investment with a great return on your investment. My associate Dan calls it ROSI: return on Staging investment!

At the time of writing, the statistics we gather at Stagedhomes.com show that 93 percent of Staged homes sell on average in less than 30 days. The homes that are not Staged are selling on average in 161 days or more. And when houses sit, prices come down. That has been proved over and over and over again, no matter what market we are in. As I said, "Longevity on the market means one thing: reduction in price!" So Staging definitely is the far, far better choice to make instead of dropping the price. By drawing a line down the center of the paper and writing on the left side "$25,000–$50,000 price reduction" and then writing the average Staging of price of "$2,800" on the right side, you make the decision very easy to make. Even if the fee is $5,000, it still is so much less than dropping the price—and most Staging service fees are between $500 and $5,000. (The fee for Staging is determined by the size of the house, how much clutter is in the house, and just what needs to be done.)

Many people don't consider terms a controllable ingredient. Sellers will sometimes say, "Well, I really can't offer seller financing. I've got to be totally cashed out of the property." But after they have been on the market for a while, all of a sudden they may agree to hold $5,000 to $20,000 in the form of a deed of trust for that purchaser. So, you see, terms can be controllable. Use this example to explain that to your sellers.

SETTING THE RIGHT PRICE

As the Agent, write three prices on the Triangle before you meet with each seller for your listing presentation: (1) the highest Staged price you would list the home for, (2) the lowest Staged price you would list it for, and (3) the Staged price you recommend as optimum price for selling time as a Staged Home. The highest figure goes in the top of the triangle, the lowest at the bottom of the triangle, and the recommended price in the middle of the triangle. For example:

- At the bottom of the triangle, you might write $480,000, the lowest price at which you think the property should be priced.
- In the middle of the triangle, write the price you are recommending for the property: $487,500.
- At the top of the triangle, insert the highest price, in this case, $495,000.

Now, you will see little arrows beside the pricing triangle, before and after the words "Time" and "Price." They go in both directions: up and down. What you want to share with your sellers, Agents, is that a price can go as low or as high as one wants it. There is no beginning and no end in pricing. However, *as you go up in price, the longer it is going to take to sell the house and the fewer buyers there are to buy it.* In the Triangle, the words "Time" and "buyers" refer to the length of time it will take and the number of buyers there are for the different levels on the price range. Conversely, the lower you go in any range, the less time it will take to sell and the more buyers you will be reach who are able to buy your home.

Here's how I would explain this aspect of the Pricing-Your-Home Triangle to sellers:

> Sally and John, here is what I call the "Pricing-Your-Home Triangle." I find that it really helps sellers understand the pricing of their home. At the very bottom I have written in the figure of four hundred and eighty thousand dollars. Now, I want to set your mind to rest that I am not suggesting we list your home at four hundred and eighty thousand dollars. But you see, at the bottom of the Triangle, we have a very wide base, which means we would have a lot of buyers at that price. The lower we price your property, the more potential purchasers there will be and the faster your home will sell.
>
> As we move up in price on the Triangle, several things take place. I've written the words "Price" and "Time" on the Triangle to show that as the price goes up, so does the length of time it takes to sell a home. In other words, the higher we move in pricing, the longer it will take to sell your home. Notice that because I visually placed buyers on the inside of the Triangle, the higher we go in price, the fewer buyers there are for your home. I've shaded in the upper section of the Triangle to demonstrate that the higher the price climbs, the more time it takes and the fewer buyers there are. At four hundred and ninety-five thousand dollars, you can see that there are not as many buyers to sell your home to. This is true in any price range.
>
> The price I recommend we come on the market with is four hundred eighty-seven thousand and five hundred dollars, which is the price in the middle. This is a fair market price where your property should sell in a reasonable period.

Notice that not only does the Triangle demonstrate how price and time are related, but it visually makes it even more clear by showing how they work together. I have found since I developed Pricing-Your-Home Triangle that it really does help sellers understand the importance of pricing their homes right.

THE BOTTOM LINE

The idea I am about to share with you has enabled me to help a lot of sellers price their property right. After you have gone over the Triangle, as depicted in Figure 9.1, move to the line drawn across the bottom of the page that is right above "Homes for Sale on the Market." This line represents homes for sale on the market today, and you can use it to get sellers to look objectively at the pricing of their homes. You can use this approach with your sellers just as I am relating it to you.

The line represents the market. Then I divide the line into thirds, which represent almost exactly the three states of our market (not shown in Figure 9.1): SOLD (rightmost), questionable to sell (middle), and *never* sell (leftmost). Statistics from all over the nation have proved this arrangement to be reliable, except in the most active markets. Even in those markets, however, homes still fit into one of these thirds. Again, I draw the line and write in the thirds right there in front of the sellers.

Let's talk about a home that fits into the first third on the right: never sell. It could be a mess or on a really busy street. The condition may be horrible. The roof might leak. The carpet is worn, or the rooms need painting. It is overpriced or in a bad location. As I talk about this category to my sellers, I lean over in front of them and I scrawl the word "*never*" on that first third. I write it in big letters, and I underline it. This third will never sell—unless the owners change one or more ingredients of the sale. They would have to drop the price or change the condition. But as long as things stay the way they are—overpriced, in a poor location, and in bad condition—it will never sell. It just sits! Houses like this can sit on the market for years, and they are out there today in every market.

In the middle third of the line—questionable to sell—I lean over in front of the sellers and draw a big question mark. This house could go either way. Somebody might buy it, but the word is "might." There are no buyers standing in line to purchase this home. The location is not too bad, but the corner is way too busy. The condition is not horrible; however, the house is priced higher than most of the others. Buyers usually won't put this property on their possibility list. It's just a question mark. The buyers looking through these kinds of properties usually say, "Well, this seller will have to get lucky, but not with my money. I am not buying it."

How many sellers have you heard say, "Let's just try it at this price. Maybe we'll get lucky"? Sharing this truth about what buyers think and say when they are looking at homes priced in this third really educates sellers about the possibility of being lucky. So I explain to my sellers this third of the market is a real question mark. We have to do our job and share our professional opinions with sellers. Look them right in the eye and say:

> There is no getting lucky in real estate. We cannot just see what happens or just try to get lucky. When sellers try this, they usually end up losing even more later on by having to lower their price even farther than if they had priced it right in the beginning in order to get the buyers back in their front door.

The National Association of Realtors statistics support this idea, and you can show the figures in Figure 9.2 to your sellers if you like. The chart simply shows that the longer a home is on the market, the lower the selling price of the property will be. These statistics prove that pricing the property right in the beginning will bring your sellers a quicker, more profitable sale.

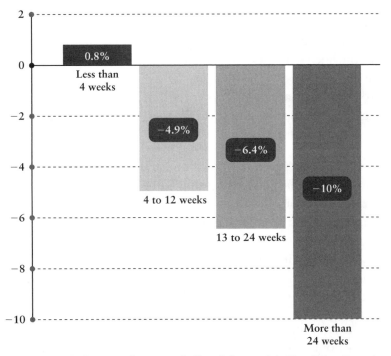

Figure 9.2   Difference Between Selling Price and Asking Price Based on Time on the Market

Source: "Real Estate Outlook" © National Association of Realtors®

Then we have the final third: SOLD. I lean over and say, "This is the third of the market that is hot. This is the third of the market that sells." I write, in big letters, the word "SOLD!" on that third. In this third of the homes, buyers go in and say, "This is exciting! This home looks better than the other two-thirds we just looked at, and it is priced equal to or lower than the other two-thirds." Tell your sellers that this is where they need to be! To have a sale in the quickest, fairest amount of time, the property needs to be priced right, be Staged, and be in a good location. The better your sellers understand this, the easier it is for you to price the property right as their Agent. This final third is where you want all your listings to be. In this third of the market, all the ingredients of the sale work together.

Using a line to divide the market into thirds turned out to be a great idea, I must say. My intuition came up with it as I working with a seller who was having a hard time understanding pricing. When I drew the line, divided it, and wrote in the words, he got it. He *really* got it!

You can talk about the ingredients of the sale as well as the length of selling time. From the "SOLD!" third all the way over to the *"never"* third, you have just moved from selling in a short amount of time to probably never selling. I always put the SOLD third on the right end of the line, the question mark in the middle, and the *never* sell on the left side of the line. This way, the *right* way to sell your home is on the *right* end of the line!

You can also adapt prices to the line, simply moving them from the Triangle to the appropriate third. As you move the prices to the line, you could say something like this:

If we set the price for your house at five hundred and twenty thousand dollars, we are going to be in the "never sell" third. If we resell at four hundred and ninety-five thousand, the sale could happen, but it is still a question of how long it takes and how many buyers would purchase at that price. We just don't know. However, pricing your home between four hundred and eighty and four hundred eighty-seven thousand and five hundred dollars, we are going to fit the *"yes!"* third: the hot category!

In the end, the price selected is the price that the seller selects because it is their home. However, as the Agent, you are a team member with the seller, and your job is to educate sellers in the best possible way that will still bring them top dollar. And sitting on the market for a long time will not make that happen for either them or you!

REFUSAL OF A LISTING

People occasionally ask me, "Do you take overpriced listings?" I admit it! I have taken overpriced listings. As Agents we all end up doing it at one time or another. The key is not to take listings that are way overpriced, that is, priced totally out of sight. If I meet sellers whose motivations I feel will change, then I go ahead and list it at the top of the price range, as long as they fit into the price range on the Triangle. (So you should give yourself a bit of leeway in the Triangle.) But if the sellers want to go far above the highest price on my Triangle, then I will let the listing go. If their expectations are way, way too high, I work like the dickens to get them to at least the top price on the Triangle. Once I have done my Comparative Market Analysis and determined the prices on my Pricing-Your-Home Triangle, this is where I professionally think the property should be listed. If the sellers want to come on higher or lower than that, my professional policy is that I will not take the listing.

Having professional policies and being honest is the only way to work, and it wins out every time. I have learned in the long run this will save you a lot of time, frustration, and money. (It takes money to market overpriced listings!) Plus, I can't tell you how many times over the years sellers listened to another Agent who told them what they wanted to hear (a price that was too high for the market) and then three to six months later called me when they weren't able to sell. At that point, they listed with me at the right price, and we got the home Staged and sold.

IF THE TIME ISN'T RIGHT

Now, this brings us to an interesting question. How do you turn down sellers? For example, let's say you have sellers who you would really like to work with. You love the house, and you'd really like to list it, but the sellers are not yet motivated to sell. How do you turn down the listing, but still leave the door open so that they will want you to list the house later?

The commitments you have made to the sellers in the marketing portion of your Detailed Report leave you a perfect solution. When you think you shouldn't take a listing, look at your sellers and say, "Sally and John, I just love your home. I really do. And I would very much like to represent you as your exclusive listing Agent. But, *at this time*, I cannot enthusiastically support listing the property at that price, with all my marketing techniques and efforts." By saying "at this time," you leave the door open for the future. And the phrase "I cannot enthusiastically support" lets you off the hook. No one would want you to list his or her property if you weren't enthusiastic about it. It is a perfect way of saying to your sellers, "Later on you may be ready to sell—and I hope you are—and I'll be there at that time to bring your home on the market with you. At that time, I will enthusiastically support it with everything that I've got." With all the commitments you have made to them, they understand you need that enthusiasm.

Then add:

> Down the road, chances are that you are going to need me. [I have found that that one simple sentence has brought more business back to me than you can realize. It seems to stay with people and they realize that they *do* need us. And you can say that as an Agent or as a Stager because it is the truth. People do need you.] And I am going to be right here ready to go to work for you. I will really look forward to that time. And I want to keep in touch. I would like for you to call if you have any questions at all. If you decide not to go on the market, and you want to look at my Detailed Report again with me, let's sit down and review it. But the important thing I want you to know is that I have enjoyed meeting you. I love your home, and I am ready to go to work for you as soon as we can enthusiastically come on the market together at a competitive price.

You have left the door wide open! I know this works. I have had sellers call me later and say, "OK, Barb, we're ready to go. Get yourself over here and list our home." "Terrific!" I say. "Is three o'clock good, or is four o'clock better?" (Please never tell them "I told you so" about pricing.)

When your sellers call you back, meet with them again and be prepared to present a new market analysis, because prices may have changed. If the figures haven't changed, take the opportunity to reeducate them. Review your marketing and pricing with them all over again, because sometimes a lot has happened in their lives and perhaps some time has passed. Educating your sellers, even if you have to go over something twice, is not a waste of time! It is a matter of service, of professional policies, and of making sure that every house you list as an Agent is Staged! And your ASP Stager is your new best friend, as you will undoubtedly find out!

CHAPTER 10

STAGING THE PROPERTY: THE OUTSIDE STORY

You can't get them inside if you don't Stage the outside!

BARB SCHWARZ

SELLER'S NOTE

Why does it matter how the outside of your property looks? You have lived there the way it looks so why should you do anything differently to sell the house? What happens when you meet someone new? As it is said, "You never get a second chance to make a first impression." That is true for the outside, and the inside, of your house, too! Buyers see everything that you have stopped seeing because of how busy your life probably is these days: the bush that never got trimmed as you had planned to do or the fresh coat of paint you were going to put on the front door that never happened. Everyone is slammed for time today just living their lives, but I remember this: How you live in your home and the how you market and sell it are two different things!

IN THIS CHAPTER

You will learn

1. As Stagers and Agents, how to help your sellers see the outside of their homes from the buyers' point of view.
2. My Tips for Selling for the outside of the property.
3. My extra pointers on making sure a house shows at its best.
4. For sellers, why buyers see your property differently than you do!

If your home is your number one investment—and for most of us our homes are—then it only makes sense to invest some time and energy and even a few dollars to get the highest return on your number *one* investment! Another pair of eyes seeing your property and recommending what you do is so crucial in today's market! Your Agent needs to see it from the marketing standpoint, and your Stager needs to see it from the Staging standpoint. Together, as ASP Agents and ASP Stagers. They make a great team. Very few of us do our own dentistry or medical diagnoses. There is no way that I can perform a root canal on myself. Yet some sellers seem to think that they can either put the house on the market the way they have been living in it or that they don't need anyone else's opinion about Staging their property. Either way, it is a huge mistake. As a seller, you are too close to your house. You don't see the overgrown bushes or weeds that have started to grow in the yard, as your Stager and Agent do. It pays to invest in your number one investment, and the return on your investment will make you very happy that you did. The ideas presented in this chapter work! I have developed them, testing them over and over again with thousands of sellers, and they work every single time. Follow what I ask you to do, and these tips will work for you, too! Your Stager and your Agent will back me up on this and why would they do that?

Because you told the Agent and Stager that you want to sell the house and not live there anymore (although I believe in Staging to live as well, but that is a story for the next chapter), you are selling a product—your house—and you need to dig in and get some things done with your fellow team members, as they guide you with their advice, which comes from their head and heart. People care when they tell you things. If they didn't care, they would just turn the other way and say, "Why bother?" It takes guts sometimes to tell sellers what needs to be done *and* to stick to it. This

I know and learned the hard way. So I am going to tell you the simple truth and what works, and I really have great expectations that you will work with your professional team guiding the way!

So let's Stage the outside of your house so that you can sell for top dollar and in a reasonable amount of time! You have signed the paperwork with your Agent and Stager, and now it is time to Stage your home, first the outside and then the inside. The way a home looks from the curb may determine how many potential purchasers will look at the inside it. So, the Staging of the *exterior* is just as important as the Staging of the *interior*.

THE POWER OF FIRST IMPRESSIONS

The inside of a home may be where most people are most of the time, but the outside of the home often attracts buyers. This feature is known, of course, as curb appeal: how good the property looks from the street. Because Real Estate Agents know this, the first thing a buyers' Agent does is to park the car with the buyers across the street from a seller's home. If a messy yard or falling gutters completely turn off the purchasers, the property has just taken a giant step backward, no matter how good the interior of the house looks. So it is just as important to prepare the outside of the house as the inside. Sometimes buyers won't go inside the house if they don't like the looks of the outside.

THE BUYERS' POINT OF VIEW

One of the best things to do as Agents, Stagers, and sellers is to go across the street from the house, perhaps in the neighbors' yard or safely on the other side of the street. I have found that this is one of the most effective ways to get sellers' cooperation Staging the outside of their homes. Everyone has to see the house from across the street. Many people never look at the outside of their house objectively after they buy it. They walk out of the house in the morning, get in their car, and drive off to work without looking back. When they return home, they whisk themselves into the garage without even looking at how their home really appears. This happens day after day after day after day. We are all this way. Some days I come home, and the drive is so familiar, it seems like I can't even remember how I got home. The longer we live in our homes, the less we see it as we did the day we bought it. We become familiar with our environment, and we don't see many times that the bushes grew taller and that the paint needs repainting, we get busy and just don't see those things: "You can't see the forest for the trees."

Getting some distance, even across the street, really helps sellers get objective. So take your sellers across the street and say, "Look back at your house, Mr. and Mrs. Seller, and I want you to *think like a buyer*. Tell me what you see." The sellers will usually stand there a second. Then, all of a sudden, they will get tough on themselves. They'll see things they haven't seen for years. For instance, they might say, "Gosh, I didn't know that gutter was coming down." Or they might say, "Wow, that front door sure looks bad. I guess it'll need a new coat of paint." From this viewpoint, they usually can't help but notice how overgrown the plants are. They'll say something like, "The plants have grown so high, I can't even see the den window." As they say these things, add them to their list of things to be repaired.

Now, if the house is overgrown by plants and the seller doesn't bring it up, you need to say something like, "Do you see how the right side of your house is buried behind the two very large plants, Mr. and Mrs. Seller? In fact, aren't those your master bedroom and den windows behind the plants?" The sellers both answer, "Yes." "Well, Mr. and Mrs. Seller, I noticed that inside those two rooms of your house it was darker than in the other rooms. Now, I don't think the problem is with the rooms at all. I think the rooms are dark inside because the plants have grown so large outside that they're preventing light from flooding into those rooms. Wouldn't you say that is correct?" Again your sellers will have to answer, "Yes."

This is when I tell one of my many Staging sayings and principles: *You can't sell it if you can't see it*. Learn this saying. How can you sell something if you can't see it? It only makes good sense! Teach this principle to your sellers, and I promise it will make good sense to them as well. But you must take them across the street to get the full impact. Telling them in their living room about their overgrown plants, which are outside, or even telling them on their front porch, usually won't work as well. Taking them across the street really gives you the power you need to teach your sellers that homes that are full of light inside are really in demand these days. Personally, I don't know anywhere in the country, after teaching my class in literally almost every state in the union (and in Canada too), where light isn't an appealing feature. Today's buyers always ask Agents to show them light and bright homes. You need to share this with your sellers so that they understand what today's buyers want.

Also, another powerful thing to share with sellers is that *plants are like kids.* When we first have them, they are so little and cute; then they get just about right and before you know it, they get so big that some of us don't know how to take care of them anymore. This is a very effective analogy with the sellers, who tell you they planted the tree that is now grown over the entire top of the roof.

Now we cannot trim our kids, but we sure can trim the plants to let in more light. We don't usually have to cut the entire plant down to the ground, although sometimes it is necessary. Most of the time trimming the branches in certain places will let more light into the room, but the plant will still look good. It works. Tell your sellers, as you add trimming to the list, that you will help them establish how much or how little to trim. Remember, the key is to let more light into the rooms and to let the house be shown from the curb at its best. You need to have the sellers trim overgrown trees from the bottom up, in other words, trimming off the lower branches so that the house can be seen past the trunk. That way you still have the main larger part of the tree at the top. It works. Also, have the seller trim the plants from the top down (the opposite of trimming the trees). Rounding off the top of the bush makes it look more compact and abundant, and the individual looks of all the plants add up to the total look of the yard and landscaping of the property.

As Agents, sometimes you will get sign calls on a listing (buyers calling the number on the yard sign), and buyers will tell you that the property is overpriced. One common reason for this is that the shrubbery is overgrown, and the buyers cannot see the house. They think that the house is smaller than it may be and conclude that it is overpriced. The fact is that you can't sell it if you can't see it!

When you take sellers across the street, several great things happen. First, they get to be the judge criticizing the house and you don't have to be. If you were to talk to them about the outside of their home while you were on the inside, it would not mean nearly as much.

Second, taking them across the street is wonderful because it gives so much more perspective, and the emotional strings are really cut from the property by being across the street. Usually, when you ask how long it has been since your sellers looked at their home like a buyer, they will say, "Not since the day I bought it" or "Never."

Let the sellers talk and name all that they can about what they see and what they think they need to do with the property to get it ready for sale. When they finish talking, bring up things you see that they missed. Remember, the first time you went to see the property, you should have sat in your car or stood across the street and really looked at the house to figure these things out, so that you know how to guide your sellers when it is time to Stage the house and make their list to get things done. Together, write down everything on the list as you talk about the actual things that need to be done on the outside of the property.

Also walk all the way around the outside of the house, continuing the list as you go. Keep your eyes open to anything and everything you think needs to be done, and talk about each item openly with your seller. Don't hold back on anything. You owe it to your sellers and yourself to bring up anything you see, even if it may be difficult. Discuss the two-by-fours piled by the house, and ask the sellers where they can be put away. Have your sellers move the pots filled with the dead plants off the deck or patio. Ask your sellers to move the old worn-out patio furniture if it is cluttering up the back yard. All of these things detract from showing the property to potential purchasers.

Staging the outside of the property is just as crucial as Staging the inside, and making the exterior list with your sellers is extremely important. Then you want to make sure that the list gets done and everything gets put away. We will talk about how to be sure that it all does get done in the next chapter.

TIPS ON SELLING FOR OUTSIDE OF PROPERTY

The pointers in this section work wonders with the outside of someone's home. Use them, because they really do work. As Stagers and as Agents, share them from the very beginning in your *Marketing Portfolio* as you work with your sellers. As an Agent, you know what kind of buyers will be looking at the property, and you need to share that with the sellers and the Stagers. By the time the sellers and the Stager actually Stage the house, your sellers will already know the general theory of what and why everything needs to be done. But remember as Agents and as Stagers, zero in on the actual items, one by one, *only* after the sellers have signed your agreements. In other words, then, trimming the plants and bushes outside the house is noted on the Tips for Selling list, and you should talk about the idea during your presentation, if it fits the situation. However, you show which bush or where to trim it only when the sellers give you their commitment in writing.

And, sellers, I certainly hope you understand why this must be so. The Stager's expertise in Staging and the Agent's expertise in marketing are what you need to get top dollar. This happens because you each make a commitment to the others. As the seller, you receive your equity, and the Agent and the Stager receive their fees for their expertise. That is why you are working with them—for their expertise, knowledge, and skills.

Tip 1: Remove All Garbage Cans, Discarded Wood Scraps, and Extra Building Materials from View

Stagers, go around the perimeter of the house with the sellers to make sure everything is cleaned out of the yard. Have the sellers put these things into storage or take them to the dump. Most individual homeowners have some of these things around the outside of our homes. And these things are in the way of the buyers seeing the yard or the property. It is outside clutter, and it has to go!

Tip 2: Look at the Bushes and Trees

One of the best phrases I have ever developed to use with sellers is, "We can't sell it if we can't see it!"

That is the truth! So have the sellers trim back any bushes or shrubbery that is obscuring the house from view. Tall plants not only make it difficult for potential purchasers to see your sellers' home, but they block light from the windows. Suggest to the sellers that they trim back the bushes and prune the trees. Sometimes, trees are so overgrown the sellers need to cut away the lower branches so that purchasers can see the front of the house. This type of trimming is called "skirting the tree," and it works like a charm. Have your sellers remove any dead plants or shrubs. Sometimes you work with sellers who have not yet removed a couple of plants that died the year before. It's just one of those things they never got around to doing. If you see any dying or dead foliage, point it out to the sellers, and put it on the list for them to take care of.

Tip 3: Weed and Mulch All Planting Areas, and Groom and Fertilize the Lawn

Many yards can use a little sprucing up before they go on the market. Be honest with your sellers about what you see and how they can make improvements. The investment is small, or it can be done with just a little extra time and effort. If beauty bark is widely used in your area of the country, then have your sellers put fresh bark in their planting areas. Different parts of the country use different ground cover mulches; whatever it is, have your sellers add a fresh layer. Or ask them to at least till the ground in the planting areas, so that there is only fresh dirt, no weeds. The lawn also needs to be kept cut, and a little fertilizer is a small investment to really make a lawn look sharp. This is true for vacant properties that you list as well.

Tip 4: Clear Patios or Decks of All Small Items

Patios and decks should be Staged as well to show off the outdoor living aspect of a home, even if it's the dead of winter. Move extra planters, empty flower pots, charcoal, grills, toys, anything like that into the garage or storage shed. If it is summertime, and they are going to use the barbecue grill, at least put it in one corner of the patio or deck. If it is wintertime, have your sellers put it away in the garage.

One of my pet peeves, which my friends kid me about, is seeing dead or dying potted plants that people refuse to throw away. We all do it, and you know the kind I mean. They have two short sticks coming out of the pot with three faded leaves just barely surviving. For example, people tend to keep poinsettias. Do you still have a poinsettia from the Christmas season before last? Yes, I thought so. Or at least we all seem to hang onto plants that are continually on their last leg. It's the middle of August, and there is a poinsettia, with its red foil wrap, sitting on the deck—half with us and half gone. Have your sellers clear away all those things. By the way, most of us keep these sick plants for two reasons: hope and guilt. Your sellers will love you because when you talk to them about the sick plants, they will be so happy to throw them out because you have just saved them from feeling guilty anymore.

Here is how I do this. I just look at the sickest plant they have, then I look at the sellers, back to the plant again, and then I say, "I don't think it's going to make the move, do you?" The sellers laugh and say, "No. Barb, you're right. It will probably croak in the moving van." Have them take it to the garbage right then. This works great for plants on the inside of the house as well as those on the outside.

If it is springtime or summer, keep flower pots to a minimum and full of live beautiful flowers. If it is winter, put all of them away or use fake flowers. Keep decks and patios cleared of lots of small things. And the same goes for the front yard and back yard. The more things there are to distract the eye, the harder it is to sell the property.

Tip 5: Check the Paint on the House—Especially the Front Door and Trim

Here is where curb appeal really works! The paint job is one of the first things a potential buyer notices. If the paint is peeling off the house, a number one priority is to try to have them repaint the whole house, but let's say the sellers can't afford to do that. Those circumstances come up for all of us from time to time. Ask them whether they could just paint the front door. I haven't met a seller yet who couldn't afford one gallon of paint for the front door and its trim. Remember, after all, a gallon of paint on sale at the hardware store is less than $15. I have yet to run into motivated sellers, no matter how poor they were, who would not buy a gallon of paint when asked in that fashion.

If sellers are going to paint their home, I suggest that you as the Stager offer the service of helping them pick out the color. If you are unsure of color, I suggest that you go to where new homes are being built and look at the colors that the builders are using. After all, they are in the business of building homes for a living, and they usually know the best and latest colors to use. Then suggest some of these colors to your sellers. Also, I have picked Staging colors from Sherwin Williams for ASPs to recommend, and Sherwin Williams gives you, as an ASP Stager, from 50 to 70 percent off the retail paint price. So, sellers, make sure you work with an ASP to get the savings on the paint you purchase. Sherwin Williams' paint brochures are another source of excellent ideas for paint colors, especially the ones that show pictures of homes already painted.

Sellers, if it is a real financial challenge having to paint the house, then do it by degrees of importance. Paint the front door first if that is all you can paint. The next level of importance is the trim and any shutters, and then paint the house. It isn't the paint that is expensive; it is usually the labor. So, sellers, perhaps you can get your relatives or friends to help you get the house painted.

Check the front door for any damage. If there are claw marks from a dog or a cat, have those repaired and painted. Is the doorknob working properly? Does the doorbell work? Your goal is to assure that the house makes a good first impression.

Tip 6: Finish Any Unfinished Projects

If a pile of lumber is lying in the yard because the sellers haven't finished putting the last planks on a new deck, have the sellers make that a priority project. This rule applies to the inside as well and to any project that has not been completed. If your sellers started it before they ever met you but never finished it, *now* is the time. Finishing projects can make a tremendous difference to a purchaser and can earn the sellers, at times, a higher selling price. The opposite is also true. That's why it's important to educate your sellers that most buyers are not interested in taking over someone else's project, and an unfinished project decreases the total number of possible buyers, usually increases selling time, and can ultimately reduce the selling price. I think it's actually better, if possible, to remove what has been started rather than list a property with a partially completed project. Of course, many times that is impossible; so have the sellers get the project done.

Tip 7: Go Completely Around the Property

For your information, protection, and Staging, I suggest that you walk around the whole property with your sellers, or without them if they are physically unable. If it is dark outside, I suggest you return during the daylight hours. This way you can be sure there are no surprises that the sellers forgot to tell you about, such as a junk pile, any building materials or firewood piled against the house (a red flag for pest inspectors!), or anything else that looks suspicious or unattractive.

Tip 8: Add Magic Trees

I love my magic trees because they work like magic. They do well in the hot weather, the cold weather, wet weather, and dry weather. You know what they are when you see them; they are a nice green shrub in the cedar family that grows nearly everywhere. In the plant world they are called Arborvitae. In the nurseries that is how you will find them. They range from $25 to $100 depending on the height of the tree. In stores such as WalMart, Target, or Kmart, they are called "Emerald Greens" (the same type of plant). The price range in these stores is usually from $10 to $40.

Sellers, I recommend you put the smaller ones in pots at your front door or by the garage between the two doors. You get to take these with you when you sell, and they add such a green touch as you have the house for sale. Green is for money, for trees, and for a prosperous look. The house will look healthier and more inviting with the green magic trees in front. Many houses have hedges out of these trees, and that is great too on a busy street to block the site of cars rushing by. I love what my magic trees do, and they help sell houses that have been sitting for a long time. That is why I call them magic!

Tip 9: Add Shutters

In addition to magic trees, I also love what shutters can do for a house for a small investment. Now, I do not have sellers put shutters on every house, but I have had them installed on high-end and lower-priced homes, too. How the house looks before putting up shutters determines whether I recommend putting them up. Stucco and cottage-style homes both look great with shutters. Traditional homes look fabulous with shutters, and any plain house that needs dressing up looks super with shutters too. It is also great to be able to add shutters that have a European look and that do not take much money to reproduce. I do not care for shutters that have what I call "frozen slats," which were used a lot in days past. The look is a bit too canned for me.

What I am taking about is shutters that you can make without even owning a saw. If you don't have a saw, have your local home improvement store cut the boards for you. Here is what you buy: six 1 × 4-inch boards cut to the height of your window measured on the outside. Do not buy cedar because it is expensive, not the quality that it used to be, and warps very easily. Buy plain old 1 × 4 boards because you are going to paint them anyway. Also you will need six 1 × 2-inch boards for the cross bars. Again, buy just plain old 1 × 2 boards. These boards need to be cut in approximately 12-inch lengths (three boards 4 × 12 inches long). Then you paint all the boards with one coat of spray primer and two coats of paint on the boards. Lay the three painted 1 × 4 boards side by side, and then put the crossbars on top. Nail, or preferably screw, the crossbars on top of the three boards, and now you have a shutter that is ready to go up on one side of the window. Make two shutters per window, and put one on each side of each window.

The colors to paint them are usually all black or all white. On light houses use all black, and on darker houses use white. Other colors are fine, too, such as a dark brown or a deep forest green, but the all-white or the all-black shutters are the safest.

Shutters add warmth to a house and also add an emotional look that really pulls people into a house. I have seen this happen time and time again. I decide to put shutters up when there isn't a lot of interest going on in the appearance of the house. For example, when there is no stone or brick on the house as trim, or when the house is all brick and not much wood, then wooden shutters look good. If the house is large, small shutters on all the windows in the front of a house or just on some of them add an attractive accent. On a one-level house they look good on the windows of, say, the dining room, the bedrooms, or both. On two-story homes, the shutters can be on the upper story or both stories. You do not want to have them ever clutter a house, so listen to your intuition and decide by going across the street and asking yourself just where to put them. And for some houses I would add none at all. But on at least 60 percent of my houses I have made sure that they were added because they were needed to make the house look more appealing!

These are my Tips for Selling on Staging the outside of a home. Do take the time necessary to go over all of them and to go through the whole house with your sellers. These will pay off in countless ways for you and your sellers.

THE DIFFERENCE STAGING MAKES

To help you get an even better Idea of the difference that Staging can make In a home's outside appearance, here are some before-and-after pictures of a house before it was listed (For Sale by Owner) and after it was Staged. It doesn't even look like the same house, but it really is! You can see the difference Staging can make. It is like a miracle, but is really so easy to do.

BEFORE STAGING

AFTER STAGING

BEFORE STAGING

AFTER STAGING

BEFORE STAGING

AFTER STAGING

CHAPTER 11

STAGING THE PROPERTY: THE INSIDE STORY

Buyers only know what they see, not the way it is going to be!

BARB SCHWARZ

SELLER'S NOTE

The time is here to Stage the inside of your home. This can be fun, you know; you shouldn't look at it as hard to do. It is work, but you also can have fun when you look at it in the right light. This is about making you money. You do want to make money, right?

Staging is about attitude. For one thing, most of us have way too many things . . . way too much stuff. We do, and our significant others or spouses do, too. Our kids have too much stuff, and the house is therefore probably cluttered and may be bulging at the seams. But even it if isn't stuffed, it still needs to be Staged. How you live in your home is totally different than how you sell it! I developed that Staging saying many years ago as I helped sellers then, and now I will tell you it is as important and valid today as it ever was *because it is true and makes sense!*

(Continued)

So where do you begin? As they say, start the same way as you would to eat an elephant: one bite at a time. You can start outside or inside, but the best approach is to start both at the same time. And you need two very important people to come into your life. One is an ASP Real Estate Agent to list your house. The Agent knows how to market Staged homes. Once it is Staged, the Agent will place your home on Stagedhomes.com, where today's buyers and buyers' Agents go to find houses that are Staged for sale. The other crucial person is an ASP or an ASPM Stager. These Stagers have been trained in the correct ways to Stage your house inside and outside. (The *M* in ASPM stands for Master, by the way, and holders of the certification have attended additional training with me in person.) Either an ASP or an ASPM Stager is trained to prepare your home for sale, and you can find either one on our Stagedhomes.com Stager directory. Stagers also can place your home on Stagedhomes.com, and they will do the work that is needed inside and out to make sure that your house is a Certified ASP Staged Home. As the creator of Home Staging and the Staging business model that is used today around the world, I say that it is really important that you are working with an ASP or ASPM Certified Stager! Training is obviously crucial because anyone can use the name of Stager, but you want an ASP or ASPM Stager to make sure that the professional *knows* what he or she is doing. As I have built Stagedhomes.com, I have also developed from day one the *Staging University* for ASPs to train and continue their training to be the best trained Stagers in the world.

As you will see in this chapter, of my Seven Cs of Staging, Commitment is really important on your part. I am serious about your making money, and your commitment to getting your home Staged for sale will show how serious you are. Every room must be Staged. That means going through your collections and going through each room looking for things to put away and to live without while buyers come through your home to see whether they feel it can become theirs. Remember, please, that Staging is about selling your space, not your things! You can live without seeing that collection for a couple of days or months, and it is far better protected, too, by your putting it away.

Some people feel that their home is Staged *just* by putting the collections away, and that is very far from the truth. We have only just begun. Concealing collections *is* a good place to start, but Staging has to do with the whole room. Everything in it has to be looked at and questioned as to whether it stays or goes. Don't get me wrong: You don't have to move everything, but at least you have to look at each item and ask the question: papers, magazines, too much furniture, too many accessories, too many paintings, and so on. When you have too many things in a room, people look at what you have, instead of at the room. Staging works on the principle that less is more. I want you to sell your space, not your things. Totally vacant rooms are not good, and rooms crammed full are not good, either. It is the balance between the two extremes that works, and our ASP Stagers can help you see the balance and, when they do their magic, you *will* see it.

After seeing their homes Staged, many of our sellers say, "We should have done that while we lived here." And the next thing you know, you will also decide that you want to live in your next house as a Staged-to-Live Home. One thing leads to another. Too many of us are owned by our things instead of owning our things. Staging lets you own your things again, not the other way around. That is another reason that it works. Your home should be the star, not your stuff. Stuff causes stress, and Staging destresses a property and lets the buyer see your house with its greatest potential. No one (except the coldest of investors) buys a house to make it a home before imagining living there. Staging allows buyers to do just that because the scene is set in each room for them. Staging doesn't cover up anything. In fact, it uncovers things, and the best thing it uncovers is your house's potential for all buyers to be able to see. That is why it works.

Now, on to Staging your home so that the buyers can see *your* house's potential and sell for top dollar in the shortest amount of time!

IN THIS CHAPTER

You will learn:

1. The importance of mutual, written commitments between the Agent and Seller and between the Stager and seller before Staging the house.
2. Agents and Stagers, how to tell your sellers what needs to be done to Stage their homes for sale.
3. How to Stage the inside of the house.
4. My Seven Cs of Staging.
5. My Tips for Selling for the inside of the home.

This is the fun part! I do not know of anything that is more fun and more satisfying than Home Staging! I love to Stage homes! And when you teach your sellers up front that this will help them get the most equity in the shortest amount of time, they will love to Stage their homes, too. It is important that you keep going back to the following truth:

The way you live in your home and the way you market and sell your house are two different things.

Once the sellers authorize you to list their property as the Agent or to Stage it as the Stager, the real work—and the fun—begins. The agreement must be filled out correctly, and the house must be prepared for sale. If you want to represent your sellers' properties accurately as an Agent, you must complete the listing accurately, too. And as a Stager you want to make sure that your paperwork is correctly done too! Remember:

Get the sellers' signatures before you begin your service of Staging their home.

Agents, if you have the sellers' property Staged before they sign the listing agreement, you put yourself in a vulnerable position. And, Stagers, if you Stage the property before you have the sellers' written commitment, you are also in a very vulnerable position. I learned that from an experience I told you about in Chapter 1, where I Staged a home before I had the owners' commitment in writing. I hope that tale will save you from making the same mistake. It takes commitment by all parties, and, sellers, you need to commit in writing to your Agent and to your Stager before they do their work to serve you. After you have gone through everything on the listing agreement (Agents) and the Staging paperwork (Stagers), and when the sellers have signed it and they have a copy in their hands, *then* you can begin you work.

FEARS ANYONE?

There is really nothing to fear at all, except *not* having the house Staged. That would surely create fear and concern for me. One of the keys to Staging is to think like a buyer. Stand in the doorway of each room, and make your Staging decisions there, because that is where buyers stand. Buyers usually just walk down a hallway and lean on one leg and look into a room. Then they walk to the next room and do the same thing. Nobody is going to buy a house without going into each room and really considering living in that room. So Staging needs to be largely decided from the doorway of each room, and then Stage the room effectively from this vantage point to get the buyers into the room.

Agents, if you have any fear that a seller would not want to Stage, I'm going to prove to you right now that sellers really do want to Stage their homes, once they truly understand it (and remember that your job is education!). Sellers who list their homes for sale expect to get the best work and service possible to get their homes sold, or they would sell the property themselves. If you have ever gone to see sellers at For-Sale-by-Owner properties, they are eager to learn everything you can share with them of your ideas and tips for selling and yet not pay a fee for your information. Here is what I want to ask you: If the For Sale by Owners want to know anything and everything that can help them sell their home, including Staging, and get the information from you for free, why would sellers who are listing with you and paying you thousands and thousands of dollars in commissions *not* want to know? Of course, they want to know! So have no more fear in sharing with sellers about Home Staging! Just asking myself the question years ago changed my life and career forever! That led to my developing the Home Staging industry. I am convinced that Agents must teach sellers how important it is to Stage their homes and that our trained ASP Stagers need to do the work to get the job done and done right! Sellers need that service, deserve it, and want it. It is your responsibility to help them.

GREAT IDEA: THE CAR STORY

When you meet sellers who do not seem to understand the concept of Staging, ask them one simple question. "If you were going to sell your car, what would you do to it before you showed it to potential purchasers?" Everyone has the same answer. They will invariably tell you: "I'd wash it, wax it, vacuum it, clean out the junk, and touch up the chips. I would detail it. Everyone does that." They may even talk about fixing other problems.

Then ask your sellers where most people's money or equity is: "In your home or in your car?" Wait for the answer, which invariably is, "In our homes." Then add, "Well, do you know that many sellers on the market today have not done with their own homes what they have done with their cars to bring them on the market for sale? They haven't gotten them ready to sell. By preparing your home for sale, you will be so much farther ahead of most of your competition." The car story works! I say that people "spend" money on a car because they usually can't sell it for what they paid for it, no matter how long they have it. But we all expect to make money in selling our homes, as long as we own it for a while. Our homes are our number one investment, not the family car. So why would sellers detail their cars and not detail their houses? In real estate, detailing means Staging! And that equals ROSI: Return on Staging investment! Sellers, it is all about making the investment in time, energy, and dollars in your number one investment of your home for your highest rate of return!

MY SEVEN Cs OF STAGING:

My Seven Cs of Staging all start with the letter C. Each of them is very, very important. Take any of them out, and the results are not the same. These apply inside the house and outside it, too. Staging needs to be done in every room, every nook and cranny, everywhere on the property for sale. The Seven Cs are:

1. Clean.
2. Color.
3. Clutter.
4. Creativity.
5. Compromise.
6. Communication.
7. Commitment.

1. Clean

Have you ever gone to see someone else's house, and when you walked across the kitchen floor, your foot stuck to it? I've been there. Properties for sale need to be clean. Clean houses are more appealing. They look better, and buyers will assume that a clean home is better cared for. Many buyers will walk out of a dirty house without even considering what's underneath the dirt because they feel so uncomfortable. Working with sellers, we need to point out where cleaning is needed, and we have to point out areas and rooms that need attention. This includes cleaning the top of the refrigerator, scouring the stove, shampooing the carpets when needed, wiping away all the cobwebs in the corners of the ceilings, cleaning the baths, and much more. Sometimes, when we are living in a house, we tend to let such things go. We say to ourselves. "I really do need to get around to that." When sellers decide to sell the house, then it is time to get around to it. Sometimes sellers are not tuned in to how dirty their houses are. A few do not really know what cleanliness is. Your job as an ASP Agent or ASP Stager is to show these sellers the problems you are talking about, in a nice way.

I'll never forget showing a seller with four children what needed to be done under her kitchen cupboards where the cookie crumbs and sticky Kool-Aid had been spilled everywhere. You may be thinking, "You really showed her?" You better believe it, and she took it in a great way. She wanted to get her house sold, so she could join her husband in another city where he had already started his new job. Motivation was the key for her! Sellers who do not want to move would probably object or be offended, but not those who want to sell and want their money.

Remember, it's not *what* you say, but *how* you say it that counts. Just like the doctor, attorney, or accountant, we must think of our clients first, do our job, and tell them the truth. Too many Agents are afraid to do that because they are afraid of offending the seller. Agents, we owe the sellers the truth! Otherwise, you may be wasting everyone's time when a problem is left unsolved and a house is unsalable at the listed price. If you are worried about a tough problem, use my analogy of the doctor who has to tell the patient something difficult. Because the doctor cares, he or she discusses it with the patient instead of simply holding back or not saying anything. Think of the tough job doctors have when they have to tell patients they are dying. Thinking of that has given me great courage many times to tell sellers that their home smells like cats, or even worse.

If we can smell it, we can't sell it!

Once I had to tell a seller that there was a smell of human urine in her home, and the doctor story really gave me courage. I told the woman about that problem by sitting her down at the kitchen table, holding her hand, and talking about how doctors have to tell patients things sometimes that are difficult to say. I told her that what I needed to share with her was very difficult for me to say, but if I didn't tell her no one else would.

The timing was also important. I told her about the problem *after* she had signed my agreement. Also, remember in my presentations that I ask my sellers to give me their commitment to Stage their home, and she had already said she would before I listed the house. It worked. We took care of the problem over the weekend before the company tour, before the sign went up, and before the buyers started coming through on Monday. The house sold immediately, and I will never forget the feeling inside when at closing she said how glad she was that I had the strength to tell her of the problem because she really did need to sell!

Get the inside and outside of the house clean! If I can tell someone that the home smells like human urine, you can tell your sellers *anything!* It isn't what you say, it's how you say it and when you say it.

2. Clutter

You've heard of the lived-in look. Usually that means clutter. We all have clutter in our homes. There is nothing wrong with that—unless you are trying to sell your house. Teach your sellers they have to unclutter their homes! Get the house clutter free! It is the number one challenge in most homes that come on the market for sale.

You can't sell it if you can't see it!

We all have a right to live in our homes any way we want. But when our homes come on the market for sale, that is something different. The public is now going to be coming through the house, and now it is a product for sale on the market. Clutter makes it difficult for a purchaser to *mentally move into a home.* Most of our homes come on the market with simply too much stuff in them. Have your sellers pack up extra things that they really don't need while they are selling and put them away. I have had many sellers rent PODS (portable on-demand storage) or storage space or store these things in a basement. If they cannot rent a storage space or if they do not have a basement, they can pack their extra things in boxes and stack them *neatly* in one corner of the garage.

So look for too many books, knick knacks, plants, or even too many pieces of furniture in a room. Tell your sellers the truth: "Buyers can't mentally move all of their things into your home until you put some of your things away. Psychologists also tell us, Mr. and Mrs. Seller, that no one will buy a home until he or she mentally moves in. Therefore, Mr. and Mrs. Seller, you have got to pack up some of your things." And one of my best Staging sayings is, "Clutter eats equity!" So pack it up, put it away, and sell the house instead of your things!

By creating space for buyers to mentally move into a house, Staging produces a look that appears sparse to some. Perfect!! It is important that that is the look you achieve. I've seen so-called Stagings done by non-ASPs who were interior decorators who brought lots of beautiful furniture and accessories into a home and produced the opposite effect—and the house doesn't sell to its full potential.

3. Color

Remember this: Dark colors on the walls make the room seem smaller; light colors on the walls make the room seem bigger. The house should flow in color, with one room leading to the next and soft colors on all the walls. This adds a spacious look to the house. Do not have one bedroom bright red and the one down the hall purple. This cuts up the space and makes the house feel chopped up and smaller.

Look at the color scheme of the house from room to room, including carpet. Is there a different color of carpet in every room? This color scheme can really give a house a chopped-up feeling. It can make the home seem smaller than it really is. Are the walls painted the same color throughout the house, and is the same soft color of carpet used throughout? If they are, this scheme gives the home more of a flowing feeling and can help it seem more spacious than it is. These are things to keep in mind if the sellers need to do any painting or replace the floor coverings. Remember, Staging usually doesn't mean investing a lot of money. So don't be confused by my comments about painting and carpeting. Sometimes a home or condominium desperately needs paint or carpet. In that case, recommend it as we are discussing here. However, at times sellers simply don't have the money. The property can still be Staged by investing little or no money. Even spot cleaning the carpets helps. Cleaning spots on walls, along with patching or touching up the paint, is easy and can add a lot, too. As an extra service, help your sellers by going with them to pick out the right color of paint or carpet. Sellers, you could pick one that is actually not right for selling the house.

When it comes to paint, remind your sellers that a gallon of paint, on sale at the hardware store, is usually less than the cost of a carton of cigarettes. I've never had a seller say no to buying paint when you put it in those terms. Even one gallon can work miracles in painting a small bath or a child's room. (Most buyers just don't buy homes with purple bedrooms or baths.) Outside the home, one gallon works wonders on the trim, the front door, or shutters to give a crisp new look, as well.

If you are working with sellers who don't want to replace worn carpet and says, "We'll just let the buyers do it when they move in," remind them of my saying:

Buyers only know what they see, not the way it's going to be!

Buyers do not have the imagination to visualize another carpet. Instead they will buy a home where the carpet has already been replaced. It is crucial that you take the time to educate your sellers that most buyers have very little imagination. This is why I don't recommend sellers having allowances for buyers to make changes when they buy. It won't happen because the buyers will take the least course of resistance and buy a home where the work is done, where the carpet is already replaced, and the paint is already repainted. Also, many Real Estate Agents remember only what they see, not the way it's going to be, and they hold the power as to which houses they show.

When you discuss colors, paint, and carpet, never tell your sellers that they will get back the cost of replacing the carpet dollar for dollar. I do tell them that it could be the thing that will help them sell their home.

You may ask, if we have more neutral colors in the background, then will the house be bland? Is any color allowed at all? First of all, the background will not be bland. The background will help enlarge the space, and we want to sell the space. Color is, of course, wanted and needed, but not on the walls or in the carpet. Use color in the accessories. Use color in the towels, in the artwork, in the area rugs, and on the beds. Color is wonderful. But use it in the accessories because the accessories add splashes of color in each room rather than in the paint and carpet. They add the punch to each area but aren't overkill, as is putting the color on the walls and in the carpet.

You want the added accent colors to go with the color scheme in the house, room by room. In other words, are there three colors of towels in the bathroom? Ask the sellers to use towels that match, or suggest that they find some new ones on sale that will complement the bath and can be used in their new home after this one sells. Pay attention to colors and color schemes in each room as well as to the whole house.

Color is not a hard subject. It is really simple: neutral colors in the background and accent brighter colors in the accessories and accents.

That is easy to do, and the sellers can take the accessories with them and typically use them in their new home. And colorful accessories do not have to be expensive; sellers can find good beds in a bag, new towels, and fairly priced area rugs in stores such as Target or JCPenney. It is fun and easy to do. Go for it.

4. Creativity

You are a genius! Yes, you are! I really believe that we all are. Research shows that we usually don't even come close to using all of our brain, talent, and creativity. Therefore, it is really important that you and I strive to grow it, use it more, stimulate it, and complement it in a good way to improve it for ourselves. This is not about being an egomaniac. This is about believing in oneself and doing so in a happy, grateful way, being thankful for the creativity that we all have. If you constantly say that you are not good with something, such as selecting fabrics, you will surely prove yourself right. What you say, you usually create. So if you say you are not good at something and believe that you are not, then you will prove it to yourself. If you say you are becoming better and better at working with fabrics, then you will prove that as well. If you think you can, you can. And if you think you can't, you can't. Either way, you are exactly right because you will make sure that the universe shows you what you believe is true. So change your thinking and change your life. Believe more in the creative you!

The very essence of Staging is creativity! That is what Staging is. I have said this all along since the day I got the idea of Staging homes back in the 1970s. Staging is *not* about spending money. It is about investing time, energy, and creativity to have each home look the very best that it can, and this is where creativity really comes into play. It needs to come into play in each room, in each case, and in each situation. Creativity solves problems, saves money, and makes you feel good, too.

Look for creative solutions to Staging room challenges. Here is a fun example of just how I love to use creativity in Staging. The young boy's room was very bare and plain. It was, in fact, very boring. The bedspread was an ugly gray, the dresser was scratched, the fabric of the curtain was torn, and the curtain rod was broken. The room had nothing going for it. Now to tell these people to go buy things is not creative. That is what most people do: spend money. That should not be done unless there is nothing else to work with in the home, garage, or property. And this is where Creativity comes into play big time. Now, remember I said that decisions for Staging begin and end at the doorway to each room. And the way this room looked, there is no way that anyone would even walk into it. It was not inviting at all. People would just lean slightly into the room, make a huh sound, and keep going on down the hall. You would have done the same.

I asked the owner to go to the garage with me. In the garage I was looking for anything that could be fun to use to add interest to the room for Staging. Sports equipment is good to use for this very thing many times, especially in kids' rooms, dens, and similar rooms. In the garage, wouldn't you know, there was some fishing equipment! Perfect! I put the fishing rod on the brackets and that became the new curtain rod. It is the same shape as a curtain rod, isn't it! I took a twin white sheet from their linen closet and draped it nicely over the top of the fishing pole and that became the new curtain. I pulled it over to one side and made a knot in it and wrapped it with rope and tacked it to the side of the window on the wall. It doesn't matter that it didn't go all the way to the floor. Who said it had to? Many drapes do not go all the way to the floor. So with the new fishing pole rod and the new white drape pulled to one side and swaggered to the side with rope around it, the room really looked great, and not one dollar was used for the improvement. I then took a fishing boot, cleaned it up, and put the ugly lamp that was on the dresser into the boot, and the shade came just over the top of the boot. Now we had a boot lamp. I took more rope, and put it around the ankle of the boot to match the rope on the sheet drape. It all started to come together. The other boot I put into the corner, put a vase of water in it and then I had the seller cut a tall limb off an alder tree in their backyard and put it into the vase in the boot. Now they don't have to buy a silk ficus tree.

By putting the bed in the corner opposite the doorway, I enlarged the room because that arrangement frees up the walls. I had them flip over the bedspread to the other, beige side, which looked so much better than the gray on top. And it looked cleaner, too. Then, we added contrasting sheets out of their linen closet. A burgundy one went on the bottom and a plaid one on the top sheet, both folded down to show them off. We had a great new look on the bed with no expense made.

Last, but no way least, we needed a headboard, and this was totally fun to do. In the garage I found a fishing net. That became the headboard for the bed. Because I moved the bed to an angle, it left a triangular space behind the bed. With fishing line, I hung the net by its handle from the ceiling corner above the bed. With more fishing line, which I attached to both sides of the net and rim, I hung a bit out over the back top of the bed. After making pretend fish out of brown grocery sacks turned inside out and then putting an eye on each one with a black felt pen, I hung them on fishing hooks and hooked them onto the front of the net as though they were jumping into the net. I added the water look by crunching up wax paper and stuffing the inside of the net with it. All in all, this looked fabulous!

Creativity like this is fun, and you can do the same thing, too. This whole room was Staged by using the magic of creativity. And it was done— the entire room—without spending a dime! This is where the fun is. This is what I am telling you to do, too. Have fun, play with it, and by doing so you will invent many new uses of things for no money. This is why as an Agent and as a seller you need to hire an ASP or ASPM Stager to work with you and to do the Staging for you. This is what I train ASP Stagers to do. This is what they so love about Home Staging, and they are experts at it. That is why they are drawn to Home Staging; so put them to work. Hire them and they will help save you money and make you money at the same time. Wait until you read the Staging success stories at the end of my book. You will see over and over again how the ASP Stager makes more money for their clients and for the Agents whom they work with and represent. And creativity is the middle name of an ASP!

5. Compromise

"Compromise" is a wonderful word! Relationships, such as friendships and marriages, take compromise, and compromise is a part of Home Staging, too! Here is a good example of how compromise works in Home Staging as well. The floor in the kitchen was damaged and was the wrong color. Down the hall was a hall bath that had bright pink tile and grout. So the kitchen floor had two strikes against it: One was the poor condition because the floor was damaged, and the other was that the color was wrong. Now, the bath tile was in perfect condition, but the color was wrong, so it had only one strike against it: the wrong Staging color. So I had the sellers put the money into replacing the floor in the kitchen. I picked the right color for them, they had the new floor put in, and now the kitchen floor was Staged and in good condition.

In the hall bath, however, we needed to compromise because the tile was in great shape and there weren't funds to replace it. The key is to use creativity and compromise. Let's go retro! Black and white are colors that defuse other strong colors. Green is the color in the middle, and it is a healing color at that. Green stands for trees, prosperity, and money. So I added black towels, a fresh new white shower curtain, and a bouquet of greenery for the counter. With the addition of a lovely picture framed in black of a pastoral scene and a lovely small rug to replace their pink fuzz rug, the whole bath looked so much more expensive and sophisticated. The tile was still the same but looked really good. The picture and the rug were already in the home in a different room. It seemed like a miracle, but it was easy to do; with a simple plan it doesn't cost an arm and a leg, and it works. Now the bath and the kitchen are both Staged, and they both are in great condition. So compromise is an important C for Home Staging!

6. Communication

Staging is a communication tool! And, sellers, what is the message that your home sends to the buyers coming through? The front of your house sends a message, and each room communicates something about itself. The room says that it is too small, too crowded, or too dirty—and the list goes on. You get the idea.

Staging sends a message of space and openness. Staging sends a message of being Q-Tip clean and of having the right colors that invite people in instead of turning them away. Staging is all about the messages that the front of the house, the back of the house, and all the rooms in the house send to potential buyers. And because that message is a Staged Homes message, the communication works, bringing in buyers and leading to a sale. Staging is communication.

7. Commitment

It takes commitment to get the house Staged! Everyone has to be committed to the process. That means the seller needs to be committed, the Agent has to be committed, and the Stager has to be committed to getting the house Staged. Everyone also needs to be committed to keeping the house Staged during its time on the market. It may amaze some of you reading my book, but I can tell you that at times some Agents don't even think that the house needs to be Staged. You will read a couple of those stories in Chapter 15. I believe that Agents who say this are afraid either that they will not be in control or that the Stager will be in control, or they don't really know what Staging is or how to talk about it. The key is that everyone has to be committed. Everyone needs to be a member of the team, committed together.

When that happens—and it will—then the house will be Staged to its very best, and that means a sale will follow for the best of all concerned.

So the Seven Cs stand for cleanliness, clutter, color, creativity, compromise, communication, and commitment. They all work together and, as you will see and experience, bring great results!

THE KEY: DO IT NOW!

As an Agent, when you first list the house, have you ever encountered sellers who somehow just don't get around to getting the house Staged? They want you to market it as the Agent, but they don't get their part done to get the house Staged by hiring an ASP Stager to work with them. They just don't get around to getting things done. You know what I mean. The property is listed, and six weeks later you are still waiting for the sellers to clear off the dining room table, paint the front door, and put away all the knickknacks on the hutch. That is not the way it should ever be, so I came up with a way that really works to get sellers to Stage their houses the right way immediately.

First, I started to think about Staging the house and how I was really Staging the merchandise or, as in Hollywood, the set. I also realized as the marketing expert that the Agent should be the director. The house is the set, and the sellers are the producers, because they own the house; they are also the actors who have to carry out the requests to get their house Staged. Think about Hollywood. Every set is staged to look great and sometimes even to look bad on purpose, which we of course would not do because we want our sets to look the very best they can. Consider the audience as well. Who are they? They are the buyers, and they decide what to offer and how many offers will come in on the house. Because of the feedback, the multiple listing, and what all Agents see on the market for sale, the Agents act as the critics. And ASP Stagers are the set designers who design the set in each room and the whole house by Staging them! Again the whole team needs to work together.

Second, I always go over these words with my sellers before we start to Stage the house: "list," "sell," "move," and "pack." I simply ask the sellers the following questions as we start to Stage: "You have listed your home because you expect it to sell, isn't that correct?" Of course, they say, "Yes." Then I ask, "And when you sell, that means you'll need to *move,* isn't that correct, also?" They say "yes" again. "And when you *move,* you'll need to *pack!* Right?" They say, "Right!" And now you finish by saying,

"So what you need to do is just to *pack* up early." Sellers get the point because it is true. It works.

I also thought about my daughter and what I have her do when I want her to clean out her room or to go through her closet to sort out clothes or toys that she no longer uses. What do you do when you go through your closets or garage to give or throw things away? We all make piles of some kind, don't we? So, as simple as it sounds (simple is always best), I had my sellers start to make piles. The approach works every time. My sellers have been making piles for years. I also want you to know that I have never had a seller refuse to make piles. Why? Because I educated them from the beginning about how important Staging really is. By the time we get to the piles, they just say, "OK, Barb, tell us what to do."

As you work with sellers and with Agents, ASP Stagers, make sure that you set out your professional polices of how you work and what you want the sellers to do. Once you know you are going to work with people and that they have signed your forms to pre-Stage before you return, I suggest that you as the Stager go through each room, asking your sellers to pile all the things you suggest they pack up in the middle of the room. Then when you leave, the sellers can just put these things in boxes, pack them into storage, and get the home cleared out of some things so that you as an ASP Stager can come back in and get your job for them done much more easily. Have the sellers leave out all items you want and will use to Stage the house and room; have them pack up the collections and magazines and extra papers themselves. Hold up a basket and say, "Pack up anything smaller than this."

This technique really works to eliminate the dominance of clutter by the time I come back. It doesn't mean that it is totally clutter free, but it is much better than it would have been, and it is ready for you to Stage the house. Do this room by room. This is what you should tell them from the beginning when you first talked about the Staging process when you said, "Let me tell you how I work." Now, a lot of real estate salespeople smile when I tell them I do this as an ASPM Stager, but I really do this because it works! No sellers are going to leave a pile of their things lying in the middle of the room if they want you as the Agent marketing the house. Stagers and Agents, set your standards, and sellers will match them and do what you ask. This is one of my professional policies.

Stagers, stay in control by educating people. Guide your sellers by educating them and getting their commitment, and you won't have to worry about those problems later. The only things that you don't do immediately with your sellers are the projects that can't be completed right away, like painting a room, and that need to get that done anyway before you come back to Stage!

As you go through a home with your sellers and you come up with things that cannot be done right then, simply make a list as you go. Be sure that everything that cannot be done right away goes on the list! That is very important. I've never had a seller tell me "no" at this point.

Go room by room with your sellers. Have them make piles in every room, and make a list of the things they need to do that cannot be done immediately while you stand there. In another chapter, I will show you how to be sure that your sellers get everything on the list done and the piles packed up and put away. Personally I have never wanted to be paid to pack. I want to be paid to be creative and to Stage! As an ASP Stager, Staging is where the money is, and you can have fun doing it, too! It really does pay. And everybody gets money from Staging: The seller gets more equity usually, the Agent gets more commission, and the ASP Stager gets paid to Stage. This is a good thing because everyone wins. That includes the buyers, too, because they get to buy a home that is detailed, clean, neat, and well taken care of; because time is money, that saves them time and money, too, from having to do all those things if the house weren't Staged.

If you educate your sellers from the first contact until it's time to Stage the property, then they will *want* to help you help them. If you follow the steps I outlined, your sellers will make piles and complete their list because they need you and trust you. And, ASP Stagers, you need them to do their part so that you can get your part done!

MY TIPS FOR SELLING

Say the following phrase to your sellers as soon as you start Staging their home, and you will have all the cooperation you need:

Start packing, because with your home Staged, you soon will be moving!

This statement really hits home, and they understand what you are talking about.

Now I would like to share some specific tips on Staging the sellers' property. My Tips for Selling are specific to the inside of the home.

Tip 1: Clear Away All Unnecessary Objects Throughout the House

This tip includes objects on end tables, dressers, coffee tables, counters, and any other furniture throughout the entire house. This doesn't mean you strip the house bare. But you do want your sellers to keep things limited to groups of one, three, or five. Have them pack away all extras.

As for magazines scattered on the coffee table in the living room, either have them remove them or stack them up, but don't leave out any more than three. Also remove the extra pillows, afghans, newspapers, and various other items from the living room, den, kitchen, or any other main room in the house. Mantels should also be cleared off, leaving only one to three items. Reduce family photos down to one or two, and reduce the number of pictures and paintings on most walls. Remember, you need to create room for future buyers to move in their own possessions mentally.

Tip 2: Rearrange Dining Room Furniture to Create More Space

We want to sell the room, not the furniture. If the sellers are using extra leaves in their dining room table, have them take them out and put them in a closet. This will make a dining room look bigger. Also, put any extra dining room chairs away. Again, this will create space. Most dining rooms look bigger with four chairs, not six or eight. One of the chairs could be used as a side chair in another room, such as by a guest bed. But in most cases the extra chairs need to go to storage.

If they have a hutch or a buffet in the dining room, have them clear any excess items from it, including anything that might be stored on top of it. Also, anything valuable should be taken out of the hutch and packed away. "Out of sight, means out of mind." I normally like to pack up all the china and glassware, put in art objects such as pottery or books, and make it more like an art gallery center instead of a china cabinet.

Tip 3: Clear Away Unnecessary Objects from Kitchen Countertops, Refrigerator, and Kitchen Table

In the kitchen, "What can you live without?" is the key question you should always ask your sellers. Also ask them, "What, in the kitchen, haven't you used for the last three months?" You'll have reactions like, "Well, let's see, I haven't used the coffee pot for a while because we quit drinking coffee." "I used to bake so much bread, but I don't do that any-more, so I really don't need the mixer." Have them pack these things up.

While you are in the kitchen, have them clear away messages, pictures, cartoons, and so forth, from the front of the refrigerator. Many times, sellers have drawings the little ones have made in kindergarten or the grandchildren have made in school. Ask them to clear those things off. You might say, "Sally, can we just pick the very favorite picture that your son did? Let's put it up and put the others away." This works very effectively. Also look at the tops of refrigerators. These can be collect-alls and need to be clean and clutter free.

Remind your sellers also that a sparse, clean kitchen—in which you can see almost all the countertops—makes the area look bigger and helps potential purchasers to mentally move their own things into the kitchen. So advise them to keep the sink clean, the countertops clear, the appliances clean, and the whole kitchen neat as long as the house is on the market. This means *every single day,* because you never know when the right Agent with the right buyers will walk through the door. Have them move such items as soap dispensers, scouring pads, and dish drainers underneath the sink. Ask your sellers to be tough on themselves and give up what they can truly live without. Once they get into the swing of things, sellers usually start to be harder on themselves than you or I would be.

Tip 4: Remove All Unnecessary Items in Bathrooms

Most bathrooms have too many things scattered all over the counter, around the tub and shower, and all over the back of the commode. Ask your sellers to put those things into the cabinet, under the sink, or in packing cartons. Have the sellers put their most needed things in a basket, and put that under the sink. Yes, I know that under the sink is already full, but most of what is under the sink they haven't used for a long time. People keep products that they haven't used for too long a time. So clear that out, Mr. and Mrs. Seller, put the basket of what you need under the sink, and bring it up and down every day while you get ready for work. I also ask sellers to put away any small garbage cans in the bathroom or put them under the sink, too, where you cannot see them. Another thing is to keep the lid down on the toilet while the house is on the market. This way it does not look like we are marketing garbage or toilets. It may sound funny, but all these things subtly affect buyers when they look at a home. Lids left up make it look like people are selling holes in the ground.

You can really straighten up a bathroom if you tuck all the necessary toiletries into a basket or set them on a tray. Baskets, bowls, and trays are great for organizing things in the bathroom, the kitchen, and on desks or dressers. Most people already have baskets and trays, and everybody has a bowl.

Coordinate towels, limiting them to one or two colors that match the room decor. If the sellers have a matching set of towels, use them. If they don't have a matching set or a nice collection of towels, then suggest they buy some. A good way to phrase this is to say. "You know, it is really a small investment, so how about going down to the department store and just buying one or two sets of towels? Then you can use them in your new home when you move." And, of course, as ASP Stagers we have these things in our inventory and can bring them in for sellers as Staging inventory so that they don't even have to buy them.

As an Agent, while you are in the bathroom, check again for any problems, like weak flooring where bathwater has spilled. If possible, things like that need to be taken care of before the house goes on the market, or they must be disclosed in the listing agreement. Check behind the toilets and under the sink for leaks. Check the shower and tub for mildew, cracks, or bad grout.

The bathroom is a room where cleanliness is crucial. Be honest with your sellers if you see anything that needs attention, such as dirty counters, sinks, toilets, shower stalls, mirrors, soap scum, mold, and the like.

Tip 5: Rearrange the Furniture

Many people have too much furniture in their rooms. That may be fine for living, but it's not good for selling. In the living room, for instance, your sellers may have too many chairs, which creates a feeling of less space for the potential purchaser. You want to create just the opposite impression, and removing a chair or an ottoman can really help. Focus a lot of your attention on those so-called emotional rooms when you are Staging the property: the living room, kitchen, and master bedroom. You want those rooms to look really sharp because those are the rooms on which most buyers will focus. All rooms need to be Staged—all of them. However, when budget is limited, the ones that should never be skimped on are the living room/dining room, the kitchen, and master bedroom.

You may face the sellers' question of, "Where do we put the extra furniture?" Of course, getting a storage unit or a POD makes it easy. However, the basement, attic, garage, or storage room are also good places to store their extra furniture and all the other items removed from the main rooms in the house. Moving pieces of furniture from one room to another really works, of course. A lot of the time just rearranging the furniture creates more space without removing anything.

Tip 6: Take Down or Rearrange Pictures or Other Objects on the Wall

We've all seen the 20 posters or more on the walls in a child's room. Those have got to go. Have the sellers take these down, and patch the holes and touch up the paint. If your sellers don't, the purchasers are going to think, "Wow, this room looks small and, oh gosh, if I got this house then I would have to patch all these holes and paint the walls." Then they buy a different house where the work has been done for them because that house is Staged. The sellers have to make this fix ahead of time because it will help sell the house.

Clutter happens on the walls of many homes. It has to come down, and you should use the pictures that work and put the others away. I love to move pictures from one room to another. Our ASP Stagers are experts at this. Sellers, hire an ASP Stager. You will be thrilled you did because their talent brings more to your bottom line!

Tip 7: Paint Any Rooms That Need It

If the paint in one or many rooms is in bad shape or is a bad color, then you must decide which rooms need painting and suggest it. Painting is one of the cheapest things sellers can do to improve their homes. As I have already explained, neutral wall colors are the best for selling a house, and off-white is definitely the best color in most cases. However, remember that whites have different shades or tones. Some whites have blue shades; some have green, yellow, or pink tints. So pick a safe color that works with the carpet and floor coverings in your sellers' home. Off-white is the safest way to go, because most furniture will work with it, and that makes it easier for the potential purchasers to mentally move in.

If you come across rooms with wild or dark colors, suggest that your sellers repaint them. Put those rooms down on the list for painting. If the hallway walls have been marked or scarred, have the sellers clean, paint, or touch them up as well. Painting is not always necessary, but it is one of the least expensive things that can be done to make a home look better than the competition. Sellers should have their rooms painted professionally if at all possible. It saves them time and money, and it will usually get done much more quickly. The light colors on the walls also give the background palette for Staging the furniture and the accessories. Then everything flows much better. If a room needs painting and it is dirty and cluttered, there is no way that the average buyer will buy that house—not when there is a clean, clutter-free, Staged Home down the street that has soft colors on the walls and that shows like a dream.

Tip 8: Clean the Carpets or Drapes

The difference that clean carpets and drapes can make is well worth the expense of having the drapes dry cleaned and the carpets steamed cleaned. It really is a small cost of selling a home.

Sometimes the drapes need to be removed altogether. For example, the drapes may be so dark and heavy that they overpower the room. If there is a sheer drape underneath, you can say, "Mr. and Mrs. Seller, let's take down these overdrapes. They are a heavy brocade and they are making the room darker than we need for selling. But leave the sheers, and you will still have some privacy at night."

Be confident. Remember, you are the expert (the director) whom they respect. Sellers want your opinions so that they can get their equity. They are not going to be there much longer. They are moving, remember? So, when the seller says, "Oh, but I really enjoy those drapes," just say, "That's OK. You're moving, remember. You are not going to be here anymore!" (Besides, if the sellers take them down now and pack them away before purchasers start to look at the property, the sellers can keep them because they will not be included in the sale.) Whenever your sellers don't like a change you are suggesting, just remind them they are moving. It works like magic!

Tip 9: Clean the Windows

Dirty windows are difficult to see through, and they give a home a poor image. I find that most sellers plan to clean their windows, anyway. But sometimes you'll meet people who just forget about it. Remind them! Put it on their list, and have them get it done. And they need to have them professionally cleaned. I never recommend that sellers do their own windows. The carpets, the windows, the draperies all should be professionally cleaned as well as the whole house. Using professionals pays in the end, and the sellers won't hurt themselves, either.

Tip 10: Eliminate Any Odors

If there is a unique odor problem such as from a pet, cooking, or smoke, this must be taken care of. As the expert, you need to tell your sellers about such problems.

One way you can handle this is to use an example that is the opposite of their problem. For example, let's say you are working with someone who has pets, but they don't smoke. You could say to them, "You don't smoke, do you!" They will answer, "No, I don't." Then ask them, "Have you ever been in someone's home where the people who lived there smoked? Did you notice how you could pick up on that smell in the carpets, the drapes, and even in the people's clothes?" Usually they will say something like, "Yes, and I can't stand it. I can't even breathe when I'm in a smoker's house." Then say, "Well, you know, Mr. and Mrs. Seller, there are a lot of qualified purchasers out there who do not have pets such as your beautiful cat [use the pet's name]. Now, you are accustomed to the aroma of your own pets, but purchasers who do not have any animals may be very sensitive to those aromas. So we need to do something about that." Use the word "aroma" when you are talking about the seller's situation. It's a safer word. But you can refer to the other people's problems as "smells," as I did earlier. Use a situation that does not apply to them to explain how others may feel coming into their home.

For eliminating smells, I recommend a product called Pure Ayre, which is made from plant enzymes and really does a great job of attacking the source of odors. It is the greatest product for eliminating smells. It doesn't cover up odors; it eliminates them by getting to the source. This product has helped many an ASP Stager and seller. It is available on www.staging-shoppingcenter.com and also in some pet stores and grocery stores. For serious problems, you can rent large ozone machines from some carpet cleaning companies. It's not very expensive, but the process takes a couple of days and the house must be vacated. These commercial ozone machines work wonders on tough odors.

Do not ever light a candle in a home for Staging because it smells good. It is dangerous to have anything lit in a home for sale. Not even the fireplace should be going unless the seller lights the fire and stays at the home. I would never have the fireplace on or going as an Agent or Stager for an open house or showings. Not unless the seller was there (and they shouldn't be there for open houses and showings, anyway). Anything burning is too risky, in my opinion.

If you don't tell your sellers about an odor problem, then who will? This can make a big difference in the length of time it takes you to sell their house. As you know, it can even influence the actual sale price of a home.

Tip 11: Clean the Fireplace

If the fireplace is full of dirty ashes or needs work, then add that to the list. Ask your sellers to leave the fireplace screen closed during showings. If the screen has rusted, have the sellers spray it with black fireplace paint from the hardware store. Most hardware stores have a spray paint that is heat resistant and that will not melt or come off when the new buyer builds future fires. If it is summertime and the fireplace is cleaned out, have wood set in the fireplace that looks ready to light (*but do not light it*).

If the outside front of the fireplace has soot on it, have your sellers clean it off. Have them test a small, out-of-the-way area on the fireplace with oven cleaner or soot remover. I have seen this take off the soot many times successfully, without damaging the fireplace. For dark fireplaces or for fireplaces on which nothing seems to be able to get rid of the soot, have your sellers paint the face of the fireplace with brick paint from the hardware store. There are paints especially made for bricks that will not come off, and it will make the fireplace look better and bigger as well. Use semi-gloss, white brick paint. It almost seems like a miracle in the right situation, especially in older homes or in homes where the bricks are not as up-to-date as those used to build with today.

If the fireplace has damage, never cover it up. Agents, make sure that your seller discloses the damage in their disclosure statements.

• • •

You will be amazed at the difference these tips can make in a house. They are easy to do and simple, and they make sense. The better the house is Staged, the higher the price it can command on the market!

STEPS TO STAGE A ROOM

As I analyze how I have Staged Homes all of these many, many years, it became very obvious to me that I had developed steps to Staging a room. I have done this in thousands of homes and in thousands of rooms. The steps work for Staging a room, are easy to do, and make sense when you read them. It is taking a room apart and rebuilding it, really. I like to work in systems. Think about it: The *Career Book* is a system to sell you, the *Marketing Portfolio* is a system to sell what you do in services, Staging is a system to prepare a home for sale, and the Steps to Stage a room constitute a system, too. Systems work, and it gives me great joy to share these steps and system with you.

1. **Stand in the doorway.** Make all of your Staging decisions from the room's doorway. This is where the buyers will stand, and this is where they will decide whether to go into the room. It is where the decision is made to enter or keep on walking. Always, always go back to the doorway as you change things and Stage the room to make sure you are on the right track from the buyer's point of view.

2. **Make a plan.** Be open to change as you go, but start with a plan and go from there. Do you want to make more space? Do you want less furniture? Is the room too dark? Make a plan of what you think needs to be done and changed.

3. **Deaccessorize.** Take *everything* off the furniture and walls, and pile it up in two main piles: things to give up and things to keep. Now the give-up category doesn't mean that people get rid of the items, but rather it should be packed or put into another room. The keep category means to keep it in the room. These things are pictures, magazines, candlesticks, lamps, mirrors, and the like.

4. **Decide which furniture needs to be taken out.** Maybe it could be used in another room in the house or go to storage. Remember, even if the same furniture has been in the living room for years, it wouldn't necessarily look worse with one less chair or without a loveseat or an end table.

5. **Decide which furniture stays *and* arrange it.** Play with it. For example, move the bed from one wall to the next until you see that it is in the right place. If you have the help, try rearranging every room more than once to get the best look. Some rooms can be done four or five different ways. Always go back to the doorway to decide on the best look.

6. **Reaccessorize the room.** Once you have the furniture where it looks best, then start adding the accessories you have kept in the room and things you have taken from other rooms. Hang up the pictures and place things on the end table, the coffee table, and elsewhere to reaccessorize the room. The key usually is to put back about one-half of what was there before because many rooms start out overcluttered.

7. **Fine-tune.** This is a big one for me. It is the icing on the cake, so to speak. What did you miss? Is the cord sticking out from behind the

TV? Are the tags on the toss pillows showing? Is the blind tilted? Fix these things because with fine-tuning you are really not done even if you thought you were. Ask yourself whether anything still can be removed? Do you need to bring something else into the room? By fine-tuning you will be even more pleased than just saying, "Oh, the room is Staged" and then later seeing something else you should have done. Fine-tuning is the extra step that ASP Stagers always do!

By taking these steps, Stagers stay organized and make their projects much easier to do. I have always said, "You put me in the middle of a room, and I will say I have to get to the doorway to start to Stage!" As the woman who invented Staging, I have seen thousands of buyers look at homes, and it is crucial that they enter the room. But if the room sends the wrong message because it is cluttered or because the furniture is in the wrong place or because there is too much furniture, then buyers won't even go into the room. So it all begins and ends at the doorway. Follow these steps, and you will see the great results that Staging produces over and over again!

IDEAS FOR SHOWING A HOME

In addition to Staging the house, you can also teach your sellers a few simple ideas to help them show their houses at their best. Share these pointers with your sellers.

Explain to all of your sellers three important points when it comes to showing their home: lights, music, action. Remember, I got the idea for Staging when I went into real estate after being in theatrical productions in college and then realizing that houses are sets, too. And in the theater that means lights, music, and action (and the action is Staging)!

I will explain each of these in detail subsequently, but sellers should know why you expect them to have lights, music, and action when it comes to Staging a home. Ask each of your sellers about where they buy things that they need, such as their favorite department store, grocery store, drugstore, or even where they would buy a car. Do these places normally have lights on, music playing, and marketing action to set the Stage for selling? Of course, they do! That is because these conditions are conducive to buying, and buying is what we want for our sellers and their homes.

The very same rules apply to showing a home. We want to appeal to the emotions of the buyer during all showings. Remember that Agents, appraisers, and inspectors are people with emotions, too, and that these people are crucial to the sale and closing. Lights, music, and action help in every situation in a very professional way. Educate your sellers on these important points so that their house will be seen in the best way possible at all times.

Idea 1: Have Your Sellers Leave on Certain Lights at All Times During the Day

Show the sellers which lights you want on because they often don't know. I recommend they always leave the lights on in the darkest spots in the house. Your sellers might object, saying, "That is going to cost too much." Ask them, "How much will it cost you if you don't sell your home?" That really helps them understand why the extra expense is necessary. The extra pennies they will invest in electricity are insignificant compared with the equity they will be getting from their home.

Let's say they have a hallway that is very dark; there is no skylight, and the light from the bedroom windows doesn't quite make it into the hallway. Ask them to spend the few pennies it takes to leave a few lights on in those dark spaces.

And for lamps in dark rooms, have the seller put them on light timers so that they can have them come on at 9 a.m. in the morning in dark rooms and go off at 6 p.m. because most buyers do not look at a house before or after these times. Sometimes they come *back* to see the house again, which is really a great thing, and they will have to have their Agent set up an appointment with the seller because the seller will be home from work then. In that case the seller can turn on *all* the lights for an evening showing!

This situation leads us to . . .

Idea 2: Have Your Sellers Turn on All Lamps During Showings

Educate all your sellers to go from room to room and turn on every lamp and light in the house for a showing. And I mean every single light and lamp. You cannot have too much light for showing a house. It's the same as when you go to a store to buy a new piece of clothing. If that store has done its Staging correctly, the lights are on bright, not dim. Nobody buys in the dark!

Idea 3: Leave All Curtains, Drapes, and Blinds Open for Showings

Again, good lighting is imperative. Have your sellers leave their window treatments open all day, especially if everyone who lives in the home is gone during the day (that is, no one is there to open them for an unexpected showing). Also show your sellers how far open to pull the drapes. When it comes to blinds, a lot of people tip their vertical blinds upward or downward, and all the sunlight gets wasted. Have your sellers open the vertical blinds so they are level. This lets the full light to flood the room!

Of course, if a window has a terrible view, such as a brick wall only a few feet away, then keep that window's curtains closed. If there are vertical blinds on a window with a bad view, tip them slightly down but not closed, so that light can still come in and flood the floor, but the potential purchaser isn't immediately struck by a bad or poor view.

I know that sellers can be concerned about furniture fading; however, it is more important to have the blinds open so that the house can be sold instead of leaving them closed and not selling the house. Again, light is crucial. I do wish that all Agents would open drapes before they showed the house to buyers, but the simple truth is that too many Agents working with buyers just open the front door and have them come right in as they enter a dark house. Marketing, did I say marketing? Having the drapes open is called marketing, and I shake my head when an Agent just brings buyers right out of their car into a dark house without any presentation at all being done first. So, sellers, you are much better off with your drapes open rather than being worried about fading the furniture. You've got to see it to sell it!

Idea 4: Have Music on All Day for All Viewings

Have every one of your sellers turn on music throughout the house as soon as they get up in the morning and keep it on all day, even if they leave. The radio can be put on a timer, too. Share this wonderful secret with your sellers! Soft FM radio station background music is best, not hard rock or so-called funeral music. You never know when an Agent might want to bring a potential buyer to the house. Agents almost always try to set up appointments so that sellers know when buyers are coming. But sometimes an Agent will be escorting a purchaser to another house, and, as they pass by the sellers' house, the purchaser will say, "Wait a minute! Look! What about this one? I like the way this home looks on the outside." The Agent will most likely say, "Wonderful," pull up across the street, ask the purchaser to wait a minute in the car, and go to the door to ask the sellers, "Could I show your home? Would this be a convenient time?" In this event, the sellers will not have time to turn on the stereo and the lights in the dark rooms.

So advise your sellers to keep the radio and lights turned on all day. And if the seller isn't home, the showing Agent will bring the buyers right in. Once again, it is crucial to have the lights, music, and action set for unexpected showings.

Idea 5: Keep the House Neat and Clean All the Time—Keep It Staged

Remind your sellers not to let the house get cluttered or dirty after it has been Staged. If they have children, ask them to be sure they pick up after themselves. Keep dishes out of the sink, beds made, clothes off the floor, counters clean, and so on. I know that it takes work and it *is* worth it! Sellers, the day you let it slide will, without fail, be the day a potential purchaser for your home will walk through the door. That's life! It is also called Murphy's law. Sellers, keep your house Staged, and the effort will pay off for you, I promise! Think of it as earning your equity day by day—as you really are!

WORK EQUALS MORE MONEY—FOR YOUR SELLERS AND YOU!

As already explained, sellers, you are earning yourself money by the time and energy you invest getting your home ready to sell and keeping it that way. Purchasers are very selective when it comes to finding a home of their choice. So, sellers, you need to make your property the very best available on the market in comparison with all the other homes.

These ideas work. They will work for you as they have for thousands of other sellers, ASP Agents, and ASP Stagers who have attended my seminars and workshops. Make the effort *now*! Stage the outside of the house. Get it done, and the work will pay off big time.

For additional creative Staging Ideas please, read my book, *Home Staging: The Winning Way to Sell Your Home for More Money* (Wiley), available at Barnes and Noble, on Amazon.com, or www.stagingshoppingcenter.com.

Also, please see the Appendix for complete details on how to order your copy of my DVD, "How to Stage Your Home to Sell for Top Dollar." Enjoy and learn from the following Before and After room photos.

BEFORE STAGING

AFTER STAGING

Before Staging

After Staging

BEFORE STAGING

AFTER STAGING

BEFORE STAGING

AFTER STAGING

BEFORE STAGING

AFTER STAGING

BEFORE STAGING

AFTER STAGING

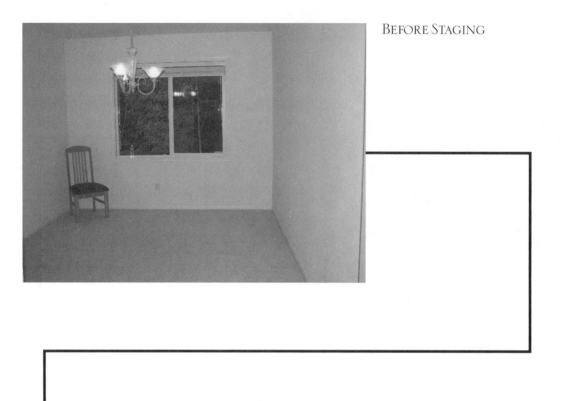

Before Staging

After Staging

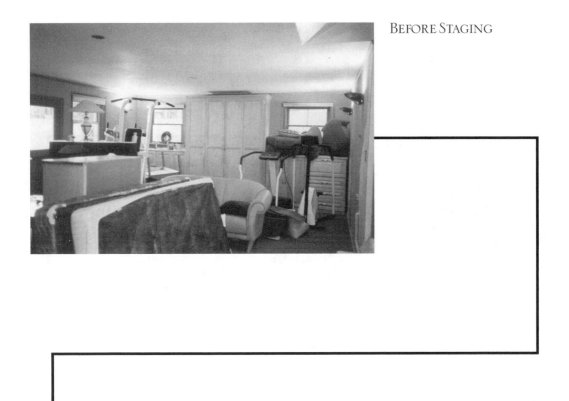

BEFORE STAGING

AFTER STAGING

BEFORE STAGING

AFTER STAGING

BEFORE STAGING

AFTER STAGING

BEFORE STAGING

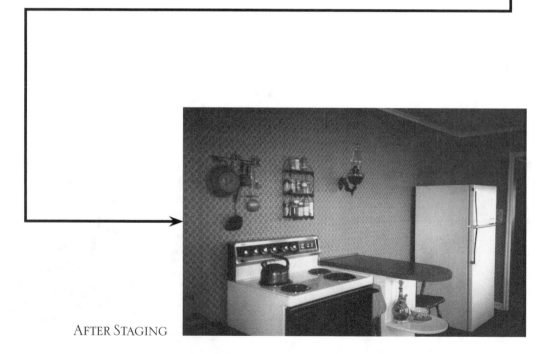

AFTER STAGING

Before Staging

After Staging

BEFORE STAGING

AFTER STAGING

BEFORE STAGING

AFTER STAGING

BEFORE STAGING

AFTER STAGING

BEFORE STAGING

AFTER STAGING

BEFORE STAGING

AFTER STAGING

BEFORE STAGING

AFTER STAGING

CHAPTER 12

STAGING COMPLETION

Commitment + Accountability = Results.

BARB SCHWARZ

SELLER'S NOTE

You've got to get it done! You have hired your Agent or your Stager. There are things that the Agent will do in preparing the house for the listing and that the Stager will do in preparing to Stage the house. And, Mr. and Mrs. Seller, there are things that *you* have to get done. I have seen through the years that people have good intentions but that many just don't come through. And the list of reasons and the excuses is long. People have unexpected company. People have to take the kids camping. The list can go on and on. The question is, "How do you plan on getting top dollar without getting the house Staged and everything done?" At first it seems easy to say, "Oh we'll get it done." I know that people mean well, but without deadlines it doesn't usually happen. Remember that one of the Seven Cs is commitment and that you are not the only one who needs to make and keep commitments. Your Agent is excited

(Continued)

to get the house on the market and to get it sold. And that is a good thing. But if it is not Staged and ready to show, then we are right back to my saying of, "Buyers, Agents, and appraisers know only what they see, not the way it is going to be!" Many times Agents want to get the pictures taken, bring over other Agents from the office, make the brochures, and get things done right away. And as much as you want all that, doing so without the house's being Staged first is not smart. No pictures should be taken prior to the Staging being completed; no other Agents should see your house, and there should be no open houses—not until your house is fully Staged. Staging is what we have talked about as the crucial S Factor, and to show your house to anyone is like having the public view the dress rehearsal before the night the play opens. Dress rehearsal is not opening night! And seeing your house before it is Staged is not your Staged opening, either.

In this chapter, I explain the steps that you and your Agent must take. I share with you what I have told my sellers all these many years. My advice is based on commitment, timing, a deadline, and starting the marketing for the sale of your home *only* after the Staging is done! This makes sense, yet participants in the real estate industry at large don't always do it this way. That is amazing, I know, and this is part of my mission to change the industry. Present practices are backwards, truly backwards. For decades, Agents have started the marketing before the seller ever finishes getting the house ready for sale; *and* this goes on in every company in every city all over the United States and Canada. And many sellers haven't finished getting their home Staged, but all the while the Agent tries to market the house. So the to-do list doesn't get done when it should. Why should the seller finish the list when the Agent is already marketing the house? When things happen in this order, many sellers just seem to feel that maybe they don't have to finish their list because buyers are already coming through. The seller's list never gets finished at all—and no wonder. Why would a seller finish the work if the Agent is already doing all the work to market the house? The buyers coming through look and don't buy because they simply cannot imagine living in the house when it isn't Staged.

So, sellers, ask your Agent and your Stager to follow the recommendations in this chapter because now you know the correct way it needs to be done. Our ASP Stagers get what I am talking about, and the key is to educate the Agent to what the team is doing and why. To get top dollar and to sell in a reasonable amount of time, nobody should see the house until it is Staged. Also, make sure to find an ASP Agent to list your house and market it as a Staged home. ASP Agents have been trained to do just that. They will put your Staged home on Stagedhomes.com, and, working with an ASP Stager, they can give you exposure through Stagedhomes.com—

and that is great because it gives you double exposure in the best and only site in the world for homes that are Staged to be seen and sold. And the ASPs do not charge you to put your house on the StagedHomes.com site. So get your work done. Keep your commitment and don't let anything get in your way.

IN THIS CHAPTER

You will learn:

1. The steps to make sure the house gets Staged and prepared for sale.
2. Why it is crucial to get the house Staged before any marketing is done.
3. Why Staging should be done by the ASP Stager, not by the Agent!

DON'T PUT THE CART BEFORE THE HORSE!

For years Agents in our industry have filled out the paperwork and then gone back to their offices and started all of their work to represent their sellers with ads and open houses. At the same time, sellers never did anything to get the houses ready for sale. Bringing a home to market takes commitments on all sides, including the commitment of the sellers to sign the paperwork to list the house and to finalize the paperwork to Stage the house. As an Agent, I am sure you have promised the sellers many marketing commitments, and as a Stager, I am sure you have promised many Staging commitments. One of the commitments that sellers should make and uphold is to finish the to-do list that you, the Agent, and you, the Stager, have agreed on. Before Stagers can get their work done, there are always things the seller needs to do first: painting a room, hauling out garbage from the backyard, and so on.

Getting the commitment from your sellers to complete the list of things to do should not be a problem at this point if you have educated them as I have explained in this book. One of the reasons I think we have had problems with this in the past in the real estate industry is that we did not educate the sellers enough up front about the importance of preparing their homes for sale. After all, if you have educated them on the importance of Staging from the very beginning, they should be eager to get everything completed.

Follow the few upcoming steps, and you will get solid commitments from your sellers without any problems, and everything they should do will get done.

DOING THINGS IN THE RIGHT ORDER

Sellers, Agents, and Stagers have to follow these steps in the order presented. Don't put the cart before the horse. These steps work, and they are easy to do as long as you stick to the order:

Step 1: Be sure the sellers have the list of what they are suppose to do to get ready for the ASP Stager.

Step 2: Set a deadline with the sellers for completing their list. After you have handed your sellers the list, you must get a commitment as to when it will be done.

Ask for a specific time. The sellers must finish their list so that the Stager can get the Staging done and the Agent can start the marketing. The Agent cannot market the house until the work gets done.

Your sellers already know how important this is, and most of them will dig in immediately and give their commitment to be ready in two days or even one day. A time has to be set. If the seller has to take off a day or two from work, then so be it. I have always told sellers that I am sure that they don't earn in one or two days' work what they will earn from Staging their house and getting top dollar.

Step 3: Tell your sellers that you will call them the night of their deadline. With a firm commitment from your sellers to finish the list, tell them that you will be calling them the evening of their deadline to check that the list got done. But it is crucial that you tell them now what you will be telling them then!

You must share with the sellers that you cannot start your part until they get their part done first. And if their part doesn't get done first, you will have to delay your work, thereby delaying the house's coming on the market Staged.

Be strong, firm, and professional about your commitment not to begin your work as the Agent or as the Stager until the sellers get their work done first. This technique works, and we have no one to blame but ourselves as Agents or Stagers if we go ahead and start our marketing or the Staging before the sellers get their prep list done.

In other words, as an Agent, you should not hold open house and you should not bring your office on tour, if the sellers don't get their list done. As a Stager, you can't get your part done if the sellers don't finish their work first. For example, Stagers, if you start Staging the house before the seller repaints the purple bedroom or doesn't get the floors refinished, then your Staging will not be as effective. Our professional policies once again come into play, as well as your standards of excellence, which you must stand by. You need to reset your time to Stage the house and not proceed with Staging. As an Agent or as a Stager, you have to tell the seller that you can't start your part and make it effective until the sellers get their chores done.

I feel very strongly about this! Agents, think about how our industry has worked in the past. For years, we, as Agents, have given sellers lists that somehow never quite got done. Do you know why? We have given sellers lists and then gone back to our offices and started all of our marketing efforts *before* the sellers ever finished their lists. No wonder they never got it done. We took away all their motivation. Don't misunderstand me: Never hold back listings from the multiple. In some areas you could lose your license if you were to do that. Certainly, turn in the listing, but do not start your marketing efforts until the sellers finish their list. Make it a firm professional policy. It works!

For years I have explained to sellers that, for them to get the most amount of their equity from all my marketing efforts, they must finish their part first. Sellers easily understand why when you explain that buyers and Agents know only what they see, not the way it's going to be. That way, everyone's effort can be as effective as possible. As an Agent, it does not make sense for you to start your marketing program, which is the best I know of, until your sellers' house is ready to go on the market.

Stagers, you might ask why an Agent would ever start marketing before the house gets Staged, but it happens all the time, everywhere. In fact, as a Stager, you are going to have to educate Agents all the time—at least those who do not read this book or who are not ASP Agents—that they should not start taking the pictures and that they should not bring over other Agents or the buyers until you get the house Staged. Mark my words: It is going to happen. It will amaze you, but many Agents will push you as a Stager to begin their marketing before you finish Staging. Stay strong and don't back down. Amazingly, an Agent may say "no" to you for six months as you talk with them about Staging their listings and then call you one day to get the Staging done the very next day. You might do the Staging the next day, but they are there taking pictures or trying to show the house all while. Educate, educate, educate everyone about the Staging process and the timing. Educate the sellers so that they gets their lists done before you start Staging, and the educate the Agents so that they don't start their marketing until you have finished Staging the house.

So. . . .

Step 4: Agents, start your marketing only after the seller's house is Staged. This is why from the very beginning you make sure that all your sellers realize Staging their property correctly and thoroughly is in their best interest. Educate them that the number one aim is to sell their home by maximizing all your efforts. You have to be working together for that same purpose. I have never yet had a seller who did not finish what we had agreed needed to be done because I took the time to educate them about how important Staging is.

The other element is motivation. Show me a seller who wants to sell, and I'll show you someone who will Stage his or her home. If you ever have sellers who do not finish the list you both agreed on, then I would seriously question their motivation. Do they want to sell or don't they? Preparing their home for sale is the best and fastest way I know to get their money.

Another important policy is not to take pictures until *after* the home is Staged. The statistics today are overwhelming. Over 80 percent of home buyers look at homes on the Internet before they buy. The sad thing for me personally is to look at homes for sale on the Internet and see how many of them look terrible! This practice is almost criminal! Instead of attracting buyers, poor pictures or pictures of an non-Staged home actually turn buyers away.

Agents, to professionally represent your listings on the Internet, you need to have *good* pictures of your listings, taken only after the house is Staged. Don't just take snapshots yourself with an inadequate camera and expect good results. Invest in a good camera with a wide-angle lens (most don't have this), and make sure you have one that either has a powerful flash (most don't) or the ability to take longer exposures to let in more light. Sadly, most Agents take poor pictures, so consider hiring a professional photographer to take your photos. A pro costs more, but the results are much more professional, and they will make your listings stand out. As an Agent, you can really set yourself apart by promising this great service that most Agents don't provide.

Sometimes, the Agents I meet in my seminar programs say to me things like, "Three months after I listed the property, my sellers still hadn't cleaned up the debris around the house. They still hadn't painted the kids' bedrooms. They never did get around to fixing the leaky shower." I ask them, "Did you get a commitment from the sellers to repair all those things before you started your marketing?" The same answer always comes back to me: "No, I didn't."

I'll tell you the same thing I tell them: You have to get that commitment from your sellers! I will not start my marketing program until my sellers have completed their commitment to get their house Staged, and they know that. If you start your marketing before the house is Staged, you just give away all your leverage, and it becomes very difficult to get the sellers to finish.

Also, markets come and markets go, and Agents may say, "Barb, the market is hot. It's a seller's market and to sell the house the sellers don't even need to Stage it. How do you feel about this?" My answer is always the same, "Can a home ever sell for too much? Tell me, would you or your sellers like to sell the home at an even higher price?" The answer is always the same: "Yes!" Agents in hot markets have already proven that Staged homes can and do sell for more. So even in really active markets, sellers should Stage their homes because they will sell for more, which means more satisfied sellers, more referral business, and more commission dollars to take to the bank. I have collected an amazing number of success stories of homes being Staged and selling for $50,000 to $100,000 more than the asking price, sometimes even in the same neighborhood with cookie-cutter homes. I personally Staged one home that had sat for nine months without selling at $1.4 million. After Staging, the home went back on the market and sold in less than 30 days for $1.9 million!

Whether the market is active or slow, the following is always true: *Staging homes makes great sense for everyone in every market!*

THE STAGING SHOULD BE DONE BY THE ASP STAGER, NOT BY THE AGENT

Specializing is the name of the game. This is true in all industries. To attempt to be all things for all people is not generally a good idea. That is why doctors specialize in medical practices. That is why lawyers specialize in certain areas of law. That is why there are escrow companies and title companies. The list goes on. So why should an Agent clean the roof, survey the property, pump the septic tank, paint the outside of the house, and Stage the house, too. Yet too many Agents try to be all things to all sellers. When it comes to listing and selling residential real estate, an Agent is supposed to list the house, market it so that it sells, review the paperwork of the buyers' purchase agreement, and close the transaction. Nowhere does it say that the Agent is to Stage the house, too. Now, it is crucial that Agents know what Staging is. It is important that they know the steps in Staging so that they can follow up on the steps' getting done. But to do the actual Staging themselves is not what I recommend for the Agent.

Stagers specialize, as a part of the real estate industry, in Staging homes! It is crucial that the house be Staged by an ASP Stager, not by the Agent. That is why I invented the industry: We need experts who specialize in preparing homes for sale. The Agent's job is to market the house, not to do the work to prepare it for sale. That is the Stager's role, and by hiring ASP Stagers, Agents save time, specialize in marketing the house and selling it, work hard to close the sale, and make more money by having their listings Staged by professionals. It is crucial that Agents know what Staging is so that they can educate their sellers about why the seller should have a house Staged. Agents should not take the time to Stage the house themselves, nor do most Agents want to do it themselves. When Agents are great at what they do, working with sellers and buyers, they are listing houses and selling houses. To try to do all things for all people isn't a good idea. An Agent should be the director of the show, as I have explained, and bringing in specialists in each area of the process in the listing and sale of the house allows the Agent to get on with marketing and selling the house.

Many Agents do not want to Stage the house themselves—a wise move, I say. But a few Agents think that they can do the job without being a trained ASP Stager, and that doesn't make sense. Agents are trained to be Agents. If you are a good Agent, first of all, you don't have time to Stage, and secondly why would you want to? If you try to do both jobs, you won't do either well because there isn't enough time and you need to specialize in one profession or the other. And if you are an Agent who wants to Stage, then you need to become an ASP Stager and Stage for a living.

A teaming-up of an ASP Agent to list and sell the house and an ASP Stager to Stage the house is where the profitability is for all concerned: Agent, Stager, and seller! Agents, go to www.Stagedhomes.com and to the directory there to find the ASP Stagers you like to work with the best in your area. Have them Stage the house, and then you as the Agent can get on with listing and selling the house. Become an ASP Agent so that you can learn how to educate your sellers about Staging and its benefits and learn how to market a Staged Home. But leave the actual Staging to the ASP Stagers.

By the way, sellers, you need to know that, in many areas, the Agents are paying ASP Stagers to do a Staging Consultation. The cost is part of the Agent's marketing program for you. The ASP Stager then does a 35- to 50-page written Staging Consultation report so that you and the Agent know everything that needs to be done to Stage the house. Then you, the seller, can do the Staging or have the ASP Stager go ahead and Stage the house.

The other option, which a number of top Agents are also doing, is to pledge to the seller in their marketing program how much they will pay of the actual Staging when the seller or Agent hires the Stager to Stage the house. This is a step in the right direction because the Agent will pay part or all of the Staging service fee instead of the seller. Agents for years and years have been put on the defensive about their commissions. As I said for two consecutive years at the National Association of Realtors National Convention, at which it was my honor to speak, Agents need to add Staging as a service for the sellers to their marketing program because they are bringing in an ASP Stager to do the work. Staging *is* a marketing tool.

Those of you Agents who decide to pay for the Staging service will bring a true value-added service to what you do to list and sell the house. This commitment takes you to the next level of service. It is a big step up. And I believe, as I have said for a long time, that Agents need to invest for the seller the dollars needed to Stage the house. Determine a dollar amount, put it into your marketing plan. Budget it as a part of your marketing plan. Teach the seller about it and how much you will commit to it. You may be able to charge a higher commission by including the Staging; some Agents do that. You could also invest the amount as part of the fee instead of all of it. Either way, you have moved up the ladder of service. As a way to protect your investment in this great service, you can also commit to paying your share of the Staging costs at closing. The sellers can pay in the beginning and you reimburse them in the end. This will help keep the sellers working with you, and you don't lose the money you would otherwise invest up front.

And having all your listings Staged will actually *save* you money on expensive advertising that doesn't need to be done when homes sell faster in a slow market instead of sitting on the market for an extended period of time!

Staging really gives you the edge in your marketplace, wherever you live and work, because it puts you at the top in giving the most service in today's real estate industry. Agents, invest the dollars in the service because the ASP Stager will make money for you as well as for the sellers. Take the lead in your market. Be the Agent who hires ASP Stagers to do the Staging for you. Then, as you hire them, you will have more time to list more houses and sell more houses. Sellers talk and their neighbors talk, and word-of-mouth is where referrals come from. Be the Agent who leads the way and who sets the pace that the others have to try to catch up with. That is how you lead. And leaders lead the marketplace every time, no matter what the market is doing!

CHAPTER 13

STAGE YOUR LIFE AND WORK, TOO!

Live a Staged life or live your life by default. The choice is yours.

BARB SCHWARZ

SELLER'S NOTE

It is important to work with a professional who is organized. An organized Agent and Stager will get more done for you and in a quicker amount of time. Commitment is crucial as you work with Agents and Stagers. They need your commitment to get your house Staged, and you need theirs to make sure that they get their part done too: paperwork, equipment, supplies, inventory, phone calls returned, emails returned ASAP, and more. In this chapter, I share ideas that have worked for me and that I suggest you check out with those you talk with. You can tell whether Agents and Stagers are organized by the equipment and the systems they use: a *Career Book*, a *Marketing Portfolio*, record keeping materials, phone equipment, and more. Companies have proven that organized people who work well with details are much more effective because they serve people well. And details are crucial in listing homes and in Staging them. It is all in the detail.

IN THIS CHAPTER

You will learn:

1. How to organize your three workstations.
2. How to get the most from your time.

ATTAIN SUCCESS BY GETTING YOUR ACT TOGETHER!

Staging is the act of preparing homes for sale, but living a Staged Life is a good idea, too. You can live your life by default, or you can Stage it! I strive daily to Stage everything that I do. I Stage my home to live in, I Stage my car to drive, I Stage what I wear, and I Stage my office and my work itself, too. I ask you to look at living and working that way also. You will find that it that helps you be more organized and have more fun. This chapter is for us all: Agents, Stagers, and sellers too because I hope you all love your work and what you do. This chapter may help you love it even more because my goal is to help us all do things just a little bit better in an organized, Staged way.

Get Organized and Be Proactive!

If you want a smooth journey to success, get organized. The best defense is definitely a good offense! Now, you may be saying to yourself, "These stacks of paper on my desk only look like a mess. Actually I know where everything is." But I caution you that, if you follow the program I have outlined for you, those piles on your desk are going to grow into monsters, which will eat you alive, because you are going to have more business than ever. The number of clients you will have will increase, and so will your paperwork and the demands on your time. You will need to be Staged for work, and to do that you have to be organized!

FOUR AREAS TO ORGANIZE

I encourage you to organize four areas to help Stage your life:

1. Your desk
2. Your files
3. Your computer
4. Your car

Your Desk

You should have everything you need at your desk. The forms, the supplies, and other day-to-day items such as paperclips, staplers, and so forth, are close at hand in a supply closet or storage area, right? But what is the condition of your desk? Do you have a few copies of all the forms you use in a desk drawer? Do you have at your fingertips more than one pen that writes? Just think how much simpler life would be if you had everything you needed right there with you. No more rushing around to find supplies. No more rummaging around for a form when you are rushing out the door! Organize your desk drawers, and be sure you have everything you could possibly need for business right there with you.

One good way to control the clutter on your desktop is to use baskets labeled "Do Now!" . . . "Read" . . . "File" . . . "My Clients." You can save your desk from sinking in a sea of paper and yourself from losing important documents.

Another important tip is to strive to touch each piece of paper only once! I know that can be hard, but be tough on yourself. The day I started acting like every paper I picked up was stuck to my fingers like glue until I did something with it, I really started to save time and change my work habits. Have you ever noticed how often you pick up the same piece of paper without doing something in the form of action to get that piece of paper put away or thrown away once and for all? Work hard to touch each paper only once. The time and energy you save by keeping your desk organized can be invested in obtaining more business and earning more money!

Your Files

It is important to organize and Stage your files. I like to color-code my files. As an Agent, I put the buyers in yellow folders and the sellers in green folders. As a Stager, I put my consultations in yellow folders and my Staging projects in green folders. It is really important that you can find any file you want at any time. Color-coding the folders helps me know which category it is.

Also I like to file by address. Therefore I have files that go from 0 to 500, 501 to 999, 1,000 to 1,500, and so on. You get the idea. Then I file the folder by the address (the seller's name is on it, too), but I file it by the address. If a buyer becomes a seller, I put the yellow folder into the green folder. As a Stager, I do the same when a Staging Consultation becomes a

Staging project. The yellow folder then goes inside a green folder. My invoices for Staging are numbered by the house number, too. My in-closing numbers that I assigned when I was an Agent were by house number, too. Then, at any time with my numbering system, I could go into the file cabinet, find any file, and know its category by the color.

Think about how you file files and perhaps you can take my idea and make yours more organized in a way that works for you.

Your Computer

Your computer or laptop can be a critical business tool, but only if you know how to use it quickly and wisely. If you are not computer savvy, do yourself and your business a favor and invest in a class or two or in a tutor to get you up to speed. The real estate industry is now highly computerized, with online pictures, web sites, uploads, downloads, pdfs, jpegs, and countless other acronyms. Not being able to communicate and use these tools efficiently *will* cost you business.

Organize your computer. Make sure you have easy access to all the forms, web sites, and software you need on a regular basis. Creating shortcuts, custom links, and bookmarks to your most often used files and web sites can be a great time-saver. There are several good contact management software programs to use to keep track of and to market to all of your business prospects. More and more of us are now using BlackBerries and Pocket PCs that will communicate and sync with your home and/or office computer so that you can do email and access files while mobile. There are lots of exciting advances that are making the use of computers easier and more productive all the time. To be competitive as an Agent or a Stager, you need to be proficient and confident using new technology.

Your Car

If you are like me, you are in your car a lot because of our work. And we work out of our car, so it becomes an office as well. Your car therefore needs to be organized, too.

Have one box in the trunk of your car that holds a few copies of every form you could possibly need. In other words, have copies of all the forms you would use in the office. I'm talking about any kind of form that you need in your day-to-day career. Have them with you so that, when you go to see your sellers and all of a sudden they decide to change something, you don't need to go back to the office to get a form to make the change. You have the appropriate forms with you at all times!

Of course, you can carry some of these forms in your briefcase. But if you run out of them, you can just go out to your car to get more copies, instead of going back to the office. Get into the habit of restocking the supplies in your car as soon you notice you are running low. Always have the forms with you.

Also in your car keep a box full of various notepads, envelopes, your company stationery, and other writing supplies. You never know when you are going to be kept waiting—maybe in a doctor's office, maybe on a ferry in your area, or on the freeway. If you have these supplies with you, you can write a letter to someone whenever you are delayed. It is a great way to keep thank-you notes going out every day and to stay in touch with prospects, sellers, and Agents!

I recommend that you also have a second box in your trunk with supplies such as paper towels, hand wipes, toilet paper, a first aid kit, dog biscuits, stapler, staples, scotch tape, scissors, hand cream, hand sterilizer, tissues, paperclips, rubber bands, straws, napkins, pens, pencils, maps, lipstick (as a female), a mirror, aspirin, stamps, scratch pads, paper punch, tacks, clippies, signs, and other things you may think necessary.

As ASP Stagers, of course, have a full array of Staging tools with you. Your ASP Caddies are typically full to the brim of tools such as screwdrivers, hammers, rope, nails, picture hangers, and the like! Keep these supplies up-to-date, and go through them often to make sure that you are not out of something. I really keep my car organized, and it saves me so much time in the short and long run!

Being prepared and organized can make the difference in your business. Be ready for opportunities that present themselves. Being organized can make the difference between securing the business and not getting it at all. Organized people usually make more money because they are more productive and save time by being that way. And remember to keep your *Career Book*s and *Marketing Portfolio* in your backseat, so that you have them as you need them, even at a moment's notice!

TIME MANAGEMENT

Being organized also means getting the most from the time you have. We all have the same amount of time: 24 hours every day. But have you ever noticed how some people seem to get so much more done in that time than others? The secret of effective time management is really no secret; it is a matter of getting your entire career organized, not just your car and desks. I want to share with you a few tips that, if you follow them, are guaranteed to help you use your time more effectively.

Tip 1: Schedule Your Time

That doesn't sound complicated, does it? Putting yourself on a schedule doesn't mean giving up personal freedom. In fact, it gives you freedom. When you *are* organized, which includes having a schedule of all the things you need to do each day, you will be amazed at how much time you can save. And the time you save is yours. You will have more time for presentations, which means more listings. You will have more time for marketing, which means more sales!

So plan and schedule your days. And schedule time off for yourself. It may be the only way you'll get it.

If you have five houses to check out tomorrow, write yourself a schedule of which houses you are going to see, when you are going to see them, and what you will do on each visit. You will find that you can keep yourself better organized when you know what you are going to be doing most of the day and in what order. Start scheduling your activities, including non-business activities. If you are having lunch with your mother, include that in your schedule. Then stick to the schedule unless something really important comes up.

One thing that has worked well for me is that I always ask myself every day, "What is the most productive thing I can do today to bring about a new Staging as a Stager or a new listing or a sale as an Agent?" Then I do it. I also strongly believe in writing a to-do list every night for the next day. I find that I sleep better knowing I have everything mapped out, and then tomorrow that is my map of what to do and I do it. Become a do-it-now person. It pays off big time, I promise you!

Tip 2: Build in Flexibility

Don't put yourself on such a strict schedule that if an appointment is canceled, you are robbed of two productive hours. Be prepared for delays and changes. This goes back to my advice about keeping company stationery and notepads in your car. Use spare time to review an upcoming presentation or to contact prospects. Don't just spend time: Invest it!

Tip 3: Use Travel Time to Your Advantage

Why not put traveling time to work for you? As I said before, most of us practically live in our cars. If you are on a trip between cities, listen to an educational CD or cassette, or use the time to brainstorm for an upcoming marketing program or presentation. Practice what you want to say out loud. No one can hear you, and I found that, if I practiced out loud in my car on the way to appointments, I had a much higher rate of success. Much of my program, which you have read about in this book, I have practiced out loud, day after day, year after year, as I worked with the thousands of sellers for whom I listed and sold properties. They say practice makes perfect, and I truly believe it does.

Schedule your appointments in areas that are close together when you can. When you are going to see three houses, work to arrange the visits so that you can see them all without backtracking; that saves time and you will get more done.

Tip 4: Keep a Daily To-Do and To-Call List

Keep a list of all the things you must do—and do them! This list is for the things that are easy to forget unless you write them down, such as dropping off a loan verification letter or picking up some groceries for an open house. As already explained, before you go to bed, make a to-do and a to-call list for the next day. If you really get yourself into this habit, you will find it invaluable.

I also find that, if I dump things on my mind out onto the list before I go to bed, I don't worry about them nearly as much during the night. You get more and better sleep that way. Try it; it works. Then the next morning you are all set. Pick up your piece of paper, review it, and get going.

Tip 5: Conquer Bad Habits That Waste Time

Work to eliminate these bad habits that can devour your precious time.

- Habitually leaving your home or office a few minutes late.
- Turning business calls into social visits. You want to build rapport, but don't forget that you are there for business.
- Not disciplining yourself to get your work done on time. It can be easy to just put off doing things that are productive and instead do things that are not productive at all. I encourage you to do the most important

thing first rather than waste time with something doesn't bring the productive results that you want.

• Spending too much time just talking about nonproductive things with associates in your office.

If any of these are your bad habits, overcome them. When you do, you will be amazed at how much more time you really will have.

Tip 6: Stop Procrastinating—Become a Do-It-Now Person

We all do it. We wait until tomorrow or the next day to do what should have been done today or yesterday. All you have to do is make up your mind to do things as they come up. If you have an ad to deliver to your local newspaper for the Sunday edition, then get to it. If you need to pick up your *Career Book* from a For Sale by Owner, don't wait until the end of the week. Go get it today, and sell that For Sale by Owner on how you can help sell his or her house.

If you have a tough call you have to make, do it first thing in the morning. The rest of your day will be a breeze and much more fun because you dealt with the tough thing first instead of putting it off to late in the day or not doing it at all.

Procrastination is the biggest killer of sales. "Do it now" is the best advice I can give. No matter what it is: Do it now!

CHAPTER 14

YOUR JOURNEY TOWARD SUCCESS

Your life is your journey of every step you take every single day . . .

BARB SCHWARZ

I haven't made separate notes for sellers in this chapter because this information is directed at everyone. Each of us can profit from the life-changing information I share with you in these pages.

Where are you on your journey to success? You need to know where you are going, or else you may never get there.

Can you imagine getting into your car, starting the engine, and driving down your driveway without having the slightest idea of where you are going? However, that's how many people approach their careers. They jump into it, work very hard, but sometimes don't make any progress. They end up running around in circles with no idea where they are headed. They have no direction; they have no specific goals.

What about you? What are your goals? What do you want? Do you have a plan for reaching those goals? Some people live by setting goals, and others are confused or afraid to try because they think they might fail. It's all an experience. We learn by being productive and achieving our goals, and we learn by not doing so. They key is to observe what we are doing, how we are doing, whether what we are doing is bringing us results and what we really want.

STEPS FOR REACHING GOALS

I believe in the power of having goals because I have literally seen what seemed like miracles happen in my own life from setting goals. I also believe in a system or program to make goals happen. This easy system works for me and has worked for millions of others.

Step 1: Define Your Goals

You can easily divide your goals into several manageable categories, such as:

1. Homes you want to list or Stage.
2. Income you want to earn.

Homes You Want to List or Stage

Agents and Stagers should include any prospects they have already talked with and names of people they have seen as possible prospects, such as a For Sale by Owner. I believe everyone is a prospect, but this list should be limited to specific people who you think are hot candidates. You should also set a goal of how many properties you want to list or Stage on a weekly, monthly, and yearly basis.

Income You Want to Earn

Set your sights on a dollar figure that you want to earn. The key (as with all goals) is to come up with a figure that is *realistic*—one that you will have to work and stretch a little to reach, but also one that can be achieved. It does nothing for your confidence if you set a goal that is unrealistically high, and you fail to reach it.

You can use one or all of these categories, or create your own. Remember, the only right way is the one that works for you. Once you have defined your goals and divided them into categories. I suggest that you quantitatively break them down into smaller increments so that you can actually see how you can achieve them.

For example, let's say that you set a goal of listing or Staging four homes next month. How can that be done? That's only one new listing or Staging a week, a much more specific target. Then analyze how you can accomplish that. How many presentations will you need to give, based on your experience, to get one client? How many phone calls, contacts, or referrals will you need to work to generate each presentation? If you work backward in this manner, you can even set goals for your daily work to achieve your weekly, monthly, or yearly goals.

Always divide your clients and goals into categories. They are much easier to manage that way. You won't feel overwhelmed, and you will be much better organized.

Step 2: Commit Your Goals to Writing

Write all your goals down on paper. Every expert in the field suggests you do that because it forces you to make more of a commitment than if you just think about something you'd like to achieve. Let's say you have met four new families, and you want to list them as an Agent or Stage them as a Stager. Don't just think about those families, write down their names. Get yourself a notebook, and write down their names under a heading that reads. "I am listing or Staging these homes." Notice the list does not say, "I want to list these homes." It says "I *am* listing these homes." Keep this list in front of you daily. Read it, say it, and believe it. The key is to feel it as though it has already happened. Really feel the feelings as if you were already working with them. This sets the universe into action to help bring about what you want to create. Your belief in yourself and your ability to create this is crucial. Feel good inside about this. Not egomaniacally good or feeling pompously good, but a good based in a thanksgiving that you have the ability to create this, and you will.

Another important thing that I have learned is that you don't want to limit yourself. When you are dealing with quantities, you need to state them like this: "I am Staging or listing four *or more* homes next month." The important thing is the "or more." Don't just say, "I am Staging four homes" because that may be all you get! What you say is what you get. Add the "or more" to allow more good to come to you!

Defining and writing down your goals in black and white gives them dimension and can make them more real for you. This works miracles. Written goals give you something concrete to work toward. Written goals happen!

When I started writing down my goals, as I have just explained, the most wonderful things did begin to happen—and those of you who have tried this know what I am talking about. The mind does the work it needs to do to achieve the goals we have expressed on paper. And that is one of the most exciting things about setting goals and the capabilities of our human mind. More on that later!

Step 3: Visualize the Goal as Reality in Your Mind

After you have defined your goals and added them to your written list, visualize the goals as reality. For example, as an Agent I have written down the sales that are already in escrow that I am going to close. If I have the sale on paper, whether I was the listing or the selling Agent, there is no reason in my mind why the sale shouldn't close. If I know I have done my work—my marketing, qualifying, and follow-up—then there is no reason that sale shouldn't close. So I will actually visualize myself with the Sellers signing the closing documents. Visualization works.

Many doctors, educators, and philosophers have written about this concept. A short explanation of this phenomenon is that the brain cannot differentiate between stimuli from the conscious mind and those from the subconscious mind. The act of visualizing your goals and actually putting them down on paper starts to create a "reality" in the brain that this thought (the goal) is real. The brain will then start to find ways to make the thought actually come to reality. If you think this all sounds too good to be true, I hope you will trust me that it really is true. If you would like to know more, I suggest you read one of the many books available on this subject. The more you see your goals happening in your own mind, the more your brain will seek a way to make them happen in your life.

So define your goals. Then write them down. Visualize the end result you want, and it will come to life right in front of you. Believe in your goals. Believe, and you will make it happen! This is because anything that your mind can conceive and you believe, you can achieve.

I hope that you will make goal-setting a permanent part of your personal and professional life. Millions of people have found that working toward goals gives them structure, confidence, success, and the ability to get what they want out of their lives and careers.

LET'S REVIEW

It is important that we look at tying everything together and also give you a place you can go to read, remember, and review my main concepts any time you want. Repetition is the mother of learning, so please review this or any other part of this book often. This is key to learning new concepts. When you review and practice, you learn, grow, change the way you do things, and become more successful. This is true of your career as well as of any new change you want to undertake in your life.

Let Me Tell You How I Work

Be sure you invest time during your first contact with any Seller to give an overview of the services you provide. Set yourself apart from your competitors and others right away. Sellers won't understand or appreciate you or your exclusive program if you don't explain it to them. When you go to another professional for help or advice, you don't know how that person works unless he or she tells you. You won't go wrong, I promise you, if you tell them the following up front: "Let me tell you how I work, Mr. and Mrs. Seller. Here is what I am going to be doing for you."

Not only will you take care of their concerns (formerly called "objections") before they come up, but most people appreciate being told how you can and will serve them. So sell yourself by telling people up front how you work.

> **Take the time to educate the sellers. They deserve it.**
> **Education = Control.**

Invest time in educating your future clients and then they *will* become your clients. The time is worth it. Tell them, "Mr. and Mrs. Seller, I believe in giving you great service. I am going to invest time with you so that you will fully understand all that I will do for you."

Put Together a *Career Book* to Help You Sell Yourself

Be proud of who you are. Remember, there is much more to you than meets the eye. If *you* don't sell yourself, then who will? No one, that's who. People don't know what you don't tell them, and that is true about how special you are as well. The beautiful thing is that your *Career Book* will do the talking for you, so you don't have to worry about bragging.

The *Career Book* will show off your professional side so that sellers will have more confidence and trust in you. It will show off your personal side, too, so that you can develop common ground with your sellers, a real key to getting more business. Put one together, and do it now. Also, when you leave it with clients and customers, you are "living" in the property, and you have a perfectly logical reason to go back because you have to pick up your book.

Remember the three steps of great service:

Step 1: Meet the sellers and see their property. Be sure you have the sellers show you their property, because no one knows the home like they do. Work to build rapport, and then leave your *Career Book*, which details your experience and how your expertise will help them. Tell them, "I'd really appreciate your taking the time to look at my *Career Book*. It will help you get to know me better. I think you'll enjoy it!" Review your let-me-tell-you-how-I-work plan with them so that they fully understand all of your great service and what's going to happen next. Then just set the appointment to return for your presentation (i.e., Detailed Report).

Step 2: Present your Detailed Report to your future sellers. Remember, the Detailed Report has two important parts: (1) your plan to market the house and (2) either the pricing of the property as the Agent or your Staging Plan and the investment to Stage the property for sale. The key is to use both verbal and visual components in your education of the seller. This is the time for you to educate the Seller. Don't take shortcuts. Invest your time, and you will be rewarded highly in the end.

Step 3: Take the time needed for signing the paperwork and Staging the house! Make sure that deadlines are set and that you hold others accountable for getting the Staging done! The S Factor is the difference that works! Staging is what sells homes in this market and in all real estate markets. Staging helps the home sell faster and for more money, no matter what the market is doing. Wait until you read the Staging success stories in the back of this book. The proof is there, loud and clear, and ever since the day that I invented Home Staging, it has always been there. Buyers, look and see how Staging allows the home to communicate with you to sell the house. Staging is real and it works.

SUCCESS!

I sincerely hope reading this book has been a valuable experience for you. You are very special. There has never been anyone quite like you. You can adapt what you have learned to your own style and career.

I truly believe there are no real failures, only experiences! You can't fail; you only experience! The only failure is just giving up.

So learn from your experiences. Learn and grow. Step out and step up! I challenge you to try something new, something that stretches you as a person. Take a risk. Even if it's just a small one to start with, and you will be taking a step of growth. When you think about it, everything in life is really a risk; some are just more scary than others. But the greater the risk, the higher the gain. Some people coast; they do things the same old way, never really changing or trying new ideas. And they usually coast downhill.

What you desire already exists. You can create whatever you put your heart and mind to. I have learned through my years that the following steps bring good things to all who apply them:

1. Believe that what you want to create already exists and is waiting for you to create it.
2. Take action to create what you desire.
3. Be thankful for it before it shows up, and realize that it may show up in ways you haven't even thought of yet.
4. Assume nothing.
5. Make commitments and keep them.
6. Hold yourself accountable for taking the actions required to create your desires and dreams.
7. Keep your faith, stay the course, hold to your vision and mission.
8. Celebrate your creativity and each successful step along your way.
9. Always live in a state of thanksgiving.

Enjoy your journey. Keep at this adventure called life. Success is the journey itself, not just an end. I want to thank you for this opportunity to share with you. Step out and apply what you have learned. Do it, and do it now!

CHAPTER 15

THE S FACTOR: STAGING SUCCESS STORIES FROM ASPs AND THEIR SELLERS IN THE FIELD

They say that the proof is in the pudding; well, here's the proof!

BARB SCHWARZ

Staging works and is the S Factor of why homes sell for top dollar and in the shortest amount of time. It is so rewarding to read the following true stories of the just some of many successes of the wise sellers who made the decision to work with an ASP and get their property Staged. They listed with an ASP Agent and/or Staged with an ASP Stager, and their success came through the actions that they took to make sure that they did it right by working with the best—the ASP *best*!

I have seen personally, all these many years, the same results with literally thousands and thousands of sellers I have represented who would also tell you the same thing: Staging works, it is like magic, and not too good to be true!

Our ASPs enter their Staging stats, data, and stories into the Staging University that I founded for ASPs to use in their real estate and Home Staging businesses. In this chapter, I share just a few of the thousands of success stories from today's market. Even in down markets, houses sell. The key is that they are Staged. Non-Staged houses are shown to sell the Staged ones. Buyers are smart and discerning, and so are the sellers who Stage their homes to sell.

So read on and learn from these experiences, too, because you will certainly see that the results speak for themselves!

My grandfather always said, "It is far better to know and do, than to know and do nothing at all." Now, by reading this book, I hope you know as a seller to take action and to Stage your home with an ASP. You know about it by reading my book, so now do something about it and Stage for evermore the *ASP way*!

ASP STAGING SUCCESS STORIES AS TOLD BY ASPs

1. We quoted using furniture from the furniture rental company, but the client was not comfortable with their credit application procedure and asked if I could just Stage using my own inventory. I explained that we wouldn't have a sofa or bed or matching furniture but that I would do my best and gave her a quote. She agreed and 2 days later we Staged the house. She was extremely pleased and could not get over the transformation. The next day was the open house, and several buyers stayed in the house for over an hour (900 sq ft house), and out of that they received a full price offer for the house. Even without a sofa, bed, or matching suites of furniture, Staging did the trick. —*Joy Waida, ASP Joy Home Design Residential Interior Design & Home Staging, Baltimore, Maryland*

2. This listing is a perfect example of how sellers need to update their homes to receive maximum value for their house. The house, first listed as is, sat for 400 days. Spent $10k on updating the wiring and other things found on the home inspection report. Refinished the hardwood floors. Professionally cleaned windows and interior. Once the updating was done, I came in and Staged the house. At the open house a previous buyer who saw the house originally came in made an offer $500 over asking price. It was sold in 15 days. —*Gail McCaffrey, ASP, Norfolk, Maine*

3. The homeowners did everything exactly the way I suggested in the Staging packet I provided to them. The home sold to the third couple

that walked through the home. —*Hanna Wynn Roppo, ASP, Naples, Florida*

4. Only 4 days! As you might suspect, my clients were elated. They became true believers in Staging & loved the results! —*Robyn Fewell, ASP Stager & Real Estate Agent, Winston Salem, North Carolina*

5. When I was packing up to de-Stage the property, the buyers came in to measure. They told me that the reason they purchased the home was because they liked the way the home was Staged. The stats on this property are as follows: 21 properties on the market between $1.2 million and $1.8 million. No pending sales at time of offer. The buyers offered $1.4 million and came up to $1,550,000. They were all cash buyers and closed escrow in less than 3 weeks. Wooo Whooo! —*Spotlight Staging, Ruthie Smith, ASP, Thousand Oaks, California*

6. This was a very limited Staging due to the limited budget of the agent. A team of two ASP Stagers worked with our inventory to create vignettes in the upstairs only (living room, kitchen, and two bathrooms). It was quick, easy, and it worked!

7. My name is Aileen Martinez, ASP; I cover Bronx, Westchester, Rockland, and Orange Counties in New York. This condo in the Bronx was Staged by myself and listed on the market. By the next day we received an offer.

8. Sherri went above and beyond her duties as a Stager. Besides doing a great job setting up the home for showings, she also alerted me to a minor problem, which came up a month after she'd Staged the home. Sherri had stopped in to check that the Staging items were still in the correct place when she noticed a minor flooring issue which had occurred since we'd Staged the home. She immediately called me so I could correct the problem and not lose any buyers over it. Great job! —*Dave Larsen, ABR, CRS & E-PRO, John Hall & Associates, Phoenix, Arizona*

9. I think people could see themselves living in the home because it was Staged. —*Carol Molnar, GRI Realtor, Century 21 Arizona Foothills, Phoenix, Arizona*

10. Met with client for consultation on Thursday evening. Her home had been on the market for 6 months prior to this. She became so excited that we Staged the property that night. When we left the home Thursday evening (4 hours later) all clients had to do was sweep floors. There were 2 appointments to show property on Friday. On Saturday morning client received full-price offer for her home, which she accepted. Client was thrilled! —*Deb Johnson, ASP, Jackson, Tennessee*

11. This was my first Staging opportunity. I wanted to use what I had learned in the ASP Staging Class to help my mother sell her home. The house had been on the market, previously, for 1 year and then re-listed after a few months and remained on the market for over 3 months. After I completed the Staging, we received an offer from the second couple that viewed it. The young woman said, "I don't want to look at anything else. I want this house!" This was 3 days after Staging! —*Renee Felts, ASP Stager, Phoenix, Arizona*

12. This is a success story for the client—18 days on the market and just 4 days after Staging, it was under contract. Staging Works. —*Laura Rogers, ASP*

13. Home was very cluttered. Homeowner rented a POD. They did everything that was on the room by room house report that I prepared for them. Left only 3 to 5 pieces of furniture in each room and cleared out *all the clutter* and put it in the POD and had the POD removed from the driveway before open house. The rest is history—sold in 21 days in the middle of December (the slowest time to sell a house in New Jersey). Thanks for teaching us well Barb. I am grateful to you for having a wonderful business. —*Barbara R. Cluck-Miksits, ASP, IAHSP, owner of BCMHomeStaging.com, Ridgewood, New Jersey*

14. The Seller is a real estate investor who buys/fixes and sells over 20 homes per year. He had never Staged a home before and found our information on REAPS, which is a Real Estate Investment Association. The home sold in just over 30 days and over the holidays. He credits Staging to bringing in the buyer, and we are getting ready to Stage his next project! —*Pam Christensen, ASP, Shoreline, Washington*

15. The Sellers were right on target. They first contacted me *before* listing the property. The Sellers followed all my recommendations to prepare the vacant house for Staging. We rented furniture and accessories and I Staged the home. It was listed after the Staging was completed. Within *five* days being on the market, the sellers received, accepted, and signed a contract! The sellers, realtor, and I were so so excited!!! The Power of Staging is what makes the big difference between sitting on the market and selling as soon as possible:-) —*Jodi Spickler, ASP*

16. This was a vacant Brand New construction condo, 2 bedrooms, 2 Bathrooms overlooking a beautiful lake view. This property sat and sat on the market with very little traffic for 219 days. Since it was new construction, the owner was competing with the developer to sell the

property. I am an ASP Realtor and from day one I was trying to convey to the owner how important it is to Stage the property. She was very reluctant but finally after 219 days of my persistence in trying to get her to realize she needed Staging, she *finally* Staged the home. We still had very little traffic after the Staging; however, the 1st person that walked in after the home was Staged put an offer on the home only $4500 less than the asking price. The owner then told me she wished she would have Staged the property long ago because it sat vacant for 7 months and she was paying a mortgage on the property all of that time! The developer was having problems also selling their remaining units in the condo development which also were vacant. After hearing her Staging success story, the developer contacted us and asked us if we could Stage the developers units so he too could have a Staging success story! *Wow!!* The buyer ended up "gutting" the place even though it was Brand new, tore out carpet and put hard wood floors; put granite countertops in kitchen and bathrooms etc. . . . I highly doubt that property would have sold for even close to what the owner got if the property was not Staged!! Somehow even though the new owner renovated they still saw the value. *Why????* Because Staged homes sell!!!! —*Lisa Shuster, ASP, Prudential Florida WCI Realty, Coral Springs, Florida*

17. This Staging took on a special meaning since it was my own mom moving. Our market has been slow and it normal takes about 3–4 months to sell these condos. I Staged it, it went into our MLS system, had an appointment to show that day and a full price offer within a 24 hour time frame. Something did the trick!! What else could explain it but the Staging. Mom was happy and I was happy and sad at the same time. Happy to see Staging work and sad to see mom leave. I totally believe Staging works, but continue to have an office of "doubting Thomases." Guess I will have to Stage and sell more. Works for me! —*Julie Jones, ASP Realtor, Columbia, Tennessee*

18. The builder was so impressed with the Staging it was like he was seeing the house for the first time! He liked the professionalism I brought to the job and the ease of working with a Stager. —*Kim Trudo, ASP, New Bern, North Carolina*

19. The agent was trying to skimp on accessories but we told her she couldn't skimp on plants because they were part of the Staged look. She paid for the Staging instead of the client and this was her 1st experience with Staging. She was totally blown away! Then, getting two

offers with one as a back-up and getting a higher price than listed was icing on the cake. —*Marti Rounds, ASP*

20. After bringing in my handyman & painter; Staging took place, dusk photos were taken. Thus, 2 competing offers & a signed contract for the asking price!

21. The homeowners lived in another state and this home was a rental. After renters moved out, I was able to help providing contacts for painting and a handy man. The home was Staged & contracted in 10 days! Agents who previously saw the home before Staging were amazed & gave kudos for the updates and Staging since it's what they say *sold* the home! I *love* helping people move on with life & this was a joy since owners were out of town! —*Jan Lawrence, ASP, IAHSP Home Stage Coach, Denver, Colorado*

22. Yes! The homeowner appreciated that his realtor suggested they have their home professionally Staged. It was beautiful and only 2 years young. The existing decor was very eccentric and would not appeal to all buyers. We transformed the house in just two days of Staging. The realtor had his first open house 3 days after Staging. Within 24 hours he had two offers for *full* asking price and the home was sold for 60K over list price!!! *Wow!* Nothing had sold for over 1 million ever in that development! Please note Staging costs of $14,000 included landscaping, paint, new lighting, Staging, and rental furniture/accessories for 3 mos. —*Mariagrace Welsh, ASP Home Stage Home, Lincroft, New Jersey*

23. The property was very formally decorated as the Sellers entertained a great deal. It was difficult to appreciate the space for all of the silver, china, rugs, furniture, and collections from their world travels. Once those items were packed away and the Seller had an estate sale, the rooms opened up and the buyers were amazed how spacious the rooms were. The Seller had been very reluctant about my 5 pages of suggestions, but completed every item, even painting the front door red. The only regret from the Seller was that they didn't *Stage* the property sooner. *Staging sells!* —*Kay Dixon ASP Realtor, ABR, CRS, GRI, Saint Charles, Missouri*

24. An investor owned and renovated this 80 year old home, but it had no color or furniture. We added color and spice to all the baths and then placed small vignettes in 3 of the rooms. The house then took on a personality that the potential buyers could see how to use all the extra rooms.

25. This is also another one where the agent wanted to see if Staging really worked as she had never used a Stager. She and the homeowner were "Blown Away." The home sold immediately.

26. This was the first time this agent ever used a Stager and she wanted to see if it really worked. They got a contract at the first showing. The agent said it would still be sitting on the market if not for the Staging.

27. Eight homes were on the market within 2 blocks of this home. All eight homes were listed with a real estate firm. Our home was for sale by owner. When we de-Staged after selling, all 8 of the real estate homes were still on the market listed at a reduced price.

28. With a minimal investment these cooperative and motivated Sellers were able to reap the benefits of ASP Home Staging by getting a full price offer in 14 days! Staging *does* work even in a confusing market! —*Kristen Coppa*

29. *Way* overpriced. Backed up on very busy road & had bad driveway. This investor did it the *right* way. Brought me in to pick colors, then did the rehab, then Staged, then priced right and *poof*—sold in 20 days!!

30. Under contract four hours after Staging was completed. Our statistics for Houston Home Staging this year: 24 houses, Staged 12, received bids within one week 5, received multiple bids 4. Had been on the market for 90 days or more before the Staging, and received contracts or offers immediately after the Staging!!!

31. This house was immaculate and needed little. However it had been viewed by over 45 possible buyers, with not one bid. I re-arranged furniture, and brought in 3 items. The next day two buyers viewed the home and both put in bids. The contract was signed in less than a week. It was a win-win for all. The Realtor hired me because she listened to the potential buyer complaints. She knows her business, her customers and she loves "the Magic" (as she says) I can perform. —*Susan Martin, ASP, Rhode Island*

32. My Realtor said that our home was fine and did not need Staging. But we know it can't be fine. . . . We had no difficulty embracing your ideas, even though some of them were not our taste or our choice, but we immediately understood the benefit of your suggestions. As you know our collaboration was a great success. We sold our house after only three days on the market and we were offered full asking price. Without a doubt, this success was a result of your input (our hard work) and we credit you and the home-Staging with the wonderful outcome. —*Home owner's comment submitted by Brit Brown, ASP, IAHSP, Chester, New Jersey*

33. There is no way anyone could convince me that the money I spent on your fee (and the painting and cleaning) isn't coming back to me

double in the price I got in this terrible market . . . and so quickly—
8 days after listing! Wow! —*Home owner's comment submitted by Brit
Brown, ASP, IAHSP, Chester, New Jersey*

34. The clients implemented the recommendations to the letter. The Realtor paid for the Detailed Written Report. She was very happy.

35. The home owners were very easy to work with. They painted and hired an electrician to update the lighting and get rid of the 70's feel.

36. This home went into contract before I even finished Staging! The buyers had been to see the house on a previous occasion, but they had been confused by a few of the rooms. This time they saw the rooms with furniture and everything made more sense to them. They signed a contract the next day before I had finished accessorizing the house.

37. I love this one! This house had been on the market for 5 months vacant. The homeowners called me from Las Vegas where they had moved. I Staged it and it got an offer the day after Staging! —*Kelly Townsend, ASP, IAHSP, Santa Rosa, California*

38. This house had been on the market vacant for at least 3 months. We Staged it and got it sold in 6 days! —*Kelly Townsend, ASP, IAHSP, Santa Rosa, California*

39. Here's the owner's email reply as I received a call from the buyer to buy some of the Staging pieces she liked so much. Please note all the specifics she is stating which say so much for Staging. The email reply: "Yes, she mentioned I did get a fair price $303K with me giving $10K in closing help. That's more than next door is getting $295K plus at least $10K in closing help (and that's a 3 BR) . . . wanted you to know the value your work brought to the sale. Also, I like a consult with you on my new house. Also, I gave your card to my girlfriend in my community since she also wants color and accessory help with her townhouse. Thanks a ton!" —*Deborah Harshman, ASP, ASPM, IAHSP, Deborah Decor Home Staging, Potomac, Maryland*

40. There were 6 homes on the market in this immediate area at or during the time in which we listed. This pocket has experienced a significant slow down in the past 6 months. Ours was the only one that sold. Two of them pulled out of the market and decided to rent, and three are still sitting on the market after 60 days or more. We Staged every room and the front and back yard. The other homes either weren't Staged or did a minimal job in the kitchen and living room.

41. This is from the agent who hired us to Stage the property for her. "Hi Barb. The home was on the market for 24 days (I had it Staged

before anyone could see it). It cost me $1979 for furniture and $520 for accessories which I paid for myself. Even though I only made a small commission on this deal I still took the listing and owed it to my client to do the right thing and sell their house. I knew Staging by you and Andrea would sell it faster. The home listed for $310,000 and sold quickly for $300,000. Besides Staging, a Seller absolutely *must* listen to their agent and price their house right . . . price and Staging are everything. The lower the price the faster the sale . . . and yes there are still buyers out there.

42. After reading Barb's books I Staged my home and received $110,000 over the asking price. The house sold the first day on the broker's open but since we advertised for two open houses the following weekend we kept the house Staged and received 6 offers by Monday. I was hooked on Staging! I knew when I moved to Oregon that I would look into Staging as my new profession and the only way I would do it was through Barb's courses and earning my ASP designation. Thanks Barb! —*Kate Jahnson, ASP, West Linn, Oregon*

43. Homeowners knew the value of Staging, wanted a quick sale and did agree to do all of the Staging presented in the consultation. Home was under contract in 14 days from date of listing. —*Staged Advantage by Karen McKinnon, ASP, Ponte Vedra, Florida*

44. This home was on the market at least 9 months. Once it was Staged, it sold in the 2nd month and closed escrow in 93 days. —*Dan and Karen Keating, ASP and ASPM, Long Beach, California*

45. Our market for un-Staged Homes is *slow* . . . however proving again Staging sells faster. It had two offers in 28 days . . . the highest bidder *won*! This property is listed on my "Staged Properties." I am going to make an *effort* to log all my *sold* Staged properties here!!!! —*Monica L. Obershaw, ASPM, Indianapolis, Indiana*

46. Second house Staged for same owner with third house (Staging to live) in a 4 month period due to success of Staging.

47. The property sold, due to Staging—even with a roof condition that had to be replaced before closing.

48. Most important—23 homes for sale in this neighborhood—this Staged Property/home was the first to sell of the 23 homes for sale!

49. This house was a mess after the occupants moved out. With very busy lives and 5 kids and 2 dogs, the Sellers did not really maintain the house that well. After a full week of Staging and contractor work, the house was gorgeous! I wanted it to be in the market longer

so I can talk more about how Staging helped this home but after one day we got a full price offer! —*Carina Slepian, PMP, AMR, Realtor, Vienna, Virginia*

50. My client had a country home with a lot of old country style furniture that needed a splash of new energy. After Staging, the house looked beautiful and very attractive to a wider audience of buyers. Staging is key to successful marketing! —*Carina Slepian, PMP, ABR, Weichert Realtors, Ashburn, Virginia*

51. Staging really works and creates a visual manipulation of space that is appealing to the buyer.

52. The owner was very resistant to packing or changing anything, but with gentle comments that they were moving! and loving care of their cherished collections, they agreed to Stage their home. With a growing family and no room to spare, I had to convince them to get a storage unit to store their extra items. The realtor paid the ASP fee up front, but will recoup his costs at settlement. Everyone is thrilled with the outcome! A sold listing! As a new ASP, this was so rewarding to watch this process. —*Debbie Franchek, ASP, IAHSP, Fairbanks, Alaska*

53. Lassen Place had been on the market almost a full year. It was run-down, overpriced, dirty inside, and vacant. The homeowner lived out of the area and was relying on her agent to market and take care of the house. After no movement the homeowner decided to consult a Stager. She contacted a furniture company to bid rental furniture and bid Staging too. The agent saw the price for the rental and Staging and urged the homeowner not to do it. He said the house didn't need it. At that point, the furniture rep and I (we work closely together) decided we should let the homeowner know how bad the house looked because the agent wasn't representing her in the best way possible. He was taking money from her every month to keep the yard and pool maintained and it was a *mess*. The homeowner fired the agent and asked us to refer a Real Estate Agent. We gladly sent her an agent who has all of her listings Staged. We all worked as a team and found a gardener, pool guy, and house cleaners. We pulled that house together, furnished it, accessorized it and Staged it. It looked *great*! It was on the market 11 days before a full price offer came in and was accepted. The agent we referred double ended the deal. Needless to say, the client was happy, the agent was elated, and we were proud of the job we did for the homeowner! —*Barbara Doty, ASPM, Staged To Move, www.Stagedtomove.com, Sacramento, California*

54. This house was a remodel and in a marginal neighborhood. The Staging helped a dated house feel "new" again—and refreshed the feel of the house so it did appeal to buyers. Average days on market for this house are 80–100 for that price range and location. —*Jennie Norris, ASPM, IAHSP, We Stage, Sacramento–Roseville, California*

55. We used what the Seller had in her house—moving things around to best feature the house—and brought in only one room of furniture in an empty living room. The days on market for this region are over 100—so to get an offer right away in this declining market is fabulous! —*Jennie Norris, ASPM, IAHSP, We Stage, Sacramento–Roseville, California*

56. This house was listed with 5 other houses with similar floor plans for sale in the neighborhood. The ASP Realtor had 2 other for sale—and had not used a partner ASP Stager to help with the others. This is the one that got the offer because of how it was presented. The average days on market for our region are over 100 for this price and type of house. To get an offer in only 8 days was wonderful and a true testament to the power of Staging. —*Jennie Norris, ASPM, IAHSP, We Stage, Sacramento–Roseville, California*

57. This house was built in 1890s and did not have a bathroom on the main floor. The closets were very tiny and no master bath or closet. Some of the rooms had wallpaper that was not removed. A few challenges to get over, however the agent and the client raved about our Staging.

58. My sellers cleaned this home and completely emptied it. I brought in my collection of Staging materials (light-weight furniture, plush towels, decor, etc.). It was an investment of about 2 hours of my time to set up this home. It is 2 hours well invested when I am able to get my listings under agreement in a month or less.

59. This was a series of 6, brand-new manufactured homes, side by side, in a depressed desert area (Desert Hot Springs, CA). The lender (who had foreclosed on the builder) hired me to fully furnish and Stage one unit—to represent the model. The project, including my design, construction and installation of all drapery/window treatments, furnishings, accessories and appliances, took approximately four weeks. I enjoyed the process, including the delivery logistics and actual design. The lender's Realtor increased the listing price by $9000, taking new pictures and marketing the properties more aggressively. Buyer interest increased but parties who presented offers were each constrained

by finance/credit limitations. Because of lender's financial risk on these properties and the current market, they cancelled the listings at the end of September (2007) and have decided to lease these properties; this to derive some income while they wait out the market. Currently under negotiation: the inventory—which could come back to me at a reduced price! ultimately benefiting my Staging business. —*Carolyn Desmond, ASP, Desmond Designs, Palm Springs, California*

60. This home was Staged before photos were taken for the MLS. When the photos hit the MLS they had calls for showings every single day that it was on the market. It sold in 30 days; the average for our metro area is 71 days on market. It also sold for more than the average price of similar sold homes in the neighborhood, and $10,000 more than the realtor expected it to fetch. —*Kristin Gilbertson, ASP, Minneapolis, Minnesota*

61. This home sold in 23 days with the average being 37 days in this area. —*Patricia Love, Realtor, Associate Broker, ASP, IAHSP, CRS, and ASP, Bellevue, Washington*

62. This Victorian Home had been lived in for the past 20 years by the same owner. I started working with the Sellers 6 months before they put the home on the market to have them get all the clutter out and paint the rooms. We Staged the home and kept it true to the period, however, that did not mean cluttered! The first buyer to walk through purchased the home for full price! —*Deborah Pawloski, ASP Stager/Realtor, Caledonia, Michigan*

63. This was riverfront property that was in need of a facelift so buyers could envision themselves living there. The buyer that purchased the property was very excited instead of the comments pre-Staging which were always that it was too much work! —*Deborah Pawloski, ASP Stager/Realtor, Caledonia, Michigan*

64. The homeowner had lived there with her parents for over 50 years. Her parents had died. So I guided her over a 2–3 month period. I am an ASP Stager and also I practice Real Estate too. I provide a Staging consultation with all my new listings. Most of what was done was to remove as much as possible. I think two dumpsters were filled up. In the end the house was simplified. The new homeowners were going to redo the house. But the fact everything was simplified made all the difference. The house had an offer in 23 Days. Everyone was happy. Staging works!

65. Market is sluggish in this area, and this home sold quickly while all the others of same style (several) are still sitting . . . they were not Staged.

66. The Realtor told me he had 3 offers at the open house which was held 1 week after my Staging.

67. Who says the Real Estate market is slow? Not when you have the house Staged. This was the first listing for the agent to have Staged and the homeowner. Needless to say they are both believers in Staging. The listing agent said that when she had the Realtors tour that she only got great reviews, *no* Negatives or Suggestions! The home owners were the best to work with, everything I suggested for them to do exterior and interior, it was done. It was a great experience for all of us.

68. Using only $100 in our Staged training, this house shows 100% better. Homeowner was happy with the results and more people are viewing it. —*Debby Hosgston, ASP, Roanoke, Virginia*

69. This was the first time I combined some of the client's available furniture pieces with mine to Stage. It was a good move—provided for lots of good will for me.

70. This was a very nice house but had a lot of clutter; we removed half of the furniture and set it up to flow with each room. It made the house look bigger and showed off the three fireplaces it had, etc.

71. The homeowner needed to move the house that had been on the market for 30 days (slow market right now). I provided a consultation for this homeowner and was very impressed with how much they jumped on board and got done! I came in and helped with furniture placement and a few little details. That was on a Thursday. By the weekend they had 2 offers and one was accepted!

72. This was my first home I Staged after going to classes. I am so excited. I have also done another home and it is currently under contract at list price also in 6 days.

73. This home was Staged, listed the following day, then received four contracts over Memorial Day weekend, and was under ratified contract by the 6th listing day. Staging a vacant home makes an incredible difference. We were under contract before the sign was even in the dirt, and did not even have time to hold our first open house. —*Shae Leighland, ASP, Washington, D.C. and Northern Virginia*

74. This single family home was vacant before being Staged. After Staging, you can really see how lovely and warm this home really is. Hopefully the potential buyers coming to the Open House will feel the same way! —*Tammi Stanton, ASP Realtor, Glenolden, Pennsylvania*

75. This owner was desperate to sell after the listing expired. He contacted us as a last resort. I guaranteed that his unit would look its best after I Staged it, but couldn't guarantee the sale of it. To my surprise, he

contacted me 3 weeks later to tell me that my "Staging did the trick" and that he wanted me to de-Stage it in a few weeks. We were able to get this property Staged, sold, and de-Staged in about a month! *—Erica Ishijima, ASP, Staging Touches, Inc., Los Angeles, California*

76. Homeowners overpriced home in spite of advice from ASP. Once they dropped price, home sold in 1 day.

77. Average days on market in the area was over 90 days. My friend in NY asked if I would come up and Stage her house. It was on the market almost 2 months and even though it was below market price, people would walk in and just walk out. I spent 4 days with her and her husband, moving furniture, clearing out closets, the basement and the garage, and cleaning, cleaning, cleaning until the place sparkled. We brought in a landscaper to clear out the property. And hired a handyman to power wash the house (vinyl siding), patio, front porch, and fix all the little things that needed fixing. That weekend, people walked in and stayed to look around. One couple came back 3 times, put in an offer and my friends accepted it. They closed on the house last week. *—Audrey Byllott, Celebration, Florida*

78. This was a single family home that had been in the family for generations. After speaking with the family they decided that they wanted me to Stage three rooms. There were some pieces of furniture left, so we used what was available and brought in some accessories. It turned out great! *—Sherri Boughman, ASP, Clarks Summit, Pennsylvania*

79. The homeowner was a saver, everything from magazines, office supplies, dead plants, clothing, etc. . . . After convincing her to "let go," she did. We helped her with a garage sale where she made over $1000 on her "treasures" and used that money to pay for her Staging.

80. This was a beautiful Victorian home that had been lived in for 20 years by the owners. It had a great deal to be gotten rid of, painting to be done, and carpets to be removed to reveal the hardwood floors. Then I could go in a Stage the property. The Seller had kept the things I told her in the preliminary appointment and we could then arrange and Stage what furniture was left. I brought in a number of things from my personal inventory to round out the look. The first couple through the home purchased it for full price in this market!

81. This was my first time giving a price to Stage a front yard so I underbid myself quite a bit. It turned out quite beautifully, just the way I envisioned it would. It gave the house the curb appeal it needed to attract potential buyers and attract buyers it did. It actually attracted several potential buyers within days of the Staging and they signed a

contract on the house 24 days later. —*Dawn Brigman, Star Quality Staging, LLC, Baltimore, Maryland*

82. I had Staged this property last year and was able to rent it out within 30 days. This year, when the real estate market got much more challenging, I was able to sell this property within 45 days, while other competing condos have been on the market for months. —*Sylvia Smith, ASP, Miami, Florida*

83. This home sold in one day, before sign was up. Full price offer! In the worst real estate market in the nation! Buyer was actually one of my new Staging clients, who saw our work in the fall of last year at a property we Staged. (Just next door to property ultimately purchased.) First time ever our work made a complete triangle!

84. Just as we learned in the training course, the house must be priced right to sell. In a down market, prices drop quite a bit. The home still sold at a higher rate than other homes on the street. They are all in foreclosure.

85. Hi all, Another very simple fix of Staging that sold a home! I took this property listing after it had been on the market almost a year. Taking the listing was contingent upon my Sellers' agreeing to Stage the home. I knew exactly why this home had not sold. It was an entirely blue exterior. I had my clients paint the house and shutters in buyer friendly colors. We added some beautiful potted flowers to the front step and a wicker chair. I minimally Staged the interior since it was vacant. It was under contract within 3 weeks for full asking price, which was more than it had been previously listed for, and closed. Staging does work!! And works extremely well. —*Lynne Pendlebury, Re/Max Realtor and ASP, Denver, Colorado*

86. Her neighbor's houses have been sitting on the market for months, not sold. People's comments as they viewed the house were how it looked like "those shows on TV that sell houses." Said it looked great.

87. The Sellers asked not to have some of the work I requested to be done (asphalting a long drive and 3 car pad) which accounts for the price being a bit lower. Every showing we had after the Staging had an offer, we ended up with multiple offers on this occasion. —*Jenny Scott, ASP Realtor, Oswego, New York*

88. In the present real estate market, the only way a home is sold is looking great and right pricing. I have gone to other realtors asking them if they have listings on the market for a long time; consider a Staging consultation instead of another price reduction. Sometimes, as little as $2500 can make a huge difference in whether a home sells or not. This

is exactly what happened in Garwood, NJ. The smaller 3 BR home was renovated and vacant. When I was called to consult for a possible Staging job, the first thing I realized was that you walked right into the living room. And all you saw was the fireplace in the middle of the room. Prospective buyers were not going to be able to figure out where to place furniture and this could be a *big* turnoff in getting this home sold. I was given the job by the Seller. At first he did not want me to make any holes in the new walls, so I was limited to furniture and accessories only. But the home did need some pictures etc. I Staged the kitchen, LR and DR with rented furniture and my accessories, and both bathrooms. When the owners saw it they were so happy but commented that the walls looked bare. They then agreed to allow me to Stage the walls. After I was finished, the home had an offer in seven days.

89. House sold to first buyer through the home on the morning after Staging! Well over asking price!

90. This was my first big project as an Accredited Staging Pro. I have been a designer for many years. I became a realtor as an adjunct to my Staging business. I do love making happy homes! I must say that SW Washington Realtors are reluctant to have their listings Staged, but I am showing them what a difference it makes. Thank you, Kelly.

91. This home was all white walls with no color anywhere. I did no painting but brought a lot of colored accessories. Got a contract on it 2 weeks after I listed it. —*Gloria Edgerly, ASP, Dickinson, Texas*

92. This was a family home where the mom could no longer care for herself. The siblings were so excited over the new photos after Staging that everybody wants copies! A daughter said that the house has never looked better! This was a house that had been on the market with another Realtor in 2006 for 180 days and was shown vacant and some thought they "knew" what the house looked like. Fortunately for me, my buyer thought differently. I am the listing Realtor and I brought the buyer to the Seller. The Staging business works!

93. This home is a high-end property for this community. In our current market the average time on the market for homes in this price range at the time of listing was 117 days. I Staged this home and held a broker's caravan the next day. By the third day we had 3 offers on the property. It was well priced—not under market. After the property went into escrow several agents with listings in the same price range called me to ask what I did to sell the house so quickly! I know that the Staging

is what made the difference. —*Dawna Thibodeau, ASP Realtor, La Crescenta, California*

94. The realtor realized the home was beautiful, but lacked color and punch. With 9 houses in the over $300,000 price range within a few blocks of this home, she recognized something must be done to get this house sold fast. A home priced over $300,000 is in the upper level of homes in our area. We went in, rearranged the owner's pieces, placing some in different rooms. We also brought in accessories, drapery and a few pieces of furniture. There were two offers within two days, and a finished sale 17 days after Staging. I had marketed with this realtor for over a year, she is now a true believer! —*Vicki Fredrikson, Staging Innovations, Fargo, North Dakota*

95. Home owners were preparing to do extensive work to modernize the kitchen in the main house to help sell this property. This would have been a sizable investment. I assured them that with just a small amount of Staging to allow the homeowner to visualize cooking in this room, it would not require any investment. One other key element was the huge porch over looking the mountains. I put a small set of furniture that would allow potential buyers time to "sit and enjoy the view" for a few moments while looking at the home and suggested that they actually suggest the people "sit" for a few moments during the showing. It worked!!

96. Please note that this house sold in a market that is extremely slow!! There are 75 other homes in the same subdivision for sale and a few in foreclosures. The homeowner accepted a low offer because the homes in this subdivision are not moving. She called me and said, "It sold because of the Staging you did . . . I don't know that it would have sold without Staging it." —*Lori Swanson, ASP, IAHSP, DeVine Home Staging & ReDesign, Eagle, Idaho*

97. This home was on the market for 90 days with no offers, at the insistence of the homeowner I was contacted to Stage the property. It sold two days after Staging, what does that tell you about the importance of Staging?! —*Chris Balch, ASP, IAHSP, St. Louis*

98. This was a house that had been flipped and completely updated. When I was hired, house interior had already been painted a really wretched color; appeared to be dark peach in the artificial light and bright yellow in the daylight. In retrospect, I wish I had mentioned the color choice. The house would have sold *much* quicker with a more Tuscan look. Even now, the owner says they had lots of negative feedback on

the interior color. In other houses, I have always chosen the paint colors as part of my service.

99. This home was on the market for 49 days. The Realtor was about to lose the listing to the homeowner's friend. He was smart and found me listed with the Maumelle Chamber of Commerce. I worked with him. The homeowner was happy. He had used an ASP and allowed him to keep the listing. I Staged it on a Saturday and they had an open house Sunday. They had two offers, the 1st week it was Staged and the second offer they accepted after being Staged for 14 days. The agent and I were both very happy, but the homeowner even more.

100. The home owner also invested in landscaping, professional cleaners for the interior and windows, and fresh paint for all the rooms. It probably cost them $6000 total with the Staging included, and it was well worth it, as the house was only on the market for 6 days! —*Jane Hagy, ASP, Wayne, Pennsylvania*

101. Cari and Dawna, the "*wow*" factor girls, Staged this home! Pictures are currently on Barb's website in the before and after section.

102. First showing, first buyer, put a contract on the property. The Realtor said, "Bobbi, Thanks for all your help in Staging my client's Streeterville studio downtown. I was sure everyone who walked in was going to want to buy it but as it turns out, we didn't get to find out! The first person through the door made an offer and my client was thrilled with you and you made me look great too, thanks, Bobbi!" Staging works! —*Bobbi Williams, ASP, Chicago, Illinois*

103. I simply used what the client already had available, bringing in only a few things such as pillows, candles and throws. —*Brenda Gonzalez, Realtor, ASP, Lake Havasu City, Arizona*

104. After taking the ASP Course, I Staged this vacant house I had listed for over 7 months. I had literally just put up the last picture at an open house I was holding and a young couple came in and asked me to write an offer right then! We closed escrow in 22 days!

105. This townhouse was new construction and had only been owned for 1½ years and although the development was now completed, the builder had sold the last few properties over the last 6–10 months at "fire sale" prices, making it very difficult to get comps supporting even the purchase price on this unit. However, because the owner of this townhouse had, shortly after purchasing it, upgraded the lighting fixtures and installed updated cabinetry hardware, custom window treatments and designer paint, *and* because the unit was literally "Q-Tip" clean, the appraiser said all of that added value. He even included

interior pictures in the appraisal! It appraised out and closed 3 weeks after the purchase agreement was signed. What a tribute to Staging!! And let's not forget, this townhouse was priced right. As a footnote, there were several other townhouses on the market in the same development at the time and they are still for sale as I write this 3 months later, plus 4 more went on the market after this townhouse sold and they are also still for sale. —*Carolyn Sommers, ASP, IAHSP, Hastings, Minnesota*

106. This home was being lived in by a couple in their 40's that had never had children. The home was like a museum of glass figurines and antique furniture. In just 3 hours time before the Open House my partner and I had wrapped and packed away most of the figurines, relocated furniture, and changed the two extra bedrooms into children's rooms. The Realtor who had come to run the Open House had never heard of Staging and was annoyed and skeptical of our presence. She loudly informed our client that her home showed beautifully and she did not feel what we were doing was necessary. Considering that the homeowners had already lowered their asking price twice and had been told that they should do so again if they did not get any bites at this Open House I felt as though the client had every reason to want to do whatever they could to increase their chance of selling their home. As we drove out of the driveway at 5 minutes until the Open House was to begin we couldn't help but to laugh at the expression that had been on the Realtor's face when she saw our completed Stage. Long story short, she asked for our business cards and the house had a contract within 12 days from a family that came to the Open House. It sold for a little less than the asking price but my client was thrilled nonetheless that they had finally gotten a bite and sold the house! —*Stephanie Boyle, ASP, San Antonio, Texas*

107. This house had atrocious colors. Painted the entire house a new rich gold (which sells in Dallas), added furniture and accessories and it *sold*!

108. This was a flipped house. House had gray walls, beige carpet, pale hardwood floors . . . all colors which normally do *not* sell in the Dallas/Ft. Worth area. Overcame this with a lot of black, chocolate brown bedding and red furniture. Truly it was stunning when we finished.

109. This home had two offers within 5 days to the first two Buyers who came through.

110. Long listing but—because of Staging—received $46,000 more than last condo sold for in the same area.

111. This home had been listed for 192 days prior to Staging by a Realtor who had priced it $25,000 too high for the neighborhood. The home owner is building a new home with a builder who has partnered with us to offer Staging as an incentive to buyers. The homeowner followed all of our recommendations, listed the home with a new Realtor at the appropriate price, and the home sold 9 days later! What a relief to the homeowner and proof once again that Staging works! —*Paige Baione, ASP, Dover, Delaware*

112. This was my first Staged home. It was very positive. It gave me a chance to create my very own "before and after" pictures, which I feel like have been instrumental in getting my next 4 Staging jobs!! I am loving every minute of the opportunity to be creative and do one of my passions! —*Deanna Gentleman, ASP, Murrells Inlet, South Carolina*

113. The homeowner was very aware of how the market had slowed down. She knew that she had to do everything in her power to stand out against the competition and to price the home right. She called me to preview the property and an appointment was set up. She had a few pieces of furniture, but had basically moved out most of her personal belongings. After looking at what I had to work with I was confident that I could make this home look great! With a few accessories, table settings, plants, art work, toss pillows, bedding and lamps I was able to turn the interior into something that any potential buyer would be proud to call home. I asked the homeowner if I could leave my fliers and cards out to promote my business and she was receptive. After the Staging she called and left me such a great message. She said this house has never looked so good and would like me to "Stage to live" her new home. For me the best part of the job is getting the wonderful comments and appreciation from the clients. It makes it all worthwhile! Thank You. —*Kelly Holland, Staged with Style, ASP, Yorba Linda, California*

114. I Staged this home on a Friday. Realtor had an Open House on Sunday and they got an offer that day! Got another job from homeowner that day as he is an investor. —*Gail Alexander, ASP, Snohomish, Washington*

115. This is a group of 20 new homes. A model had been previously been Staged by someone in the Realtor's office. Not one of the homes sold in 9 months. The Realtor called me to Stage from a referral in his office and they sold 5 homes in the first week! All the homes were sold by June 1st but one. —*Gail Alexander, ASP, Snohomish, Washington*

116. This home had been seen by the buyers before it was Staged and they didn't like it. When their Realtor took them to the home after it was Staged they immediately fell in love with it and submitted a full price offer and waived the inspection. Sale closed in 15 days! —*Gail Alexander, ASP, Snohomish, Washington*

117. This house was sitting vacant and unsold for months. The REALTOR shared about Home Staging with the Seller and they decided to have the house Staged. The house was located in a marginal neighborhood with lesser quality houses at the entrance to the neighborhood—and nicer ones closer to the house for sale. This house sold 3 times before a buyer finally was able to see the entire financial transaction through to the end. Over all, the house sold 3 [times] faster than when it was vacant—and is in a declining market. Staging helped bring a buyer—and the Seller is very happy with the results. —*Jennie Norris, ASPM, IAHSP, We Stage, Sacramento–Roseville, California*

118. This house was very bland before ASP Staging. The homeowner had to declutter but had little in the way of color and decor to help at the "*wow*" factor. Our ASP Staging worked magic in the house as we combined some of our inventory with what the Seller already had. The house was listed for sale, and within 1 day had multiple offers coming in. This is virtually unheard of in our current market where prices of houses are going down 1% per month, and the market has been in a decline for nearly 2 years. The REALTOR was so excited and all the Realtors that toured the house during an office tour commented on the Staging—and how it played a *key factor* in the presentation of the house. Most of all, the *sellers* are very excited to move to their new home. —*Jennie Norris, ASPM, IAHSP, and Diane Cahill, ASP, Sacramento–Roseville, California*

119. This homeowner had a Staging consultation. He listened very carefully, asked lots of questions, then went to work on the undecorating, decluttering, and a little furniture rearranging. He laughed when I told him opening up the Living Room curtains would earn him at least $500. He finished his list of "homework" and then had the open house June 16th. His ERA-Richmond Realtors, Linda Peters & Leslie Berger, knew I had been there and had been talking about and promoting the house to a number of people—but not showing it. Eleven couples showed up for the open house. One offer came in that night and two more in the next two days. It sold in 3 days. The owner worked hard, but it paid off. Staging consultation on June 4th. Moved out

and closed by July 6th. "Staging—It's Positively ConSTAGEious!"
—*Tracy Susick, ASP, Room Works, Meadville, Pennsylvania*

120. The home had been on the market with the previous owner's dated furnishings. It sold at an open house two days after we Staged it. —*Ann Waters, ASP, Naples, Florida*

121. My clients are very good friends of mine & they have 3 very rambunctious boys under 8 yrs old, and were planning on living in the home until the day it closed and keys were handed over to the buyers! Basically, I had a challenge! Not only to Stage a home that had a lot of *stuff*, but also to be able to keep the stuff out & the house & light colored carpet clean & keep the house Staged, especially during showings, when I was not around. The best part about this challenge is that I had Motivated Sellers, ready & willing to do what it took to get the house sold! The day before the house went on the market, they were leaving for a week, a perfect opportunity for me to have the carpets cleaned & the house Staged! So, I was prepared. I gave them a list & a week prior to them leaving & the house going on the market, I went on-line to ASPBOXES.COM & ordered a wide variety of boxes for them & had them shipped to their front door, so that they could begin the daunting task of de-cluttering, packing, & dumping what they didn't need & give me a clean slate (house) to work from the next week. Guess what? It worked, they did it! They de-cluttered & I Staged, and it worked! From photos to open house presentations, the house showed so well, it sold on the second day from someone who came through the open house with their agent! The house also appraised at selling value, even though other homes in the same neighborhood had been on the market for 60 days or more w/no sales in the past 3 mos. It sold in 9 days & closed in 30, God is Good!

122. This house was ASP Staged and listed on the MLS by the ASP Realtor. The *same* floor-plan house was for sale up the street—sitting on the market for over 4 months and still no offers. The house I Staged got an offer in 2 weeks of being Staged and listed—while this other house continues to sit. The Staging helped attract the buyer who was eager to make an offer—even in our slowing market. The ASP Realtor has the sign-rider hanging from this sign and is featuring the fact that the house is ASP Staged as a key marketing tool! —*Jennie Norris, ASPM, IAHSP, We Stage, Sacramento–Roseville, California*

123. There were two homes on this street for sale at the same time. One home—Not Staged—went on the market in February and is still on the market as of July after several price reductions. This neighboring

home was Staged first, went on the market in June and went under contract after 42 days. —*Debra Wallace, ASP, Portland, Maine*

124. I sold the home to these clients 9 years ago. The only updates were a new roof and some new windows. Everything was original (1986). We brought in rugs, artwork, lamps, and accessories, and made it look fresh and inviting. I held an Open House the day after we Staged it and the next day I sold it to the first couple that came through the Open House. I had listed the property for $599,000 knowing that it should be listed for $549,000 but it sold before I could reduce the price. —*Betty Cunningham ASP, Realtor Schaumburg, Illinois*

125. This home sat on the market for 8 months. I Staged it on a Monday, the first showing thereafter was the following Saturday. That couple bought the house! —*Lara Hoey, ASP, This Staged House, Fairfield, Connecticut*

126. As with most of my Sellers, after I take the listing I give them 2 weeks to do "their" Staging homework based on my room by room recommendations. In this Seller's case, they painted rooms, cleaned carpets, landscaped w/mulch-flowers-pruning, removed furniture, added room fresheners, bought Staging bathroom towels, area rugs. 2 days before we go on the market, I come by and "tweak" the home by meeting with the Seller and doing last-minute adjustments such as rearranging furniture, adding fresh/natural flower arrangements, plug in deodorizers (I only use apple cinnamon) etc. At this point, I do my virtual tour and photos for the multiple listing service. I believe in the value of having the client involved in the "Staging" process. They have a vested interest and often it is fun for them to learn all the techniques I have taught them while I am working on their house—they can move on to their new home and see it with their new "Staging" eyes. Also, all the realtors in the area know our homes are the best (and they make appointments to show them because of it!). They know our Sellers have been coached about the value of Staging and these homes will stand out above the rest in the marketplace.

127. This home was Staged and sold during January in Connecticut, which is traditionally one of the slowest sales months. The Realtor and homeowners were both concerned about the property, as it had some quirky features and was not a "traditional" Connecticut property. They worried that it wouldn't sell quickly. We updated the powder room with new fixtures, painted several rooms, decluttered, and rearranged quite a bit. The results were fabulous: they received and accepted an offer for full price on the first day.

128. Barie, Well, all of your hard work and advice have really paid off for us. We are closing the [sale] of our house today. The price is just under the list price. We are moving this weekend. The traffic and interest in the house [have] been incredible. We really feel it was due to the Staging effort. Once again thanks for all your hard work. —*Client testimony from Shelly W., home owner, submitted by Barie Pinnell, ASPM, Plano, Texas*

129. This home was purchased in May by a lady who is an Interior Designer. We became friendly neighbors and I had just quit my career of 25 years to do what I love the most! *Staging*! At the end of March she got an offer in another state and she decided to sell, in the beginning I Staged the home with her things! 2 weeks after she had moved to South Carolina and needed her furniture and asked me to please Stage it for her since she was aware of the Value of Staging, especially with 3 other models of her townhouse on the market, and she wanted to be above the average. Now, she is the only townhouse for sale that is Staged! And that makes it above the rest of the competition. That is how got my first Staging job. —*Fernando Rosado, ASP, IAHSP, Palm Beach Gardens, Florida*

130. The [number of] days on the market in our area is presently at 143 days. Our area doesn't see Staged homes very often. The agent remarks during the Agent Tours [were] very positive. Comparable homes are selling for around $185,000. The house was originally a 2 bedroom. I explained to the Seller that by investing $500 and adding a closet he would be selling a 3 bedroom house. The value went up over $10,000 for a $500 investment.

131. This home was on the market for 5 months. After working with the clients and encouraging them to move into their new home, they left me with some of the essentials of Staging and within 9 days it was under contract. Another Staging Success!!! —*Laura Rogers, ASP, Home Staging and Design, Surprise, Arizona*

132. I did a consultation at this home, and then came back with a team of ASPs to Stage just the main floor of the home. The homeowners received an offer after their first showing, which was during the week of Thanksgiving (not the most popular time to buy/sell a house!). —*Michelle Yackel, ASP Stager, Atlanta, Georgia*

133. This was my own home, at the time I was going through a divorce, was diagnosed with cancer and had a 6 year old to care for. In the beginning I thought I would just keep it clean, as I was too tired and ill to do anything else. Well, as time went on and I'm putting my mortgage on my credit cards, after 3mths of nothing, I took charge. (At

this same time am taking the ASP course), took it off the market, got a storage unit, decluttered, painted, added some new plants, worked on my hardwood floors and fixed a few bad tiles. Put it back on the market after one month, *boom!* the first person that walked through the door gave a firm offer! —*Jody Stetson, Sacramento County, Fair Oaks, California*

134. As an ASP realtor I offer to all my clients education on Staging during my listing presentation. I provide them with a free full Staging report, after I've attained the listing and gone throughout the home, that recommend needed changes. Works like a charm! Have not lost a listing presentation yet! Thanks Barb! —*Linda Bull, ASP Realtor, Central Coast, California*

135. This was a flip and fix by the Realtor that was Staged as a vacant house. The house went pending in 21 days–the average days on market for our region are over 150 for this area and this price range. —*Diane Cahill, ASP, IAHSP, We Stage, Sacramento–Roseville, California*

136. This house was dated (80's) with older tile and features. The Seller is an ABC Reporter with our local station, and his wife is the morning news anchor. After we completed our Staging, he said, "You are amazing! The true test for me of Staging success is that I want to move back in!" His wife who had lived in the property prior to their marriage was "stunned." The house received a full-price offer the same day it went on the market when our days on market for our region are at an average of about 120 days. —*Jennie Norris, ASPM, IAHSP, We Stage, Sacramento–Roseville, California*

137. This was my first official Staging job. It looked so great and sold in only 35 days in a slow market. There were 11 other homes for sale in the same sub-division and the buyer's agent said it was the Staging that made them decide on this home over the others. —*Deanna Gentleman, ASP, StagerASP, Murrells Inlet, South Carolina*

138. The Realtor told the homeowners that $380K would be the best price at the market they were in. The McCamy's, the homeowner who had researched Staging on their own, had insisted they could probably get more since they had invested in Staging. They listed it at $397,500 and ended up selling it at $390K—five thousand *over* what the Realtor wanted to originally list at. —*Marcyne Touchton, ASPM, Charlotte, North Carolina*

139. As the owners of this lovely home, Bob & Kathy's goal was to move back to their hometown in Tennessee after Bob retired. With 8 months on the market and no offers, they knew they had to try something

else to get the house sold. Their excitement and appreciation for what I was about to do through Staging was so refreshing and encouraging. I just loved Staging their home because I knew I was appreciated, but the highlight was seeing the transformation of this home and how much Bob & Kathy were enjoying it. I was so happy when I heard the news that the house *sold* in 8 days, after Staging it. They now could return to their hometown and enjoy their new retired lives. —*Margie Gregori, ASPM/IAHSP*

140. This home was 15 years out of date. I helped them choose hardwood flooring for the first floor, tile for the kitchen, and carpeting for the second floor. Most of the kitchen appliances were replaced. They filled a relative's double garage and a storage unit with their extra "stuff." The house went from lovely but needs work to *wow*! —*Janice Ankrett, ASP, Burlington, Vermont*

141. This development has other homes that are not completed and the Seller has been trying to sell these units for over 3 years. This town home was Staged and sold within 9 days. As a result of this Staging, the builder was able to solidify 3 sales after buyers viewed this unit. Due to this town home selling within 9 days, the builder took one look and asked to have his model Staged as he sees the value in Staging and how it can help him to sell his units faster. —*Darbi Comparetto, ASP, IAHSP, Bella Interiors & Staging, LLC, Rogers, Minnesota*

142. This home was in need of updating. After my consult, they painted the kitchen cupboards and replaced the hardware. A mismatched tub in one of the bathrooms was reglazed to match the other fixtures. Several pieces of furniture were stored to enlarge the bedrooms and the living room furniture layout was changed to open up the room. The front door was repainted and the front porch was repaired. The main bathroom was repainted from top to bottom. A computer area built into the front hall closet was removed. The Staged home looked much more up-to-date and flowed beautifully. —*Janice Ankrett, ASP, Burlington, Ontario, Canada*

143. This home had been on the market for almost a year. When the agent took over the listing she called me in right away. The house was on a busy road and was set up to suit the life of a single business woman. The dining room had to be set up as a dining room again. The kitchen eating area needed a table and the resident parrot in a large cage needed his own room. The Yoga room was turned back into a bedroom. The family room furniture was recovered and rearranged. The whole house was decluttered. When the Staging was finished the buyers could

see the many beautiful features of the house. The agent started getting much more positive feedback about the house. It now showed as a family home. —*Janice Ankrett, ASP, Burlington, Ontario, Canada*

144. This Beach Cottage, along the coast of Maine, had been on the market since April and was taken off for the winter at the end of December. When the owner was ready to put it back on the market for the spring we Staged it first and the results were amazing! The property went under contract with the first showing after six days back on the market . . . needless to say the owners were so pleased and felt that the results of the Staging were really what sold the property. —*Debra T. Wallace, ASP, Cumberland, Maine*

145. This property had been on the market for 9 months without a single offer. Within 3 weeks of Staging it . . . *sold*!!! —*Christine Fuscaldo, ASP, Fishers, Indiana*

146. The homeowner was very willing to do what it took to sell his home since it had been on the market for quite some time. After Staging his home, he wrote me saying he couldn't believe how good his home looked. I was thrilled for him that he received an offer soon after it went on the market. —*Patricia Holiver, ASP, Mansfield, Massachusetts*

147. This house was a shambles, so there was extra cost do to the above-and-beyond cleaning. It was impossible to see the beautiful $10K tile floor with trash, gum that had been thrown and left as well as dog, bug and mice droppings. However, the pictures of it when finished says it all. It had offers on the first open house and sold in less the two weeks. *Staging works!* . . . Now the Realtors can't wait to have me Stage more of their listings. *Yeah!* —*Deborah Heise, Eye 4 Design Staging, Roseville, California*

148. We had an investor who asked us to Stage this vacant home and he auctioned it off during an open house the next weekend. He is sold on Staging—the house went pending is less than 2 weeks! —*Kathy Dyer, ASP Stager, Roseville California*

149. In addition to Staging the homeowner had the home painted on the interior, carpet removed and all hardwood floors refinished! Staging made all of the difference as the market was starting to change and other homes were sitting on the market. —*Shannon Howard, Realtor, ASP, Petaluma, California*

150. This was my third Staged property that was sold within a week or days after being Staged. I firmly believe in Staging and I see that it is helping homeowners sell their house not only fast but for more money. —*Monika Wassel, ASP, Richmond Hill, Ontario, Canada*

151. This Beaumont, CA home was one of the first homes that we Staged after receiving our ASP designation. It was on the market for 90 days with *no* activity at all until we Staged the property with small vignettes. With what little inventory we had, some from our personal home and a little creativity, we Staged this home on a Thursday afternoon preparing it for a Saturday open house. The clients had an offer by Sunday evening. Our first proof that this technique really works! —*Michelle and Justine Pimentel, ASPs, Empire Home Staging Solutions, Rancho Cucamonga, California*

152. Property had been on the market unsuccessfully for eight months. Client approached me to Stage the property that same day for a hard-to-get MLS tour scheduled the following day. The client and I worked until 11:00 pm. As a result of a successful MLS tour the property sold eight days later! —*Sheree Ashapa, Total Home Staging & Organizing, Minden, Nevada*

153. This was a "blended" Stage, using both my and the owner's furnishings. He was an absolute pleasure to work with, and was very happy with the results of my Staging. He was especially happy with the outcome! —*Cynthia Seager, ASP, Lake Forest Park, Washington*

154. The vacant house had been completely remodeled and every room was painted a buttery yellow. I had my doubts about the color appealing to buyers but I furnished the living room with earthly colors like moss green and beige. The colors really helped to ground the room. I used burnt reds and greens in the master bedroom. The house sold in 6 days and I was a little sorry to have it sell because I *loved* what I created and really enjoyed going to the house for touchups. —*Karen Negrete, ASP, San Jose, California*

155. I am so jazzed; I was just finishing this job when a realtor with his clients arrived at the door. I let them in myself to look around. I called the listing agent to tell him that people are showing, he said he just entered into MLS; the sign was not even up yet. The next morning was a broker's open, which I was at when 2 more couples stayed for hour looking around. By the afternoon 2 offers came in, the first couple I showed through offered $10,000 more than asking price. Its was so exciting to be in the middle of all the action. I have already been phoned by the wife that is purchasing the home; she wants to buy my Staging props because she loved the feeling of the home when she walked in the front door. I work on this project for 2 weeks; [brought] in painters for the interior of the home, installed window treatment to 4 rooms, made artwork for 3 rooms. Transformed the master bedroom to beautiful romantic get-a-way. —*Suzy Legier, ASPM, Bainbridge, Washington*

BARB'S REAL ESTATE WORDS AND TOOLS THAT WILL WORK FOR YOU!

BARB'S SAYINGS THAT WORK

PRELISTING PHRASES

- "Let me tell you how I work."
- "I work in steps, and I don't go to the next step until the one before it is completed."
- "Should we decide that we will be working together?"
- "I'd really appreciate your taking the time to look at my *Career Book*. There are ideas in it to help you sell your home and lots of ideas about who I am and what I've done in real estate. It will help you get to know me better without my sitting here bragging about myself. I think you'll enjoy it!"
- "You are hiring me to perform a service for you."
- "Ads don't sell houses—Agents do. Ads make the phone ring for the company and make the seller feel good!"
- "If I didn't know of your earnest money presentation and wasn't there when it was presented, it would be like you hired an attorney and he sent you to court alone."

- "Just like the product on the shelf at the store, the purchaser of today buys the best available product, at the best price, in the best wrapper, to meet his or her needs."
- "As soon as we are ready to go to work together as a team . . ."

GETTING THE HOUSE READY TO SELL

- "If we can't see it, we can't sell it!"
- "Start packing because with me working as your Agent [Stager], you will be moving."
- "Would you consider selling a car without touching up the chips, washing and waxing it, vacuuming it for each showing, and fixing any problems?" [Wait for answer.] "Well, do you know that many Sellers on the market have not done that with their own homes? They haven't gotten them ready to sell."
- "Detail your house as you would detail your car."
- "I'm so proud of you . . ."
- "The way you live in your home and the way we market and sell your house are two different things."
- "Buyers and Agents only know what they see, not the way it is going to be."
- "You are earning yourself money by the time and energy you invest getting your home ready to sell."
- "By preparing your home for sale, we will be much farther ahead of our competition."
- "If we can smell it, we can't sell it."
- "The Seven Cs of Staging are clean, clutter free, color, compromise, creativity, communication, and commitment."
- "Appeal to the equity."
- "Clutter eats equity."
- The investment of Staging *in* your home is far less than a price reduction *on* your home!"

PRICING AND SELLING THE HOME

- "This is not the market to come on the market and *just* to see what happens."
- "If you are too high in the price range for your home, other Agents won't show your house, but if you are being shown and are not getting

offers, then the buyers think you are overpriced compared to the competition they are seeing!"
- "What do you think would happen if you overpriced your home?"
- "Location, condition, price, terms, the market, and Home Staging—these are the six main factors that sell homes, and of these price and Home Staging are the most influential—based on the other four."
- "The best time to sell a home is in the first three weeks!"
- "When homes are listed on the market, some are always used to sell others—I don't want us to be the one being used. We can be the user, not the used."
- "Longevity on the market means one thing: reduction in price."
- "Most qualified buyers are working with Agents."

GETTING THE LISTING FOR SIX MONTHS OR LONGER
- "The average selling time in this market has been between the third and sixth months."
- "As a business woman (man) it doesn't make sense for me to list a property for three months based on the above fact."
- "As a team working together we ask certain things of each other. The commitment I ask of you is a six-month listing agreement because of the extra work I will do for you (beyond the average Agent) and the average length of selling lime."

USE THESE PHRASES IN EVERYTHING YOU DO
- "With your permission . . ."
- "Working together as a team, we can . . ."
- "Trust me, . . ."
- "You may not always want to hear the facts I have to share with you, but 1 will always give you *my honest* professional opinion."
- "People sometimes go to the doctor for a diagnosis and then throw away or don't fill the prescription. I will always give you my honest professional opinion, and it is up to you to accept or follow my recommendations."
- "Tell me about that . . ."

BARB'S STORIES THAT WORK

Here are a bunch of stories proving that this method works!

Where Are the Buyers? The Top Agent Story

Question: "Where are the purchasers of today?"
Answer: "Most qualified buyers are working with Agents!"
Question: "Which Agent?"
Answer: "The hard-working, full-time Agents in our area!"
Question: "Well, who are they?"
Answer: "I decided to find out!"

I got on the phone and called every major broker in the area and asked, "Who are the top three Agents in your office?" They gave me their names immediately, and I compiled a list of the top Agents in our area. My idea was to simply drive them crazy (in a nice way) with my listings (and/or Stagings) so that hopefully they would show them first because:

1. My listings/Stagings look good!
2. My listings/Stagings are all priced right!
3. My sales close!

It worked, and this list has helped me sell more of my listings than any other way.

This list has now grown to the top 685 Agents in our area!

The Market Story in Thirds

During my career in real estate I have always felt you could divide the number of homes on the market for sale into thirds. (This is continually born out by statistics available through the Multiple Listing Association.)

If I were to draw a line on this paper, to represent the market, and divide it into thirds, we would *see* the market fall into the following categories:

First third—Never sell: This third will never sell! All of the ingredients of a sale are out of balance because the property is in a poor location and/or the property's condition is bad, it is not Staged, and/or it is grossly overpriced with no terms available, other than cash-out. Until they change one or more of the ingredients, so that they are in balance, these properties will never sell!

Second third—Questionable(?): This third of the market is a real question mark! These are the sellers who insist, "We could get lucky," when discussing the pricing of their home. The ingredients of a sale are out of balance in one way or another, but not quite as dramatically as with the never-sell group. In other words, they may have great condition or be in a super location, but still be overpriced in comparison to what the market will bear.

Third third—Sold! This group is hot! The homes in this third of the market are priced to sell! They are Staged and in super condition, with great locations, and they are priced at or even sometimes below what the other homes (the other two-thirds of the market) are listed at. This is what it takes to sell in today's market, and the closer you are to this one-third of the market, the more money you will sell for and the more quickly you will sell!

The Apple Story

Purchasers of today are very selective about finding the home of their choice. So many homes being on the market for sale today reminds me of going to the store to buy an apple. If there are three apples for sale at the store, you would probably pick up each one, look it over, and select one out of the three apples to buy. This is just what the purchasers in yesterday's real estate markets used to do: buy one home after looking at very few—even as few as three.

But *today's* market is *different*! We don't have three or just a few homes for sale. On the contrary, we have an *overabundance* of homes for sale! So in going to market, purchasers look not at one or two or three homes, but many, many homes, sometimes as many as 50 or more homes, before deciding on one to purchase. Then it's just like when we go to the store to buy an apple and there are not just three apples *but* hundreds of them. We pick up one here, look it over, and put it down and pick up one here, look it over, and put it down, and this goes on and on until we find just the right one: *the perfect apple* out of all the other apples for sale. In the same way, today's purchasers in this market select homes the way they buy apples: only after looking many of them over. We, then, working together as Agent and Seller (or as Stager and Seller), need to make your property the *very* best apple available on the market today in comparison to all the others for sale.

CLOSING A REAL ESTATE TRANSACTION: STEPS TO CLOSE A SALE

After a purchase and sale agreement is finalized by both buyer and seller:

1. The Agent deposits the earnest money in a trust account.
2. The buyer makes loan application at a financial institution of choice, if necessary. The financial institution then:
   a. Orders an appraisal of the property from a certified appraisal company.
   b. Processes the credit report for the purchaser.
   c. Verifies the purchaser's employment.
   d. Verifies the purchaser's bank accounts or other monies necessary to close.
   e. Orders any required inspections and oversees any necessary repairs.
   f. Oversees that all conditions of the purchase and sale agreement are met before closing.
   g. Consolidates all of the preceding documentation into a loan package that is presented to the loan committee for final approval.
   h. When final lender approval is completed, all the necessary information is conveyed to the buyer.
   i. Designates a closing agency.
3. The lender selects a closing agency to coordinate the closing of the sale. The closing agency then:
   a. Orders a preliminary title report.
   b. Oversees and coordinates the solution of any problems revealed in the preliminary title report.
   c. Files documents to clear title of all liens, encumbrances, judgments, clouds on title, or easement questions.
   d. Orders title insurance policy.
   e. Verifies that all work orders are completed and reinspected.
   f. Prorates any rents, taxes, or utilities to the date of closing.
   g. Prepares all documents and closing papers for the buyer and seller to sign.
   h. Arranges for both parties to sign the closing documents.
   i. Files all documents with the local government to close the sale.
   j. Upon closing, disburses funds per the closing instructions.

As your professional Real Estate Agent, I will be working hard on an ongoing basis to ensure that all of these steps take place in a timely manner as we work together toward a closed sale.

STEPS TO MAKE YOUR LOAN APPLICATION EASIER

To speed up the process of making your mortgage loan application, please make sure you have all of the following information. Incomplete information will delay the process and could even delay your purchase. Please compile the following:

1. A copy of the sales contract on the home that you're buying.
2. A check for $_____, payable to the mortgage company for your credit report and/or appraisal fee. When the loan is approved, this is credited toward your closing costs. If for some reason the loan is not approved or the house does not appraise, this money will *not* be refunded to you.
3. Social Security numbers for husband and wife or for all purchasers.
4. Savings account numbers, addresses, and balances. Gift letter for any monies received from relatives to purchase home and placed in checking/savings account. Mutual fund account numbers, addresses, and balances. Serial numbers and face values of any U.S. savings bonds and other stocks.
5. A list of account numbers for all checking, savings, and credit union accounts. Please have the current balance of each account as well as the complete address.
6. Credit card account numbers, balances, and monthly payments.
7. A list of any debts you have. Include the name of the creditor, address, telephone number, account number, the monthly payment, and current balance.
8. A list of assets, including insurance policies (cash value), cars, and furniture (and an estimate of their value).
9. Name(s) and address(s) of employer(s) for the last five years. Latest earnings statement or pay vouchers.
10. If overtime is a substantial part of gross income, provide W-2 forms for the last three years. Commission sales usually require three years' W-2s.
11. If you are self-employed, tax returns for yourself and your business for the last two or three years will be required, plus profit-and-loss statements and balance sheets.
12. If you are getting a Veterans Administration loan, your certificate of eligibility if you have one, or a statement of service or discharge papers if you don't.
13. Name and account number of credit union and balance.
14. If you presently own or have owned a home in the last three years, the name and address of the mortgage company or lending institution, the loan number, and balance.

15. If you are obtaining your equity from the sale of your previous residence, a copy of your closing statement is required.

16. If you are a landlord, bring a copy of your tenant's lease with you to substantiate income derived. (If no lease is available, bring copies of checks, receipts, etc.)

17. Any divorce papers and property settlements where property was involved in a divorce. If alimony or child support is being used as income to qualify for a loan, provide proof of amounts received.

18. If you or your coapplicant is receiving or is obliged to pay alimony, child support, or separate maintenance, bring a copy of your divorce decree and/or agreement.

19. Information on any retirement benefits that you or your company have. Provide addresses and account numbers. Also include all IRA and/or Keogh data.

20. Any bankruptcy judgment papers.

If you need further explanation or have questions about your unique circumstances, please contact me, your Real Estate Agent, or your lender's representative. Being *totally* open and honest about all of your credit history is the best way to help you secure your mortgage in the shortest amount of time.

YOUR PERSONAL MOVING CHECKLIST

SIX WEEKS BEFORE MOVING

- Make an inventory of everything to be moved.
- Collect everything not to be moved for a garage sale or charity.
- Contact charity for date/time of pickup. Save receipts for tax records.
- Contact several moving companies for estimates.
- Select a mover, and arrange for the exact form of payment at the destination (cash, check). Get cartons and packing materials to start packing *now.*
- Contact the insurance agent to transfer or cancel coverage.
- Check with your employer to find out what moving expenses they will pay.

FOUR WEEKS BEFORE MOVING

- Notify all magazines of change of address.
- Check with the veterinarian for pet records and immunizations.
- Contact the utility companies for refunds of deposit; set turnoff dates.
- Dryclean clothes to be moved; pack them in protective wrappers.

- Collect everything you have loaned out; return everything you have borrowed.
- Service power mowers, boats, snowmobiles, etc., that are to be moved. Drain all gas/oil to prevent fire in the moving van.
- Check with doctors and dentists for all family records and prescriptions.
- Get children's school records.
- Check the freezer and plan your use of food over the next two to three weeks.
- Remove all jewelry and other valuables to a safe deposit box or other safe place to prevent loss during the move.
- Give away or arrange for the transportation of house plants (most moving companies will *not* move plants, especially in winter). Plants also can be sold at garage sales or are perfect thank-you gifts for neighbors.

One Week Before Moving

- Transfer or close checking and savings accounts. Arrange for a cashier's check or money order to pay the moving company upon arrival in the new community.
- Have the automobile serviced for the trip.
- Fill out the post office change-of-address forms; give to the postmaster.
- Check and make an inventory of all furniture for dents and scratches; notify the moving company of your inventory and compare it to the furniture on the delivery day.
- Dispose of all combustibles and spray cans. (Spray cans can explode or burn; don't pack them.)
- Pack a separate carton of cleaning utensils and tools (screwdriver, hammer, etc.).
- Separate the cartons and luggage you need for personal and family travel.
- Mark all boxes that you pack with the room they will be going to in the new home.
- Organize at least one room in the house for packers and movers to work freely.
- Cancel all newspapers, garden service, etc.
- Review the entire list to make certain that you haven't overlooked anything.
- Check and double-check everything you have done before it's too late.

Moving Day

- Plan to spend the entire day at the house. You must make last-minute decisions. Don't leave until after the movers have gone.
- Hire a babysitter or send the children to a friend's house for the day.

- Stay with the moving van driver to oversee inventory.
- Tell packers and/or the driver about fragile or precious items.
- Make a final check of the entire house, basement, closets, shelves, attic, garage, and every room.
- Approve and sign the bill of lading. If possible, accompany the driver to the weigh station.
- Double-check with the driver to make certain that moving company records show the proper delivery address for your new house. Verify the scheduled delivery date as well.
- Give the driver your phone numbers both here and in new community (or cell numbers) to contact you in case of a problem.
- Get complete routing information from the driver and phone numbers so that you can call the driver or company in case of emergency while en route.
- Disconnect all utilities and advise the Realtor who sold or is selling your house.
- Lock all the doors and windows. Advise your Realtor and neighbors that the house is empty.

Moving takes a lot of time and energy and can be a stressful experience for some people. Use this list. It will definitely help. There is no substitute for good planning. Plan ahead! Roll with the punches, and things will go more smoothly. Try to relax and enjoy the adventure.

BARB'S TOOLS FOR SUCCESS: BUSINESS TOOLS THAT WORK!

The Staging DVD: "How to Stage Your Home to Sell for Top Dollar!" This 50-minute DVD teaches the proven, best way to Stage Homes to sell for top dollar. It is a *must* for Stagers, Sellers, and Agents.

The Pricing DVD: "How to Price Your Home to Sell for Top Dollar!" A new 20-minute DVD that educates sellers on the importance of pricing their homes correctly from the beginning so that they sell faster and for more money.

Books:

Home Staging: The Winning Way to Sell Your House for More Money (Wiley).

Building a Successful Home Staging Business: Proven Strategies from the Creator of Home Staging (Wiley).

The *Career Book* Marketing System Kit: Includes a binder, CD of divider pages to print, sheet protectors, and a DVD to teach you how to put the *Career Book* together and how to use it to market yourself.

The *Marketing Portfolio* Presentation Book: This is a wonderful tool for you to use in your listing or Staging presentations. It comes with a stand-up style binder, sheet protectors, a CD with all the printable divider pages, and detailed directions for how to build and use the *Marketing Portfolio.*

ASP courses for Real Estate Agents and for Home Stagers: To learn more about my ASP Courses so that you can become an ASP, please call Stagedhomes.com at 800-392-7161, and we will be happy to send you detailed information about my two- and three-day ASP courses.

For more information or to place an order for one of my tools for success, please call 800-392-7161. Or visit our web site at:

www.stagingshoppingcenter.com
www.Stagedhomes.com
Stagedhomes.com
Iahsp.com

A BRIEF HISTORY OF STAGING AND THE STAGE TRADEMARK

Barb Schwarz entered the world of residential real estate as an Agent in Bellevue, Washington. Prior to being in real estate, Barb had owned her own interior design business, so she quickly recognized the challenge that existed for all Agents of how to help sellers prepare their homes for sale without upsetting or offending them. She started educating her sellers on how to set the scene and how to set the stage in order to get their properties sold for top dollar. She created the phrases "Staging" and "Staging Homes for sale." This was the first time the word "Staging" had been used in the real estate industry, and since that time she has explained the meaning of the word over and over to both Agents and sellers. Since 1985 Barb has taught over 1 million Agents what Staging is about all over the United States and Canada. Barb's term is now accepted and understood internationally, and homes that are Staged have an immediate advantage in any market. Homes that are Staged sell faster and/or for more money.

Barb Schwarz federally registered the Stage trademark in 1990 in the United States and in 2004 in Canada. She has developed the **Accredited Staging Professional (ASP) Course**® and the **ASP** designation for Stagers and Real Estate Agents. Accredited Staging Professional Stagers have the training and the skills to effectively Stage homes for their clients and give them the Staged Home advantage. Accredited Staging Professional Real Estate Agents have the training and the skills to effectively Market

Staged Homes for their clients and give them the Staged Home advantage. Agents market the house, and Stagers Stage it; together, they make a great team!

The **Stagedhomes.com** web site was developed to provide information for sellers on the benefits of Staging and a place for the public to search for ASP Stagers and ASP Real Estate Agents. The site has many valuable ideas, suggestions, and before-and-after photos to help sellers understand what needs to be done to effectively Stage their homes.

The **Staging University** portion of the web site was developed to provide information and support for all active ASPs. In addition to the many ideas and instructions to help educate ASPs, the site has an extensive document center with professionally designed materials that ASPs can access, download, print, and use with their sellers.

Simply put, Barb Schwarz is . . .

- **An educator,** teaching clearly and effectively a program of proven keys to success.
- **A performer,** fascinating, lively, aware, and powerful on stage.
- **A motivator,** infusing those around her with renewed energy and enthusiasm.
- **An innovator,** using her creativity and finely tuned perceptions to design elegant and easy-to-use ideas and tools to solve everyday problems.
- **The Creator of Home Staging,** having created the concepts of Home Staging and the Home Staging industry as it exists today.

PROFESSIONAL SPEAKER

As a seasoned speaker, Barb Schwarz has logged over 18,000 hours on the platform in over 2,000 full- and half-day seminars. More than 1 million people have attended her live programs. Her wonderful gift for speaking and her ability to educate, motivate, and entertain were recognized by the National Speakers Association in 1990 when they awarded her the coveted designation of **Certified Speaking Professional (CSP),** earned by fewer than 300 speakers worldwide.

Barb Schwarz, ASP, ASPM, IAHSP, AB, RLS, is a leader, an innovator, and a truly gifted speaker who shares the wisdom of her personal triumphs. Those who experience Barb are always struck by her incredible energy as well as the valuable substance of her programs.

AUTHOR, RADIO, AND TV PERSONALITY

Barb Schwarz is internationally known as the Creator of Staging. Recently Barb has been featured on:

- ABC's *20/20*.
- NBC's *The Today Show*.
- CBS's *The Early Show*.
- CBS's *Evening News*.
- *FOX News*.
- PBS.
- NPR radio.

She is the author of the best-selling *How to List and Sell Residential Real Estate Successfully*, and her new books, *Home Staging: The Winning Way to Sell Your House for More Money* and *How to Build a Successful Home Staging Business*, have received rave reviews nationwide.

Barb's DVD, "How to Prepare Your Home for Sale . . . So It Sells," won the Consumer Education Product of the Year Award from the Real Estate Educators of America, and her newest DVDs "How to Price Your Home to Sell for Top Dollar" and "How to Stage Your Home to Sell for Top Dollar," are used by ASPs throughout the real estate industry and Home Staging industry.

Barb is named as one of the top 50 Most Influential Women in the Real Estate Industry in 2008 by *The Real Estate Trends Report*.

Barb has also been featured in a variety of newspapers and magazines including:

- *The Seattle Times*
- *New York Home Magazine*
- *Smart Money Magazine*
- *Fortune Magazine*
- *CNN Online Magazine*
- *Realtor Magazine*
- *The New York Times*
- *Time Magazine*
- *BusinessWeek*
- *Cosmopolitan*
- *Washington Post*

- *US News & World Report*
- *Money Magazine*
- *Wall Street Journal*
- *New York Magazine*
- *The Home Magazine*
- *Southwest Airlines Spirit Magazine*
- *Woman's Day Magazine*
- *New York Magazine*
- *The Wall Street Journal*
- *Consumer Reports*
- *Kiplinger News*
- *Washington Times*
- *South China Morning Post*
- *Mortgage News Daily*
- *Entrepreneur Magazine*
- *Home and Living Examiner*
- *San Antonio Express*
- *Chicago Tribune*
- *LA Times*
- *Orange County Register*
- *Puget Sound Business Journal*
- *Woman's World Magazine*
- *Home and Garden*
- *Work Bench Magazine*
- *Real Estate Business Magazine*
- *Shop Smart Magazine*
- *Christian Science Monitor*
- *Associated Press*
- *Arizona Republic*
- *Boston Globe*
- *Wellness Magazine*

INDEX

Note: Figures and illustrations are indicated by "f" following the page number.